Scourged

©Michelle Dooley Mahon 2015

Michelle Dooley Mahon
2017

All Nature is but Art, unknown to thee,
All chance, direction – which thou canst not see,
All discord – harmony; - not understood,
All partial evil; - Universal good,
And spite of pride,
In erring, reasons spite; -
One truth is clear,
Whatever IS, is right

Alexander Pope

You need chaos in your soul to find the dancing star

Friedrich Nietzsche

First published 2015 by
Shellshock, Wexford, Ireland

Printed in Ireland by Creative Design & Print

ISBN – 978–0–9932773-1-3

For
Siobhán Philomena Salomé Dooley
And
Thomas O'Connell Mahon
My Parents

But nothing is forgotten. It follows you from the city to the country, stoops with you as you bend to tie your shoelace, trots into the shed where you get the hose, even pursues you down into the bowels of a ship, if you happen to be a seafaring man.

Time after Tide

"Sometimes one word can recall a whole span of life."
The Lonely Girl - **Edna O'Brien**

It's whirling she said
and her fingers curled around the shower frame.
"It's whirling".
I was in the bathroom with her then -
which to my naive mind
was as shocking as I thought it might get.
O, the innocence.
On an outlandish shopping trip
where the extent of the fizzing synapses had first revealed themselves -
a Victorian Madam displaying slim stockinged ankles,
a hint of the debauchery
beneath the crinoline and corsets,
still to come.
The Trinity of us in the Supermarket
Father, Mother and Prodigal Daughter,
morphing from *normal*
into a nightmare scenario-
the contents of the trolley -
meat, vegetables, biscuits, teabags, bread, butter, milk
abandoned - as I ran for the baby aisle
to get wet wipes and pads after
an accident.
In the stifling cubicles I watched her smile at herself in the mirror,
and push the wrong glass,
pushing, pushing on the cold glass,
and I put my hand on her arm,
the brown suede coat,
as it was wintertime,
and lead her into the tiny toilet,
and bend her between the porcelain bowl and the sanitary disposal bin,
and make her stand out of one leg,
and then the other,
to change her like a toddler.
Out at the sinks I watch the teenagers smirking as they apply eye liner and I want to shout
and bash their heads together,
I want to scream until the clouds crash into the spires silhouetted against the dark teatime sky,
"She has *ALZHEIMERS*"
And I don't know what to do......................
"And I don't know what to do either".
We walk back out to my Father,
who is standing forlornly at the Customer Service Desk,

his coat collar turned up,
his flat cap on.
We go home.
In the shower, where I know I will have to undress and bathe her for the very first time,
she has a dizzy spell and is momentarily weak.
I am quite lightheaded myself.
I brace her against me
and tell her to dip her head to her knees,
and gently push on her bending neck to show her what I mean.
It was her who taught me this.
"What do you mean it's whirling" I ask
and she tells me -*it goes all black and fast and whirls*
and then smiles at me,
embarrassed,
like a child.
In the Doctors surgery,
where I am being prescribed Sleeping Pills,
I mention this incident.
The GP slides herself from one side of her room to the other in an office chair on wheels.
- "Oh, that's Syncope " says she pulling a prescription pad from a filing cabinet and
   sliding back
- should there be a temporary disruption in the blood flow to the midbrain,
the reticular activating system may turn off, causing syncope -
It's why little old ladies faint when they are hanging clothes on a line, stretching."
She hands me the script and I stare at the word ***Stílnocht***
Silent Night in German
I lived in Stuttgart once.
The same time as Joxer.
She had ascertained that sleep was not something I was on more than nodding terms with,
having been christened "*The Night Owl*" as a small child,
and having been sent to bed,
would creep down and sit on the stairs in the dark,
with the wind whistling around my knees and ankles
from the 2" draught under the old front door
listening to the sounds from the TV
and the soft murmur of my parents voices,
knowing when to run soundlessly on frozen feet
to my attic bedroom when they raked the fire,
and washed their cups,
the water banging in the pipes
as I hopped into my *Holly Hobbie* bed.
It is Ten years since diagnosis.
Ten years of love and loss
Of yearning and learning

And silent nights
Tonight I put the radio on as I wiped the ice-cream from her face.
The singer was **Paul Brady** on *The John Creedon Show.*
The song was "*The Long Goodbye*"
How can I write this I wonder?
How can you not?
"N' God, and I could write a book about it."

Wexford October 1964

Thunderous rain took my mind off the pains.
Lightning struck in the afternoon, lifting the gloom of the 22nd, as I stared out from the Bullring rooms over slanted slate roofs at seagulls screeching to town for the fireworks. Tom hung a *"**No Stir – Yet**"* sign in the window of the attic flat He thought it might placate the queries of the general public and spare them - (and him) - the trek back up the 4 flights of stairs. On that night - as the soprano in **Lucia di Lammamoor** by Donizetti was screeching her way to the top notes in the closing Aria - I began pushing all 7lbs of a baby girl into the world. It was 2am when she finally screamed her way onto the planet, outdoing the performance in the Theatre by a country mile. Tom was beside himself with delight.
I was beside him with relief.
It is indeed a miracle he didn't burst.
It was often noted that the Mahons behaved more like an Italian family, warm, demonstrative, affectionate, hysterical. Every member of them cried like babies at our wedding the year before, while my Dooley contingent in the opposite pews looked on in quiet bewilderment and some considerable amusement.
I am one of 12 children, eight Brothers and three sisters. Maura, Seán, Tom, Pat, Micheal, Eugene, Eamonn, Oliver, Madge and Ann. My brother Brian died of Diptheria as a toddler. I was the first girl after six boys and called the white headed girl by my sisters.
The Father refused to allow me the freedom he afforded my siblings so it was only when my younger sister Margaret Catherine Grace (Madge) made a break for the next county that the reins were loosened and I followed suit. My best friend at this time traded under the moniker of Nancy D. "Mrs Dooley, will you ever let Siobhán out, she is forever baking" she would enquire chewing her hair.
Mrs Dooley came into the cool kitchen where I was rolling out pastry with a milk bottle and told me that Nancy D was below swinging on the gate.
I went to school in St Leos in Carlow town where I was born and reared, loving art and literature, moving swiftly from comics to classics, and was a homebird who helped Mammy with the younger ones, and kept the secrets of the older ones for a lifetime. The Father checked his pocket watch every night and sighing
    - *Let them that are out stop out*
then locked the front door, Madge (who was called "Keyhole Kate" after the cartoon character due to her height, plaits and ability to see through the fanlight over the paneled door when we

were foostering in the hall) lay in the small front ground floor bedroom we shared, in an agony of wondering whether he would open the door to say goodnight and spot me missing from the bed. I tapped on the window to climb in having got the last bus home from the dance in Tullow, putting the heart crossways in her. I was married before I dared to order a glass of shandy in the father's company as drinking was completely frowned upon for females. This was a complete departure from the behavior of himself and his sons. My own Mother never drank, but took up smoking ten Gold Bond in her 70s, using the firebin lid for an ashtray. If he came in 3 sheets to the wind from the club his standard response to his inebriation was

-    I swear to God Missus, I only had the two small bottles.

Men didn't get within a hundred feet of the delivery room in Dr Furlongs back then. It was a tough station, and one where a midwife was fond of pronouncing "oh, it's not as much fun NOW is it?" through the worst of the pains. There was also the medieval practice of "churching", where a woman post partum was seen as "unclean" in the eyes of God, and had to be brought to the church to be blessed. This may explain why the soft child was removed from the ward wrapped in a blanket by her Father, and taken to the church to be baptized into the Catholic faith of our forefathers and christened Michelle Margaret. (Michelle for the Beatles hit I loved, and which I insisted upon, despite the protestations of the priest who advised on calling the infant after a saint like Concepta or Attracta)

-    It's Michelle, I informed from the bed.

  (It's a Hebrew name meaning Gift from God)

Margaret, as a nod to both our mothers.

Maggie Mahon was a charmer with a sharp mind, a woman you wouldn't cod twice, a devoted Mother of Kathleen, Mance, Tom, Rosaleen and Michael and a stalwart on the bingo bus.   She played cards like a demon. Whist, Patience, Poker, 45, Bridge, and numerous others, holding court at a table and dealing like greased lightning, remembering everyone's hand and the trumps.

They played for matches as any spare shillings around the house were kept for St. Anthony's Offerings.

She had a great devotion to Saint Anthony and the Franciscan Friars and was a regular in the very last seat of the transept -beside the copper radiator with the ridges - at 6.15 mass, sweating on number 11 in a suede coat and fur trimmed boots. If it was said by Fr. Leander it was a rushed affair, which he flew through without drawing breath, starting the prayers in the vestry, a phalanx of altar boys struggling to keep up with him at the rails with the patten, and his shortest mass ever came in at 9 minutes. The longest was by Fr Charles, a friar who was so elderly, that he nodded off at various intervals for minutes at a time and we often wondered if he would make it through the mass at all. It reminds me now of a quote from Noel Coward on aging where he said he was mildly surprised if his colleagues made it through luncheon. Father Charles could bring an evening mass in at around the hour mark. Old age is a terrible thing. The first time we bathed the big eyed baby we fussed around like clucking hens, checking the temperature of the water with our elbows, laying out all the creams and powders and a soft furry towel to wrap her in. Alas, we were so busy being perfect that each thought the other had a hoult of the child, and so she was dashed head first onto the tiles, sliding with the suds out of our soapy hands. After a heart stopping moment we didn't exhale until we heard the roars of her and sighed with relief. Tom constructed a home -made wooden cot with collapsible sides. Wrapped like a Russian Doll I would put the infant down into a nest of baby blankets and go back downstairs only to then hear mewling similar to a kitten and find her perched in the hallway, the front of her sleeping suit manky from crawling down the lino on the stairs. Tom checked and re-checked the hinges while scratching his head in disbelief. One night we stood on the landing waiting. Through the crack of the door we watched as she sat up and went rummaging in one corner of the cot, lifted the foam mattress and plopped down through the webbing underneath.

- Aha, me lady

Tom picked her up and put her back into the cot while she howled her disapproval. A halt was literally called to her gallop when he placed a sheet of plywood under the mattress and so her fate and escape were sealed.

I recall tip toeing up the lino stairs to see if my husbands Great Uncle Nick was asleep in the big brass bed or dropping with the droot for goodie and tay. He had come with the house when we bought it. I had an elderly man in his dotage spending his days issuing orders and instructions from the bed and tapping his stick on the floor to demand attention or food or the bucket.

Her ladyship was in a Tansad in the kitchen doing similar.

There was a crucifix and a Sacred Heart lamp on the bedroom wall, a picture of Pope John and a gas tap. I warned her under pain of death not to touch this or the whole house would blow sky high. For years this tap would come between her and her sleep as she wondered if an errant arm had knocked against it and it was slowly seeping out the colourless, odourless poison that would choke us all to death as we slept in our blanketed beds.

When she wasn't making good her escape through the webbing of her cot, she was a fairly biddable toddler. One not prone to too many outbursts and who graced us with not just a first word but a complete sentence. Back in those days infants were still swaddled – chick or child – in gloriously named matinee coats and sleeping suits and a veritable trousseau of a wardrobe was laid out on the bed daily, with a pile of terry cloth nappies that were steeped in a bucket in the yard prior to washing. I still remember a giant pink tipped nappy pin that I used on the 3 of them.

It is probably still in a drawer at home.

I first laid eyes on Tom at a table tennis match. Of course he won it in style and pausing only to run a comb through his oiled quaff, winked at me and smiled shyly every time I walked by. I was doing what all the country girls who came to Wexford in the 50's did, and like thousands before me rented a small flat with a work colleague named Betty and joined clubs. Unfortunately, the flat mate had a personal problem and a Peggy Dell off her that would open pups eyes. I placed a basin of hot water and soap on the kitchen table and told her to knock herself out.

Tom was already knocked out.

He even used to go the long way round to work to catch a glimpse of me, and ended up having the tay in the homeplace in Carlow after a match before we even began doing a line. He thought my Mother was crying when she laughed sideways, her shoulders shaking, and he knew he had the permission to court me when he heard her say "Give that man more meat" The girls and I stood around in **Corry**'s in the knots, wearing tweed suits, unwrapping giant unwieldy rolls of fabric for ruckers who never bought or manhandling heavy women into corsets and Playtex bra's in the lingerie department, keeping an eye on the clock to run uphill home and get ready to go the C.Y.M.S. for the competitions. Tom started by giving me advice on my backhand and would hold my hand to show me how to use the bat more effectively and was loth to let it go.

- Let me show you again till you get the hang of it eh? he smiled.

One morning he missed me at 8am mass and called to my flat to see what was up, and I answered the door crooked as I had fallen and hurt my neck and shoulder, and yet responded "Nothing" when he asked what had happened. I have never been one to make a fuss.

I held his hand for over half a century.

I'm holding it still.

My son was born in the January of 1966.

There were ructions when we brought him home as she was demented that another baby would wipe her eye. Inadvertently she named him, as although he was christened Martin, she instantly called him Bartin and I gave up trying to correct her so it stuck. He was a different animal altogether and a quiet baby, and actually content to lie in his cot or around the house in baskets or on mats in the sun, getting aired. She was kneeling on a cushion peeping out the back kitchen window at her Great Uncle Billy Rossiter letting his Jack Russell terrier loose at a rat in the yard. Tom's Aunt and Sister lived across the road.

There was always some diversion or devilment to be had in Carrigeen and Auntie Nellie had an open door policy which explains how her Pomeranian pooch Peppi was savaged to death one fine day by a passing Alsation. When they added their extension they didn't level the floor so there was a hump in the middle of the kitchen. Nellie, of the house coat and blue rinse, a splash guard on the frying pan, sat at the top of the table dispensing nuggets of gossip and strong tea, while Kathleen whom I called Katie Daly after the song, of the drama club and immaculate clothing, picked the fat off her chop and reached for the batch loaf which she beat into submission with lumps of country butter. She sat at the bottom of the hill wedged in beside the leaning fridge door to keep it shut.

Their doorbell rang a multitude a tunes ranging from the Yellow Rose of Texas through to Greensleeves passing Happy Birthday and Auld lang Syne on the way. A parade of characters yoo hooed themselves up the dark hallway through the open door.

The child sat on the hard chair against the wall and gave out the information as to who was entering.

"It's the woman with the purple hair, it's the man from Bride St, it's a priest, it's the child who gets the dolls from America with another doll."

Amongst the women calling in for cups of tea and news, Friars from the Friary came to chat and confess, one who had a problem with his nerves would sit squirming his horny toenails in his sandals with the china cup rattling off his dentures. Nellie always had a joke, or a toy, or a walking talking puppet from Japan or a light up Santa that walked up and down the mantelpiece, or a tin that you opened thinking it was sweets and a coiled springy snake bounced across the room while you screamed. On New Years Eve they and all the neighbours came out into the street and toasted each other with sherry schooners and gave each other lumps of coal for good luck and sang Auld Lang Syne at the doors. Tom's Aunt Molly lived a few doors up the hill with her husband John. She had a stroke one night (in the middle of a card game)

— "Quick, Molly is having a turn" —

and came to permanently sit silently in the corner of the kitchen, faintly smiling, but never speaking. Wexford people like to "place" you, as if once they know the place you are from, they will know you, and everyone knew everyone and their children, by name. Placing appears to be a custom particular to this town and everyone above 50 will know people by their maiden names. Tom and his family could while away hours going back through every seed and breed for generations till they find a single random connection and go

      – *"Oh, yis   – I have you now".*

I have you now.

As a small child, the scourge was allowed out to play "on the island" and was admonished severely not to even think about crossing the road. Considering the only traffic back then was the occasional Morris Minor, or a horse and trap, the fears of her imminent plastering on the street proved unfounded. So she contented herself with nosing around other people's houses and finding out news. The hallways of every house in the Square were different and ranged from a glimpse of a rubber plant on a half moon telephone table, to bare boards and plaster hanging off the walls. It seemed every house had a giant black **Pedigree pram** *with a gurning baby alternately chawing on, or shaking a rattler behind white netting. Putting the babby out consumed a considerable amount of time, and meant checking and re-checking that it was still alive, not swarmed by midges, or fecked by Gypsies. There was a preponderance of prams outside the shops on the main street as people would park their offspring, put the brake on and then casually shop for hours. One of the kinder things we said to her as she was being chastised for any or all misdemeanours was the fact that she was a changeling baby and that she had been swapped for a Traveller child.*

"Oh, there is a lovely quiet child sitting in a Tinkers camp wondering where we are".

She could pass a number of hours scavenging around the house, rooting in presses, sitting on the path dragging a lollipop stick around the cracks, watching people, or eating the bottom bits off the fuschia that grew outside the Garda Barracks. Someone else showed her how to do this. They said it would taste like honey.

It didn't.

She doesn't even like honey.

"Ketch me hand" Tom would say as he retrieved her.

She was forever being told to" stand up straight, arms be your sides, be a good girl". It was also at this time that we began to call her Little Mrs Up and Down as her moods varied wildly from elation to despair often in the same hour.

Then she started school.

I brought her by the hand wearing the infernal crocheted bonnet to the Presentation Convent School where she was welcomed by Sr. Gertrude who minded the babies. She was a tall thin Nun with surprised eyebrows and a pale sad face with two scarlet poppy cheeks who was pushed to the pin of her considerable collar to contain the massed roaring of forty small children who wanted their Mothers. All the painting in the world was not going to silence that din and she was prostrate across the tiny desk with desolation and despair as I left with my heart beating in my throat. She was barely in the door before she had taken another child by the hand to show her where the toilet was, and where the buns came out, which was not the same place. I remember the huge ragged breath of relief when she saw my face appear around the door to bring her home and she informed me that she was glad that THAT was over and the sobbing higs as I responded she would have to go back again the next day, and the next.

She learned to read quickly.

Then devoured the stories and chapters long before she was supposed to be on that page.

She read night and day, in bed and on the toilet.

"There's Maggie Ann going with the Dandy up the leg of her drawers".

She took Christmas money down to the Book Shop negotiating the pall of smoke and picked out the *Annuals* that she wanted. Sisters ran the business, one chain smoking while she marked off the papers in the book, her gold wrapped wrists jangling and her nicotine stained nail marking the place. The other sister wore a built up shoe and a shop coat and hecked up and down behind the counter serving comics and sweets. There was a mild assistant in a nylon shopcoat with a disconsolate air, as if she had been pressed into service in a big house against her will. She moved about the shop like a wraith, ineffectually dusting and reading penny dreadfuls and Mills & Boon romances.

By this time I allowed her to go down town alone for messages. Initially, with a note either pinned to her sleeve or in a pocket. As she got braver, these were dispensed with. Crossing the square she went down Gibson Street, stepping over the stream of scutter and blood that poured out from the abbatoir when they were butchering. She would hear the mooing and bawling of the cows as they were herded up through the streets by men wearing flat caps shouting "Hoosh, Geddap, Hoosh" as they laid out all around them with their sticks at the shit covered haunches of the terrified animals. She asked me why there was so much poo.

- Those cattle can smell the fear, it's in the fresh blood, it's in the rivers of piss and somehow they know they are next.

November 2013 - Year 8

One month away from the 4th Christmas his wife will spend in a nursing home my Dad sits home alone.
He has finally hit a wall.
It had become apparent lately that he was low –
Unable to sleep, with no appetite and no interest in things, and a new departure - tears.
It is not easy to watch your Father sob.
I cry at the drop of a hat. It is as much a part of me as having green eyes.
The girl with green eyes.
Seeing my Father cry in a restaurant while the waiter hovered was tough.
Having a conversation across a kitchen table with a pen and paper to draw a rough sketch of the human brain and the endorphins and *seratonin* that regulate mood was much harder. We both cried.
Having a talk that drew on an arsenal of religions, spirituality, acceptance, depression, naivety and *Lazarus* was infinitely harder.
He has begun to talk.
In fact he has talked more, and to people more qualified than me, more often and for longer in the last week than in the last decade.
Our attention has been so focused on Siobhán that maybe we have been remiss and overlooked the strongest link in the chain.
Any chain is only as strong as its links
As a family I feel that we are in a giant cement mixer being cleaned at the end of the day. After the soft sloppy cement is finished, rocks and water are thrown in to chisel away the dirt.

It is in this phase of cleaning and polishing I feel we are being made braver, brighter, brawny,

I feel I may come out the other side shining like an Emerald, ten foot tall and bulletproof.

We are minding and spoiling him and begging him to take time out to nourish the soul.

I think he may actually listen and these weeks may be cathartic.

Siobhán would understand.

We are Eternal.

> ...."to morrow, and tomorrow, and tomorrow ,
> creeps in this petty pace from day to day,
> to the last syllable of recorded time,
> and all our yesterdays have lighted fools,
> the way to dusty death, Out, Out, brief candle!"
>
> *(Macbeth)*

Christmas 2013 - Year 8

Tonight I sang *Killing me softly* with *Roberta Flack.*

She didn't know, but Siobhán did.

I gave her a fair skelp of **Baileys** and the pointy thin bits of a chocolate orange.

Perfect for posting into her mouth and for melting.

I had a root in the press and saw the tiny fibre optic tree that we will be plugging in again this year.

I went home and googled *Pale Blue Dot* and used the last of my coloured inks printing it, holding it between fingertips as I bent to place it on the caravan size fridge that rarely contains anything but the light, and *never* milk, with a ceramic magnet of a woman wearing a fruit basket as a hat.

I have never been to the country it came from.

But I am reminded that we although we are minute, we are the fabric of stars.

Wexford October 1974

Tom's Mother was always warning her about church yards and not to be hanging around in there playing on the grass. The church grass was the only kind we had as the yard at the back of our house was barely big enough to put a bin in. Years later, Tom would move to the flat roof and begin to potter there with his pots and plants, always berating whose ever legs came out the window to "Mind the roof, will you MIND the roof, you'll go through it".

All houses in Ireland had their back kitchen extensions which were usually thrown up by the man of the house and a friend, without a screed of permission, and had flat felt roofs that were never entirely sealed. In a land that has a monsoon season for at least 8 months of the year it meant there

were always saucepans and bowls dotted fetchingly about the floor to catch the water.
"The roof is dripping again" –
"Christ Almighty".
The reason she was not supposed to be trick acting around chapel yards was "Quare Fellas" and
The Boogey Man. Nana brought her down to Chape Charlie to buy her a monkey on a stick and
remind her. Charlie kept a stall in the Bullring that sold all-sorts -   china ornaments, toys, pot
scrubs, plastic flowers, school copies and wind-up clockwork things from Korea that broke the
moment you paid for them. He had a shock of white hair and a line in patter stolen from a soft
shoe salesman.   Forty Coats was slumped in the corner by the statue, a man of the road who
literally wore about 37 jackets and a grey Mack.   I remember still the redness of his lower lip,
glistening through the white beard, his haunted eyes.
 Between all the Boogey Men, Quare Fellas, Chancers, Gougers, Tinkers and Nuns she was lucky
to escape with her life. Back then the summers lasted for about 4 years and in my minds eye I see
pictures of a little girl in a knobbly jumper, whiling away the long hot days and nights tormenting
us and plotting where she would bring her smaller brother the next time she was allowed out.
He was not exactly an unwilling accomplice, as the joys of the path had worn off for him quite
quickly.
It was in the spirit of discovery and innovation that she escorted him by the hand, firstly across the
road, and then when their impudence was not immediately discovered, running faster until it was
safe to explore. She knew what she was doing in that she only went a distance that they could run
back from quickly, and so it is in this vein they managed to attend mass, a wedding, and the circus
This was the late 60's and children were as welcome anywhere as the flowers of May, which may
explain why she was found waltzing in an old man's arms at a wedding in Whites Hotel while
Barty made himself sick eating the hard white icing off the cake.
Everyone simply presumed they were everyone else's children.
Ditto the circus, where she took the daring step of heading to Harvey's Field with the massed
throngs of the town and thrust her brother under the flap at the back of the big top to do a recce.
When he was not unceremoniously flung back out she raised the flap and followed him in.
They sat on the benches ringside, smelling sawdust and animals and chewing gum. A woman
beside them, enquiring for their Mother and general welfare took pity on them and bought 2 tubs
of HB Ice-cream. By the time they were running back down the hill home, he sprinting ahead as
if to disown her and any or all part in the adventure, and a crowd around the doors of Carrigeen
wrung their hands and cardigans and sent up of a cry of – Oh, HERE they are!! A neighbour,
propped in the doorway gave her a mournful eye and intoned
    -   Oh, hun, you're going to be kilt
and she looked up at her and said "Eff off".
It was the shock.
Tom's mother wore a cameo brooch on a scarf and sheepskin gloves and a pleated kilt with a giant
pin. It was **not** the pink one that was used for nappies. She wore a housecoat in the house, over
her clothes. Not since Victorian times has there been so much dressing and un-dressing as there was
in a Mahon house. You had your getting up clothes, your round the house duds, your good clothes
that you wore down town and then immediately removed when you came in the door, re- hung and
when complimented said
    -   What, this old thing? I have it the last 20 years.

My sisters and I who have always believed that breeding is better than feeding would be mortified when we met them on the town, dressed up to the nines, as we would have only stood up from the table and thrown a coat over ourselves and run out the door for a few messages.

There would be a foot of ash hanging off the fag Nana kept in the corner of her mouth, her eyes screwed up against the smoke as she cleared the table while people ate. The **YR** *sauce would be back in the press before you had salted the potatoes. Every school day the child went for her dinner there, and would be given a drink of diluted orange in a red plastic mug that lived under the sink and was frayed at the edges from years of teeth. Her Godfather Mance would be shaving at the sink mirror in a string vest, lathering his cheeks with a soapy brush and whistling songs. He was a complete character and known to tog off after a feed of pints, or put a squealing baby pig from a farm in the back seat of a hire car when they were out on a spree.*

"Drink to me only with thine eyes" He sang in all the bars and all the joints and as Town Sergeant once stood behind an American President - holding the Mace - as the tanned man with the Hollywood smile laid a wreath at the statue of Commodore Barry, only a number of months before that President took a bullet in the side of his handsome head in a Dallas Motorcade. When Mance grew too sick to sing, he called her into the bedroom they were nursing and feeding him in, and asked the child to sing what she learned in school that day. She climbed up easy on the bed near his feet in case she shook the tubes and trying not to look at the hole in his throat sang "Nearer My God to Thee" before she was brought out again fairly lively. He was 42 when he died.

When her Nana was answering the door one day she hopped up to where she kept the cordial and re-filled the red mug to the brim.

Nana caught her and with her cheeks as scarlet as the mug she threw it down the sink.

"I'll tell your Da on ya" her Nana said.

Her face burnt with shame and she whispered it was only water.

Which was a lie.

I already knew this woman was no slouch when it came to kids. As a small boy Tom was a sickly child and had asthma and was mollycoddled and wrapped in cotton wool. One day, when they were drawn to go to Ferrybank to cool themselves in the water, Nana admonished Kathleen – who was in charge – not to let Tom in the water no matter what. Of course he screeched and roared to get in with the rest of them and he got his way. Then they dried him within an inch of his life, combed his hair to dry in the sun, and swore him to secrecy.

- *Did you let that child into the water?*
- *No*
- *I'll ask you again did you let that child into the water?*
- *NO, Mammy, honest to God.*

Then she walked across to him, lifted his arm and licked it, tasting the telltale salt.

There'll be a black mark on your tongue when you wake up for telling lies.

Another time a coin went missing from St. Anthony's pile on the table she stood at the bedroom doors and shouted –

- *Whoever took that half crown, the hand will fall offa them.*

My husband was 9 years old when WW2 broke out and he remembers the terror as they listened to planes, waiting for the whistle of bombs that never came. One of the things he also recalls is the sadistic cruelty of the Brothers who taught him and who laid out at all around them, once getting a box in the side of the head for himself for writing with a scut of a pencil. There was little for them to do and they made their own entertainment, and he remembers with the delight of a child when they got shop bread again

-    "Snow white bread" he called it 70 years later.

Any time they got sweets or books or treats they sooleyed them out by keeping them for the bed. They referred to this practice as **Passee.**

Passee was keeping a few squares of chocolate, a peggy's leg, a comic, or a hambone, for the bed and he fondly remembers the skitting and laughing that went on while their parents were busy, his Mother knitting and crocheting dresses and blankets for babies and dolls, his Father in a waistcoat, with his shirt sleeves rolled up marking out squares on velvet - a pencil behind his ear, to make bonded velour cushions. Tom had a Fox terrier called Kitty who was his constant companion. Until she got off the lead one day and disappeared on the quay side. He searched high and low for her and went to bed crying. The next day and the next he called and looked until he was told she was gone and to stop. And then a week later when men were doing work on drains that led into the silt bed of the river they pulled up a pipe with Kitty perched inside it with not a bother off her. The story made the papers and his photograph was taken. It looks like a still from a Fellini Film now - the small boy in the cut down pants, squinting against the sun, gleaming white plimsolls, the cock eared dog at his feet.

Nellie was the woman you rang when someone died, and she would be around to wash and lay out the body before you had replaced the phone in its cradle. In the laying out of her own father, in what was considered normal at the time – a habit – similar to a Friars robe with a Cowl– she was heard to remark –

-    Oh, don't put a hood on me Da

They were inveterate tricksters and would play the most outrageous pranks on each other. Once when the great Grandmother was above in the bed trying to die, a man with a cork leg called to the door and asked how she was.

-    She has just passed says Nellie blessing herself, stalling at the door so her sister
      Molly could leap into the waiting coffin and frighten the tar out of him.
-    Oh, I'm terribly sorry says he removing his flat cap and calling in to pay his respects.

The "corpse "was laid out in the parlour in a habit and as he bent to kneel and bless himself, his cork leg stretched out straight behind him, Molly sat up in the shroud with talcum powder on her face and began to shout as he almost collapsed.

Because I had so many brothers, and my sister was gone to London to Nurse, I spent most of my time with Mammy, and was barely allowed down town without her. The Father made us kneel on the kitchen floor every night to say the Rosary and we would try not to catch each others eye or burst out laughing.

The family that prays together stays together.

Kathleen told the child that she would bring her somewhere lovely if she kept her nose clean. I saw her rubbing it with a tissue in the mirror and told her it was just a figure of speech. There was a great kerfuffle about what to dress the child in – (in this family you are a child till you are about 50 years old, and a girl in your 70's) and through an onslaught on various wardrobes she was kitted out like a Dickensian orphan with delusions of grandeur. She ended up wearing a fun-fur and my "Going Away" hat tied on with a silk scarf as if she was about to go about the roads in a shooting brake. She was taken off to **"The Good Old Days"** where she disgraced herself by being called on stage as a stooge and then announcing to the hysterical audience how your man was doing the tricks. The old pro that he was, he didn't miss a beat and tried to continue with his act despite the presence of a minor, albeit dressed as a miniature Lady Bracknell hamming it up to the Gods.

She was up and down the road to the Arklow Music Festival like a fiddlers elbow and came home with certificates and medals and plaques. She stood on her mark and spread her arms wide while she entreated the audience, and specifically the judges, to listen to her case of the old woman. "She's SOMEBODY'S Mother, boys, you know, although she is old and feeble and slow" – She milked it.

We paid a nun to teach her to play the piano. It may not have helped that Sr. Helen had a stick she had named Harry and was liable to bring same crashing down onto one's tiny knuckles if you hit the wrong note. It was enough to unsettle Liberace and was to prove too much for her sibling, who cried and refused to go back. She became a homebird.   If she had to sleep in another house she lay awake all night in a strange space, listening to the sounds of snuffling and snoring, crying quietly under the blanket for home.

"Are you toasty" said her Nana Mahon climbing in beside her in a floor length flanellette nightie and turning off the light, and she responded yes with a lump in her throat, while she waited for her eyes to adjust, so she could see the Spanish doll in the layers of red and black net on the dressing table, twirling her fan in the crack of light from the hall.

"Night, night, don't let the bedbugs bite"

The photo of us as a family taken when my last baby Nicola was only newborn, shows how we are all bunched up in a corner of the living room by the piano. It was to let in the light as this was 1970 now and light was at a premium.

And scarce enough in a room that was wood panelled and had dark drapes and furniture.

Strike a match someone in the name of God till we read the clock.

Our neighbor was a gentle lady who some years later would be forced to call us to come home from holidays and retrieve her, as herself and a boy in a Donkey Jacket with bumfluff on his cheeks had carried the huge stereo player upstairs and were playing "Stairway to Heaven" on repeat on the roof all night. It was her first taste of freedom and a free house, which she had responded to by listening to the lectures ad nauseam, hanging her head in silence, nodding at respectable intervals and looking as if butter wouldn't melt.

And running amok as soon as the door closed behind us

Another neighbor had a mouth like a cut turnip , dressed in layers of grey and black shawls, always bare legs and broken down shoes, Summer or Winter, I recall the mottled purple shading against the milk bottle legs, the blue veins, the diamonds on her shins from sitting on top of the fire. The man down the street had a Honda 50 and a half face helmet and he would be ning ninging up and down the roads, his sister perched primly on the back, her helmet on over her perm, her handbag over one arm, the other arm extended in a genteel fashion, holding on to his shoulder all the way to Benediction as the church bells rang, and the horn from Pierces streamed the black faced cyclists up the slanted silver streets for their supper.

June 2010 - Year 5

When I worked in the West End of London as a pub landlady - a regular customer called Peter had the worst case of *Arachnaphobia* I have ever witnessed. If he saw *pictures* of spiders he would come over all unnecessary. Taking a bath was a nightmare. Ditto if he saw a cobweb and screamed like a girl for it to be removed in a tissue. Came out in a flop sweat if a money spider fell on him in a beer garden.

Of course this meant that his friends took the right royal piss. But one took it to a whole other level the day he brought in a small cardboard box with holes in it and fired it up on the counter amongst the drip mats and ashtrays and ordered himself a pint of best bitter. I had inherited (along with a mob of truculent disaffected staff happily dispensing drinks to all and sundry for free) a pair of Rottweilers who were the pub security and spent the day shitting on a roof garden and the night patrolling the bar. I had to feed *and* walk them. One woman almost threw herself under a bus when she saw me round the corner of *High Holborn*, all 3 of us straining at the leash. The screaming from the bar alerted me to throw the food in the general direction of the dogs and run down the stairs fairly sharpish, where I saw Peter pale and prone, in a pile of pork scratchings with a crowd around him.

There was a Tarantula named Diana, after a Princess, sitting in a blue plastic *Ruddles County* ashtray on the counter.

Tarantulas are noteworthy in the fact that they shed. They sneak off to a corner of their tank where they quietly step out of themselves over a number of hours and when you wake up in the morning there are two of them. One marching around - one lifeless. I had to show no fear or the braying throng would hurl it in my face. After I ascertained that Peter was alive and coming to, I picked up Diana and had a *goo*.

It is a unique experience to be eyeball to many eyeballs with a creature like this.

It looks the very same as its doppelganger.

Same markings, same hairy legs, but the difference is the weight.

The presence is gone.

Like a banana skin without its fruit.

Like an envelope without its letter.

Only the husk is left behind.

The dessicated twin of a tarantula.

The other night I remembered this event as I moved my Mothers arm

and felt the lightness, the absence, the otherness.

They have asked me to talk about her on the radio.

I feel if I start I may not stop and will deflate like a fat balloon bouncing around the studio as I actually have a head like Holyhead today.

My brain may finally leak out my ear from trying to suppress feeling and I just want a massive remote to press **STOP** on the whole world so I can catch up.

My heart breaks to see Siobhán in the *Stephen Hawking* chair, and to find it so inaccessible to reach her - or lift her head. Dad is lower than a snakes belly at the moment.

7 days a week he watches her disappear.

We all cried at a family lunch today.

In a restaurant.
I cried trying to talk and Dad cried trying to wipe his glasses.
His grandson cried because his Grandad was crying
Damn Emotional Incontinence strikes again.
I am at a loss to offer any words of comfort to him and the blinder I played today was to inform him that she will worsen, and we have to accept it.
Go me.
My sister bought him a budgie.
A beautiful budgie in a "*Tweetie Pie*" cage which made me feel even worse as it seems to underpin the poignancy and loss that someone has only a bird in their kitchen for company. I feel I should have the fire lit for him, or a hot dinner under a checked tea towel, or visit more and document and record his memories, on a Dictaphone, in notebooks. Last night the carers used a hoist to get Mam to the commode and elevated her about 4ft in the air to swing her across. I stopped them for a minute while I held her hands and swung her gently to and fro singing
"*See saw Marjorie Daw, sold her bed to lie in the straw*"
Dad refused to take the bird home.
He is a legend.
I don't tell him enough.

Wexford October 1979

W e lived in grainy grey in Ireland then. A landline was a luxury and colour TV only a whisper, we watched the snooker in black and white, hazarding a guess if Dennis Taylor was on the pink or the blue for the century.

I was known to respond **Inging and Sheeps thinging** when they asked me what was for lunch. It was a time when Travellers would call to the door with a battered tea pot and ask you to "make tay" and try to get a shilling for the babby or sell you a floral carpet and a continental quilt.

We rang payphones in pubs and listened to the resigned plodding of the bar man back up to the roaring crowd inside, where his question would be greeted with howls of derision and laughter. We rang phone boxes at appointed times, rang relations from neighbours houses and vice versa and if someone died the Gardaí called to your house with their hats in their hands to break the news. Nobody but a Bank Manager had a credit card and clothes were let out on "Appro" which meant parading up and down the front room in a succession of coats and anoraks to hooting and applause. Appliances were bought on HP and a book was run in the grocers, not the bookies.

We watched Bunny Carr saying "Stop the Lights" before we found out he had run away with the charity money, we tried to **"Draw along with Blaithin"**, and learned the price of Bullocks and Heifirs on **Mart & Market** with Cowjack - (So named for his baldness) - **Count John McCormack** was singing Panis Angelicus on Radio Na h'Eirinn, and **Frank Patterson** was singing "She is far from the land"

We would shout ...."And she can't swim a stroke"

The boy was listening to Radio Luxembourg at full blast, playing a pretend saxophone to **Baker**

Street *and air guitar to* **Dark Side of the Moon***,*

Beckett was alive and well and hating Paris, Edna O Brien had left Ernest Gebler and walked from Chelsea to Wimbledon to start a new life minus the sons she adored. Women burnt bras and started to challenge church and state,   dispensing contraception from the North out of suitcases filled with french letters and pills.

I was standing in the kitchen with the bowls of water plinking plonking on the floor wrapping school copies in woodchip wallpaper.

One day in 1970 when my baby Nicola was only a few months old, we went on a glorious day trip to Slade, a fishing village on the coast. The Hillman Hunter was packed with all the kit and the 5 of us, a Tansad for the child, rods, reels, bait, blankets, sunhats, cream, a picnic, drinks and pretty much the entire ground floor of the house had been rolled up and placed in the boot or under their feet in the back so that their knees nearly touched the roof. We established camp and like every other children in the world they ate the picnic as soon as they got out of the car. Tom took his small son across the rocks by the hand to teach him to fish and we girls stayed in the sun.

"You can't go in that water for an hour, Shell" I called over as I removed the toweling nappy to air the child.

She wouldn't let me teach her to swim and screamed in my arms as I supported her tummy and kicked and sprocked till I released her. She got a bit of a fright one day, I think.

"I'll just go and play over there" she announced and indicated a huge flat rock up behind her on a slope.

"Be careful, and don't go out of my sight".

On the rock, I watched her as she watched me and as soon as I began undressing and rubbing lotion into Nicolas extremities, she seized her chance, and went a little further, and then a little further still. Suddenly she was high up on the cliff and then lost to sight. My heart raced, more in fear of what Tom would say than what mischief she could possibly get up to in a field.

Exhausted from her climb in the hot sun, she sat on a small stone wall that moved with her. There was nothing holding that wall together, only the laying of stone on stone, lengthways, a huge pile of overlapping dominos. She tried the first one and it fell easy enough and then she set to with a vigour placing stone after stone in a neat pile on either side as if she was constructing a gate. Despite the sun beating down on her she commenced to working like a pack mule and was hurling stones to the left and the right of her with gay abandon when she heard the shouting.

"Hi, You, Hi, HI, HI!" said the farmer as he bounced across the field in a Massey Ferguson. Deciding that discretion was the better part of valour, she took to her tiny heels and ran and skipped and dropped till she arrived breathlessly back. I was scanning the cliff for her before my husband came back, my hand shading my forehead having placed the sleeping baby in the shade with the hood up. All that could be seen was a bundle of white lace and a pair of chubby knees.

"You look very guilty" I said. "What have you been up to?"

"Nothin' "says she with her heart bursting and flopped down beside me for a hug like a limpet. It took the farmer 30 minutes to drive down by the roadway and with his tractor idling on the hard damp sand he proceeded to actually hopscotch across the flat rocks to us, where he began without preamble or ceremony to mime her actions to me while he beat his own thighs with a cap.

"Your language is choice in front of a child" I said and got to my feet.

"SIT down, DON'T move, watch the baby" I said and followed him up the cliff.

She had done the work of ten men and had laid waste to the wall with a speed unknown to a

communion child and I sighed quietly as I began to rebuild it. At the corner of the field I bent and straightened with armfuls of the warm flat stones and re-built her destruction, quietly and without fuss, or a word, till even the farmer fell silent, and as I stood to ease my back, I saw her - with the baby in her arms - edging closer and closer, documenting and witnessing, till I finished and the farmer drove away muttering, bouncing the tractor across the furrows into the sunset, and I lifted the baby from her arms and took her by the hand.
We never mentioned this again.
Don't tell Tom.

November 2012 - Year 7

Imagine being on the most interminable aeroplane flight in the world.
Not just long haul somewhere outrageous and remote, but staying on the flight.
Forever
First the journey is not too awful.
The stewardess is accommodating and friendly, the food is almost edible.
The other passengers are not a bad bunch. The ennui is stifling though - the endless view of clouds rolling past - Cumulus, Nimbus, Blue Stratus, - sometimes you can almost recognise a face or a figure in the white fog.
You visualise your loved ones, and snatch memories out of the wide blue yonder.
At some point 50,000 feet in the air and months and months into the journey, you realise you are not getting off, or going home, or even landing.
Ever landing.
In fact there may be an impending awareness, a sense of doom, or dread. As time passes - as time slowly does - the other passengers start to become an unruly bunch. Shouting and crying, walking up and down the plane, rattling the panic bolts of the doors with the stewardess urging them back to their seats and strapping them in again.
The food gets slowly worse. The seat becomes more and more uncomfortable. Impossible to find a position that even remotely passes for something bearable as your joints stiffen and ache. The stewardess adjusts your headrest, and you would give a kidney to stand up and stretch, or feel air that has not been breathed in and out tens of thousands of times. After another endless block of time has elapsed the passengers become stoic, or resigned. The jury is out. They revert to silence and watching. They sit in lines, staring. They don't look at the view. Some still pluck hopefully at the stewardesse's sleeve as she walks at speed down the aisle checking her trolley. The heat is unbearable, your clothes pasted to your back and the seat- until it is impossible to know where one ends and one begins.
Imagine that you wear a nappy and now feel it.
Imagine that your nose and eyes and whole body itches and you cannot scratch
Siobhán has been on this flight as a long haul passenger for 8 years
Terry Pratchett describes living with Alzheimers as like
".......driving a car with everything working, lights, indicators, wipers but knowing that somehow, someday you will still end up going through the windscreen.

Wexford Summer 1976

Tom always loved to take his family out for "Mystery Drives".
     Sunshine spilling into the car heating the seats until it was an oven on wheels, sunsplitting the stones in the Square with Paddy Byrne whitewashing walls in anticipation of the Corpus Christi procession. Tom, in a short sleeved shirt, standing whistling at the raised boot of whatever car he was driving at the time. He has always been a petrol head and believed in the old adage that it is better to be looking at it than looking for it.

I remember the cars now from their registration plates.

53 EYI - A Blue Hillman Hunter

695 UZO - A Navy Ford Fiest

VZR 211 - A luminous Yellow Renault 4

YMI 37 A Beige Austin

He probably spent the night planning these sudden trips but conveniently never mentioned them. Least of all to me.

The first I would know was when he tipped me the wink to get the flasks out and to make about a thousand ham salad sandwiches using rock hard Kerrygold.

Unbeknownst to any of us, he would have been scavenging around upstairs for a motley assortment of pyjamas and nighties flung around warm bedrooms while we were busy chopping spring onions, soft tomatoes and shelling eggs.

And sending someone to Hughie Moores for salad cream and sliced pans.

(The wrappers being immediately re-filled with the quartered sandwiches)

Sighing - "This knife wouldn't cut butter" as the tomato buckled and oozed pips and juice.

"Here's a visitor" as the same knife dropped to the floor from a small greasy hand.

The same greasy hand that would rub butter all over the dials on the constant radio to make it shine.

The constantly broadcasting radio from which we heard Uncle Gaybo and Harbour Hotel and Dear Frankie.

Alongside mismatched bedwear, bottoms with no fork in them, tops that were only fit for dusters and an eclectic bunch of toothbrushes (the first to his hand - whether they be ancient and used for scouring grout or the dogs matted arse) were wrapped in a Dunnes Stores plastic bag and hidden under the spare wheel, along with buckets and spades, and a bulging packet of Lug worm.

Spontanaiety is his middle name, and far more apt than O'Connell,

I give you a packed car in the baking heat with windbreakers, windcheaters, wet weather gear, tartan rugs, tents, poles, sleeping bags, fishing rods, unruly children, and a unique aroma of eggs, onions, and bait and allow you to draw your own conclusions.

Of course she got sick.

She spent her youth getting sick out of car windows and shouting "Pull over, pull over" to no avail. Tom would check her pallor in the rearview mirror till it turned from white to lime and then skew to a skidding stop on the grass verge.

Where of course she would be fine as the motion had stopped and she could bend over retching and inhaling lungfuls of fresh sea air instead of worms, onions, and her brothers feet.

"I told you I was sick!!"

They used to fight in the back seat.

"God, give me strength" Tom would cry foaming at the mouth while I calmly advised him to mind his blood pressure AND the road.

Because they were wearing shorts and the leather seats were scorching they did not want to be pressed up against each other.

Or "**Hawing**" on each other.

"If I get BACK to yee", he would shout flailing his left arm into the gap between the seats and inadvertently clouting the bare leg of the wrong child.

These trips were often and usually to beaches - where on inclement days we would sit on a hummock of thistly springing grass on a stripey rug and listen to the roars and bawls of Micheál O Hehir commentating on the hurling on the radio from the open door of the car , watching people reading newspapers, the condensation trickling down the windshield, the tannin tea tasting tainted from the plastic flask. Sometimes, further afield the light would be growing dim as we pulled into some far flung town looking for a B&B, where we would be disgraced marching down the corridor to the communal bathroom at midnight in our rags. Back in those days Irish children were as welcome in pubs as your average alcoholic and spent the night trickacting around pool tables and scourging large bottles of **TK Red Lemonade** (free on the bar as a mixer) or cokes with pub crisps and bars of plain in a fug of smoke, country music, and diddly eye sessions.

Her ladyship would be out bawshocking around with a crowd of hare baiters, mullocking around in the car park, showing off in front of strange children who were fresh meat.

Tom told her he had a surprise and they we were going for a drive. He drove up hill and down dale until finally they ended up in a field where ginger men with freckled hands and sovereign rings were selling caravans. She peeped in at the lines of sparkling new motor homes with excitement but it was another one entirely that had caught his attention. She was flabbergasted. There was a lot of pants hitching and change jingling and whistling going on, as much as there were offers and counter offers and laughter and then finally Tom said "I'm walking away" and there was spit and handshakes and luck money and he had bought it. "Mam's going to kill you" she said to him as soon as he closed the car door. He wasn't listening. He was already planning how he could get a trailer and hitch to get it off the site without it collapsing.

"Do it first and then work out how. "

He found the tiny fridges and gas burners, and I ran up loose covers and doonshey pleated curtains. Tom is the kind of man who has never wanted to do things the normal way.

If there was a great site, with play areas, and toilets and showers, and a shop, and the beach a foot from the step of the caravan, then we would NEVER be there.

We would instead be on slob lands at a wildfowl reserve in The Burrow with a gang of feral children and wild dogs. Or we would be behind a farmhouse in a field where the sons would glower at us from under their heavy dark fringes and make disparaging remarks about Townies. Or in the side of someones garden with an old whitewashed mine planted with geraniums.

Her ladyship stuck out like a sore thumb.

In almost every photo she looks like a boy as I never let her hair get overly long, preferring to keep it short and combed into a D.A. (Ducks Arse) It is weird that I always said D.A. because as a child I was nicknamed Duckarse from my little waddley walk when I told the lads at home I wanted to be a model when I grew up and they said not with that duckarse on you. Tom was called Dickett as a child because of the go of him, done up to the nines in his little suit, his kid gloves.

My siblings who were still at home, (there is 20 years between the oldest and youngest girl) also had their nicknames. "Key Hole Kate ", "The Long One", my brother who couldn't say Turnip was called "Tawnish ", the brother who loved trifle was called "Birds Custard" My brother with the sticky out ears was called "Handsome" or "Joe Scaff" when he was going through the worst of acne ridden puberty and the lad with the cromby coat was called "Girly"

My brother Seán was a barber in a town called Trim.

My brother Tom had a breakdown in London and came home to hospital.

When the Father took bad and needed minding, I brought her ladyship with me to Carlow, as she had been referred to by a sister in law on a long walk as a sticking plaster, and appeared loth to leave my side. This happened almost overnight, as she was normally as wild as a March hare, and now wanted to hold my hand everywhere. The roads were potholed and dug up, in winter locks of frozen water and gravel, in summer the tar bubbled and she stirred it with blackened lollipop sticks in the dead heat of an inland town, miles from the sea. I got lifts with a commercial traveller named Rossittor who sold minerals, and who would chain smoke **Sweet Afton** the whole way, the window open a bare crack as a nod to politeness and he would eyeball her ladyship in the rear view mirror as she made strangling noises.

"Is the child alright, missus" he would enquire while we were being overcome with the smell of fags and hair oil, sparse grey strands plastered to his head in shining waves. There was a sheen to the collar of his suit, flecks of dandruff speckling his shoulders. She would be *wake as a kitten* by the time we pulled into the crescent. My mother was still in the kitchen then and there would be a smell of gas from the Super Ser, and a spread laid out on the oilcloth of the kitchen table. At the kitchen tap geyser, a sister in law would be getting scalded washing willow pattern saucers, and another would be laying out plates of cooked meats and **Crotty's** white sliced, the bread so fresh and delicious, it was worth eating half a pan on its own, and being called "Murder the Loaf". There was always a jelly setting in a bowl on the pantry floor, and a tub of pouring cream on the shelf beside it. The vanity cabinet held shaving brushes and carbolic soap and I slid seamlessly back into the fabric of my home life as if I had never been away. We never went into overt public displays of affection, and rarely kissed or hugged but there was an affinity between us, and a way of carrying on a conversation as if it had been hours since we had met, instead of months.

There was an abundance of offerings on the altar of the long press, as each sibling brought in and laid down something for the house. A pound of cooked ham, brawn & hazlitt, a jam and cream sponge, tipsy cake, battenburg, gur cake, half a dozen bottles of stout, baby powers in brown paper bags, Corcorans Lemonade. On the wall above the window was a **Kellistown Meats & Poultry** Calendar.

Oliver Tawnish was at the table in shirtsleeves and braces pouring tea that would stand up by itself.

"You can always tell him that her ladyship was sick and you could not bring her back tonight" he says in a conversational undertone, which was not meant for her ears.

"I AM sick, anyway" she responded horsing into sponge cake, but not missing a trick, while we laughed.

The back door had a latch and everyone came and went all day and night by opening the link chain on the front gate, walking around the side and down the back steps. We knew who was coming by the sound of their shoes, the tips of the soles of Eugene Girly, with a Cromby coat shrugged around his shoulders and a red carnation in his pinstriped buttonhole. He had a cigar that always *seemed to be out and would say*

— Light, me Ollie as he came in.

For about 30 years he greeted her every single time with the same line - "Who burst your ball?"
— this relating to an incident where he punctured a soft ball that she was playing with, but which
event none of us could actually recall.

Eugene was called "Girly" by his siblings as his ablutions in the pantry took forever.

He laid out a selection of pomades, hair oils, after shaves and ties and despite the entreaties of
all who wanted to get in for a lick and a promise would take his sweet damn time about getting
himself perfect for the carousing he would later enjoy in the club. Everybody smoked. Even the
ashtray on the mantelpiece bore the legend —

"En fumant, pensez a moi."

In the shaded evenings I would stand in the front window and watch the children of the Crescent
playing heck-the-beds and skipping, their voices shrill in the sloping sun, and see her ladyship
sitting alone on the grass with a comic, smelling a laburnum leaf she had shredded with a
small thumbnail. She was a little old woman, leaning over the hedge chatting to Mrs Butler
and yoo hooing across to Mrs Farrell — (who had the only telephone in the street) hearing adult
conversations she had no business hearing and being brought everywhere we went, whether to
a Pattern in Killeshin where she danced across the graves on a day of inland heat where you
could have fried an egg on the stones, or to the club where she was ruined and gorged on bars of
Cadburys chocolate and bottles of minerals with a straw.

*When I took her downtown to **Haddens Café** for a banana boat, the entire town would smile*
and stop and say hello, and give her ten shillings or a kiss. In marked contrast to the exchange
between Tom's Aunt Nellie and a lighthouse keeper from The Old Head at Kinsale, who when
asked who the child belonged to replied "Tom's" and when pressed about whom Tom had married
replied-

"Tom married a stranger "

Summer 2014 - Year 9

For someone who could talk the hind leg off a statue I am finding it harder to communicate lately. I am answering questions with one word - a minor miracle – somebody ring the Vatican quick. It is too exhausting to explain. I wrote a piece recently called "**Do She know ya, hun**?" about the stereotypical question that people seem to find fascinating, as if this disease was comedic, or as if *THAT* was the worst possible scenario.

Oh, if only.

A brain affected by Alzheimers is like a kettle element covered in limescale. The plaque that coats the brain, piece by piece, closes down each part of the entire organ so that the memory shuts down. It does not mean that you have forgotten if it is Tuesday or Easter, or night or day, or put your shoes in the fridge- it means that you forget how to do *everything*. Remember, walk, talk, eat, swallow, open your bowels. Yep. I went there. The Nun with the white veil who has a Samsung Tablet asked me a mundane question this morning, something about weather, or aliens, or the third secret of Fatima - (I have no clue) - and I just stood blankly staring at her. I am a hamster on a wheel that knows it just has to keep running as there is nowhere to stop and scream.

Carpe Diem.

La vie est belle ...... awful, shocking, heartbreaking, messy, unfair, random, but beautiful. And short.

Be gentle with yourself says the woman from Las Vegas who wants to send me a silken poncho from her songbird cottage, as she draws on her eyebrows and reads about the Irish woman she will never meet.

October 2010 - Year 5

Tonight was like a scene from a Marx brother's movie in Siobhán's room.

The one where they are on a ship in a tiny cabin and people keep turning up with stuff - hard boiled eggs, shoeshine kits, manicures.

The only thing *not* in Siobhán's room was hard boiled eggs.

I brought fizzle sticks, chocolate, a Dictaphone, lucozade and roses.

The room which already contains an air bed, a Surita hoist, 2 armchairs, a footstool, Stephen Hawkings chair and a commode - (and where moving around becomes like a very advanced nerd-level of Tetris) had a parade of people too.

Because we have been there so long the staff has changed as much as the patients, we describe them to each other by whom they look like.

Thus the carers/ domestics / patients rejoice in the following descriptions

The blonde one with the eyes -

Amy Winehouse and Lindsay Lohan -

Michael Winner - Hairnet -

It all started when I went to get a vase.

I was breasted by a number of people en-route to the kitchen.

(It's a Dublin phrase for when people come up to you and press their chest against you to make their point)

and ended up having at least 19 separate conversations about life, death and the Universe.

When I got back to Siobhán I found not one, but 2 other patients sitting in the armchairs chilling with the TV.

One kept trying to return a book she has not borrowed and the other had his pants fall down down around his ankles as he tried to manoevure his zimmer through the furniture.

Then Michael Winner came in to ask could someone ring a hackney.

I gave anyone with teeth a walnut whip.

A tea trolley arrives and the girl who dispenses the beakers and plates of digestives.

Then, a nurse dispensing the evening medication arrives.

I am at this point melting, having been reversed into the scalding radiator.

The woman with the pale raisin eyes tells me she is afraid of the *darkness* and crippled by a fear of the *unknown.*

I wanted to be able to open an **I-pad** and show her the clips of *John O Donohue* lying on the

Cliffs of Moher, talking about facing the fears of the Universe and knowing we are eternal.
I wanted to paraphrase the tome that is *Moriarty's* **"Dreamtime"** down to one pithy beautiful line about *"standing Grand Canyon deep in the Karma of the Universe"* - I wanted to show this lovely little woman **Eckhart Tolle** holding an audience spellbound and hushed, as he explained about the presence being in the stillness and the silence and the *NOW*.
I wanted to show her the clip of the scientist *Jill Bolte Taylor* documenting her own stroke on **TED** and *feeling* the beautiful void as her consciousness shut down.
Instead I had to use words.
I thank God I was born into an era where people can open their minds before they make them up, and where they can access such beauty and wisdom in the click of a page.
Or else they can look at videos of cats playing the piano.
I hope the words I used were enough.

August 2011 - Year 6

Tonight I have mostly been behaving like Randall P. McMurphy in "One flew over the Cuckoo's nest". I marched into the nursing home with a 99 cone in a paper bag and a box of chocolates and set about causing my usual chaos
When I was a regular visitor in the hospital, I used to take it upon myself to do stuff to and for the long term patients that shared Siobháns ward for 7 months.
Oh you know , stuff - like going to the shop, or reading outrageous titbits from the paper, or washing and blow drying their hair –
(*YES, Nurse, I KNOW she is "assist by two" but there is only one of me*) –
A number of patients actually thought I was a hairdresser and would give me complicated instructions.
I had to inform them that I merely had a neck like a jockeys bollix and was only trying to help.
AND I did not charge - (well not after that perm went disasterously wrong anyway.)
On one occasion I was caught rapid by a team of consultants with an elderly lady as high up as the bed would go , laughing that she was on the *"hurdy gurdys in Tra - More"*.
Oh, what fun we had. I also played a lot of music and opened the windows as fast as the staff could close them.
I digress.
 Siobhán was being toileted when I arrived and so I sat on the armchair in the hall watching the ice-cream melt down the bag.
Dear reader, I am sure that by now you will understand that the temptation to try and move Siobhán in the Stephen Hawking chair proved too much and that when I had sated myself with ginger cake, we took off at a rate of knots down the hall.
I could barely navigate it out through the door.
After shaving a few dints into the woodwork and extricating the blanket from the wheels we resumed.

While Little Thomasina manfully played the violin at a gig for pensioners, I took over his shift and lined up a procession of lovely things on the padded armrest so I could throw the bowl of lukewarm gloop that comes on the tea tray down the toilet. Siobhán and I had a very chilled out afternoon, watching UTV, chewing gum for the brain, - soft northern accents and a programme about icing cakes, hat decoration and the series finale of Downton. Nothing too taxing as I was in the process of sewing buttons on a blanket. They were the exact buttons that Siobhán would have sorted and stored when she worked in Corrys with De Groot - (Wexfords answer to *Grace Brothers* where the staff wore green tweed suits and looked like Aer Lingus crew) - . I put the buttons in her hand and told her the story of how I have them. Instead of semolina she had trifle, instead of the apple sauce she had a tub of ice cream, instead of meds she had melted chocolate. And instead of tea in a beaker she had half a glass of ice cold coke.

And if Little Thomasina is reading this then I am officially killed.

I laid my knitting on her lap and told her what I am making and described the colours and ply of the wool.

Her eyes are usually closed

I watched the parade of Sunday afternoon visitors arriving wide eyed and awkward as they scan the dining room for their relatives and tried not to look shocked. The day room of any nursing home should be compulsory viewing for teenagers and makes people want to do cartwheels when they leave. An occupational therapist came to assess her today and so tonight she is in Stephen Hawkings chair - I gave her a thimble full of whiskey and left her listening to Mick Flannery singing about *Boston*.

There is not whiskey enough in this town for me.

Wexford Summer 1971

On Sunday mornings Tom and the children sing at home on the steps of the stairs like some demented Von Trapp family. He had an acoustic guitar with **Bob Dylan** carved into the body of it. For years, they thought he was a personal friend of their Dad's. He also had a 7" vinyl single he had recorded in a booth in Dublin with his name on it, with "The Big Rock Candy Mountain" on the A side "The Streets of Laredo" on the B side. They sat on intervening steps in height order, Tom at the bottom, balancing the guitar on one knee and leading the proceedings. Barty and herself sang **Bohemian Rhapsody** as their party piece, complete with all the high notes and sound effects. Nicola, the youngest with her Purdey hair cut sang Al Jolson numbers complete with jazz hands. If they were morto or the house was full, they would open the living room door and sing in the small space behind it so as not to be seen, the disembodied childish voices coming out from the crack while the adults listened and clapped. They sang Puff the Magic Dragon in the car on long journeys, never realizing it was about drug ingestion, and watched The Magic Roundabout where both the puppets AND their creators were out of their nuts on mind altering substances. She ate golf balls of chungum when we were not around as this was a banned substance. She used to pick it off the street with a penknife with a mother of pearl handle and chaw on the "gradgey" bits. It may have been this that made her sick, but she was a martyr to sore throats and coughs and would know she was about to start wheezing when her chin started to itch.

- The child is itching her chin again, get the stuff

The stuff was her Grandmothers antique inhaler, a contraption made of rubber and smoked glass which delivered a puff of medicine and dust after much assembly and tomfoolery. When, at one point, she had been itching and wheezing for a number of days, I brought her to the new Doctor at the bottom of the street who sent her to the old hospital to have her tonsils and adenoids removed. An ex-workhouse on a hill, it was run by Nuns, who never left hot water running or a sheet unturned but left a lot to be desired in their bedside manner. The ward sister took her details and watched as we fretted, placing crinkly cellophane bottles of Lucozade and soft jellies in her locker and then she summarily dismissed us so she could resume her reign of terror unchecked. She was stripped and hoyed into the small metal bed as quick as Johnny wrote the note. She lay very small and quiet in the high bed taking in her surroundings and trying not to cry to go home. The starched sister rustled over to her bed and produced a small white chamber pot from behind her back.

- Make water says she.

She drew a blank.

- MAKE Water!

    says she again louder as if it is her hearing that is suspect and not the command, and indicates the pot which she has placed in the middle of the floor, in full view of all the other beds, whose occupants alternately ignore or stare at her.

She was beside herself with frustration and self pity and began to bawl.

The Matron sighed and hung a **Nil by Mouth** sign over her bed and walked away. She squirmed down into the creaking bed with the rubber sheet and stared around at her fellow inmates. Directly facing her was a bed with white screens around it, bags of blood and fluids on stands beside it. This was the bed of a little girl who had been knocked down and driven over after walking out behind the Bingo Bus without looking. She never properly saw what was behind those screens which in many ways was worse, and became the stuff of nightmares for many years. She would get a glimpse of a swollen bloodied head, and a lot of bandages before the screens would be adjusted after the Doctors departure. Her visitors used to sing "Down by the banks of the Ohio" which she could never listen to again without thinking of her. At night, she could hear the injured child humming the chorus.

- "And only say that you'll be mine, in no other arms entwine – "

The seams in the corridor clicked rhythmicially as the metal trolley wheeled her down to theatre, a porter at her head and feet, pushing through the swing doors and into the tiled room with the bright lights that smelt of medicine and paint. There is a ring of masked heads upside down above hers and all is business. She was wearing a small paper gown and hat and was shocked to think people might see her in her nudiness. There are rows and rows of metal things laid out on trays. The Anaethetist is fiddling with the pressure gauge on the old upright cylinder and they try to put the big black mask over her face.

She fought like a mule.

In the end they held her hands and shoulders down and placed it across her nose and mouth and she tried and tried so hard to twist her head, to not breathe, to not think of the gas tap on the wall at home, to not think of home and with a last bursting lungful, she was under.

She woke vomiting blood and with the thirst of death on her and proceeded to drain the first of the *lucozade bottles. When the bed was awash with blood and lumps, they made her get out and stand by the side while it was re-made, and removed any liquids from the locker. She instantly made friends with a blonde child, and then drank a half bottle of hers. When the bed was in the same state again, the sheets were stripped and she was left lying on the rubber base.*

Hours later, when the tea trolley had passed her by and the bell rang for the visitors I flinched when I saw her as she spotted Tom and I coming in through the glass doors. Tom had the most amazing book under his arms. It was called "A Childs Compendium of Stories" about the size of a 1000 piece jigsaw, green, with beautiful illustrations, and perfect shiny pages, and she ran her little fingers across it in delightful anticipation of all the wonderful reading she would do, and how she would have a new story to read every night to the baby as she was surely getting bored of "Ukulele and her New Doll" by now. I was aghast at the state of her in the blood stained nightie. "Why is the child lying on a rubber mattress?" I enquired sharply of the Sister.

By the time the bell rang again, and she had been forcefully unwrapped from my neck, that book had been removed from her locker, placed on top of a high wardrobe, and it never came down no more.

October 2012 - Year 7

What was in you is now on you says the lonely Sioux Indian from the *Hunk Papa* tribe in South Dakota by email, as he criss-crosses the States in his truck, driving through Hollywood sunsets and technicolour dawns, writing songs in a **Walmart** notebook, stretching the photo of the knitted patchwork blanket bigger on his phone by the side of an endless dusty road in New Mexico, dreaming about buying a ranch.

On the morning of my birthday I met my Father for lunch.

It was the first one in 3 years that I did not spend sitting in a chair beside my Mother in her room.

And I missed it hugely.

It's a childhood nostalgic thing.

Yesterday, I was wrung out -   hips and bones aching.

I have become aware of a condition where you are incapable of masking feeling or emotion and can burst out in spontaneous bursts of crying –

Emotional Incontinence, like I need any more.

Ditto *"Ambiguous Loss"* where you grieve the loss of something not gone. It may explain the fact that I am now a fully fledged hermit.

And a recluse - and am seriously considering shopping online.

Everything seems unbearably poignant and I am snappy and exhausted and difficult to be around. (I can only conjecture as I am capable of *oscar* winning performances of hilarity)

Although as I type I am mellow/numb, quite peaceful. Maybe acceptance and surrender are the words I should be focusing on.

This tiny haven rescues me, and I spent last night slumped awkwardly watching TV - in a symbiotic gesture of co-dependancy.

Siobhán was in a deep heavy sleep.

The kind of sleep where your mouth ruffles and blows softly.

I sat and watched her for a while as I was wrecked and then snapped out of it and did the usual stuff, moving limbs and joints gently, rubbing feet before the donning of the massive pink furry moon boots I got for comfort and warmth.

She would always say " I just *can't* get the heat into my feet"

I reminded her of a story about being at the Twins 21st party in Kildare where my then lover was under orders to wear a long sleeved shirt to disguise his tattoo from the family.

The Football Club Bar where the party was at was like a cross between New Years Eve in Times Square and Croker on an ALL -Ireland Sunday.

The place was heaving.

My tattooed lover was sent to the bar by all the women.

He was weaving his way back through a scrum with 2 trays of pints, shorts and mixers (held aloft) begging everyones pardon in a thick Double Inn brogue, when a young lad from Prosperous charged into him headfirst.

Laughing boy lands on his back with a crash of glass, lying dazed and drenched amongst the fag butts and lemons, he is rescued by the barman - who gives him a "*Carlsberg*" t-shirt to cover his modesty that barely comes to his belly button - displaying his ink for the whole shooting match to see. He looked like an angry, camp Luke Kelly.

"*You can't bate a Clane woman and a Prosperous Man*" says I to Siobhán as I wipe her face and only realise she is laughing when I see her shoulders shaking.

Carlow Summer 1975

Girly had a pork butchers on *Tullow Street*, where he entertained the women with risqué jokes and an infectious laugh as he threw slices of crumbed ham and corned beef around the shop straight from the meat slicer, to whoever could catch them the fastest. Ollie took the children to the park, getting himself into a lather in case they crashed off the slide onto the tarmac underneath.

He fussed over them like a mother hen.

Summer or winter he wore the suit and braces, removing the coat only when the temperature soared. "Oh, it's savage today, fierce to the worlds end" he would complain as he dug away at the hard crumbly soil, or mowed the grass with the beads of sweat flying off his forehead, and a damp patch in the small of his back, his beloved rose bushes shedding soft scarlet and dusky pink petals, scenting the warm evening with their perfume. Ollie was a bachelor who loved his few bottles and attending funerals an hour before the mass started. He once drove away muttering and cursing without his siblings who had been up half the night toping and could not be roused from the beds they had collapsed into. Carlow must be the only town in Ireland where a surfeit of porter and a long life are described in cricketing terms.

"Begod and you'd a good innings last night" being remarked to a crawsick brother, and "Begod and he'd a good innings" as he blessed himself on hearing a 94 year old man had gone aloft. He worked as a pork butcher in Athy and being the only mankind left in the homeplace, had to care for the Father when he was in the grip of dementia.

Back then someone would be described as "gone a little bit senile".

Which may explain why he was found wandering on the train tracks in his pyjamas.

The child was more concerned that he might give out to her and bang his cutlery on the table and say in a loud voice, "Eat UP your dinner". He would enquire what book she was in, and she would look to me for clarity.

"He means what class"

"First" she said.

Oliver always had a procession of bangers that he drove around the county full to the gills of children and in laws. One scorcher of an afternoon we were heading out of Graiguecullen and up into the hills in a black Morris Minor to visit relations. Her ladyship was watching the grey road flow by under the car through a hole in the floor, a metal tool like a spanner inching closer and closer to the edge of the hole. In fascination she watched as each bump brought it nearer, till suddenly it fell out never to be seen again. She knew she should possibly have mentioned this at the time, but was beginning to exhibit traces of boldness, which would evolve into being called a scourge and a rip by frustrated adults in the future.

Richie and Nellie were my cousins who lived on a farm in Killeshin which was known to all and sundry as the Hill. Just when you thought the eyes might burst out of your head and you had to yawn to pop your ears on the steep drive in the groaning car, we turned left and went back on ourselves downhill to where the house was nestled under an overhang. The view from the back door was spectacular and panoramic, and the cousins swore you could see 5 counties on a clear day. Someone built a hotel with that name and the same claim. We were too busy negotiating the stringy collie dogs and the hens with murderous eyes and claws to appreciate the view and would run from the car to the sanctuary of the shaded kitchen. Nellie had a voice like human sandpaper and wore a navy house coat sprigged with white flowers as she mashed tea and cut up brack and scones. We sat around the giant Welsh dresser, under its assortment of painted china plates, souvenirs and gifts from Blackpool and Lourdes. Richie had a massive pair of hands and walked the land whistling, the dogs at his feet and he shouted at the hurling on the radio, his ham hands hanging on his knees as with bent head all the better to listen, he roared "drive it in boys" and went to mass and confession in his good suit. Nellie wore a Mantilla and a Navy Crimplene suit when she went to church with her brother.

They were great people for the devotions as their sisters were Nuns called Mercedes and Cathaldus, whose given names were Noreen and May. My cousin May has been a professed nun for 78 years now and is almost 100.

We took our leave that day armed with soda bread and eggs with henshit on them, wrapped in newspaper and it was trying to get back that the loss of the tool became apparent. The car stalled at a crossroads, Oliver standing at the open boot scratching his head.

"Name of Goddle Mighty, where is the cursed Jack?"

It was to be all shoulders to the wheel when she piped up and informed of its whereabouts and Olivers face turned purple.

"Jazus, that's fierce to the world" said he as he panted up and down the road looking in the ditches. We were heroically pushing the car off the crossroads when we spotted a man lying up against one of the road signs, fiddling with himself.

She had finally seen a Booshey Man and was told to get in the car quick and we chugged off with a spluttering engine and picked up speed going downhill. We were in the higs.

"Who the hell was that" I said turning around as the man casually saluted us with his free hand. "Paddy Matthis" said Oliver. "He's soft in the head".

When we got back to the Crescent Mrs Butler was out clipping her perfect box hedge and called the child over for news. She proceeded to tell her in detail about Paddy Matthis and what he was up to until I had to intervene in her prating, and took her by the hand and brought her inside hurriedly, apologising.

"Get her IN "says Oliver wiping his forehead with a polka dot square.

When my parents were 50 years married, they called their Matron of Honour, Best Man and the Priest who married them, ordered a horse and trap – as they had the first time – and booked an Anniversary Party in The Towers of Ducketts Grove. The place was packed to the rafters and there was great applause when the trap came clip clopping up the drive. After the meal and speeches the party was in full swing and noble calls were being asked of everyone, and the cry went up for Tom Mahon of Wexford for a song. Tom Mahon of Wexford could certainly carry a tune and was a great singer with a vast repertoire but was painfully shy when asked to perform. He will sing and laugh and tell jokes all night, each better than the last, but God forbid he should have a spotlight shone on him.

He stood on the stage and messed around with the mike for a while, and then finally, inspired called upon his small daughter to come to the rescue and duet with him.

They sang **"Peggy Gordon"** which is an old Irish song about a lovesick alcoholic singing to a woman who is ignoring him. It went down a treat, as did the encores, and he was only getting into his stride - about 6 songs in- when the band came back after scourging their dinner in the interval. She was being passed across heads and toted about the place like a talisman, fed to the back teeth with sweets and crisps.

I never forgot the pair of them singing that song.

- **"Oh Peggy Gordon, you are my darling, come sit you down upon my knee,**
  And tell to me, the very reason, why I am slighted so by thee"

Christmas 2011 - Year 6

Siobhán is in a medical electrical recliner now so we can raise and elevate her legs which were very swollen and lay her neck back which was extremely stiff. She is layered with air cushions and soft throws, and is still listening to the voices around her which I try to make John Creedons' or something beautiful from lyric or Radió Na Ghealtacht - gave her half an inch of a half one earlier as I thought it would aid sleep and put hair on her chest, Nice warm room with views of a purple sky and a scented candle of forest berry, lemongrass burning on the window sill amongst the green plants that my Father will not water.

I feel I cannot be trusted to speak now, as if one word comes out I will rant and rave and foam at the mouth until I fall over like an empty sack.

I am woman, hear me roar.

Yesterday every bone ached and I was dragging myself around like a sack of spuds.

Today I am just like ten bastards.

Have not left the building and am behaving as if it is Stephens Day, wandering around the house in pyjamas, looking in the fridge every half an hour (nothing has changed) and trying to stay warm. The blue of the sky in the kitchen skylight has been mocking me and calling me out to play.

On paper, there is nothing really *wrong* with me. But on my list, I have the following

A headache

an earache,

a pain in several teeth,

exhausted,

moody,

depressed,

nostalgic,

starving (but not even bothered to eat)

and in a mood where my Dad would say -

"Leave her alone, she could chop straws with her arse today"

I know these lows are cyclical, and that I will be grand by tomorrow, but they are so frustrating as I can't seem to get motivated. I lay down on the couch earlier wrapped in a woolen quilt and listened to the sounds of the shoes going past the window, and tried to make up lives for the faceless feet. Then I got bored counting my breaths and trying to calm my thoughts, and cooked a heap of pies - (which I then forced into my nephews schoolbag despite his protestations that he is not allowed to have 2 dinners)

I knew a man once that ate 2 dinners every day.

Wexford 1975

*S*teptoe and Son were trickacting around the streets of London with their horse and trap, Leonard Rossittor was trying to screw his tenants, seduce Miss Jones and deal with Rising Damp. Wanderley Wagon was on RTE with Judge, O Brien, The Crow, Forty Coats and Slightly Bonkers. In the States Cannon could hardly get out of an armchair, McCloud was riding down 5th Avenue on horseback with a Stetson, Macmillan and Wife were crime busting, Columbo was gesticulating in his dirty Mac and Caligula was disemboweling pregnant mothers in a bacchanalian orgy of blood letting.

So we turned over to The Riordains in Leestown.

John Cowley was saying Grand Cake Nora and teasing Minnie about her hair. Benjy was having a breakdown by a broke down Tractor and promising strangers he would buy them a packet of mints, and Tom was up and down like a dog at a fair changing the channel manually as it would be another decade before a remote was invented. Nobody had a video recorder in their house and instead went to a local store to hire both the film and the equipment to play it on. It cost a king's ransom and meant half the street came in to watch "Close Encounters of the Third Kind" or "A Clockwork Orange"

Due to her sparkling evereffescent personality she was picked to play one of the babes in the eponymous woods in the Pantomime and she could hear Barty crying from the balcony when the wicked witch caught them. She had the privelege of dousing the male leads with a balloon full of water during one act.

Fill it up hun, says one of them - I have a head on me tonight that would kill a bull after last nights gallivanting.

She was complicit with the audience, gurning into the dark, sighing and blowing her fringe off her forehead and at an eventful matinee , handing back the plastic leaves that were supposed to be strewn over the sleeping babes, to a distraught child who had run out of hers and was miming the throwing. When the final curtain call came down on the last night the entire cast and chorus and choreographer came out on stage to take their bows. She waited for Hansel to come from the opposite wing and pausing longer than a Kardashian at a mirror, milked it until they could run out on stage hand in hand to roars from the crowd.

The canteen in the parish hall smelt of egg and onion sandwiches and stewed tea and was full to the gállyogues at the interval where she liked to wander around as if she was looking for someone, wearing full make -up and her costume - to show off.

Pssst says the Principal Dame from the stage door.

- Come back in here and don't break the spell for them.

Due to nervous tension and adrenaline by the time it was all over - rehearsals, shows and after parties —she was wrung out as a dishcloth, and would have to repair to the bed with a stye the size of a gobstopper on her left eye. She was like a sponge left out on a windowsill in torrential rain.

An hour later she would be mooching around the kitchen with a cold tea bag held to the offending eye, rooting in the fridge to see what she could reward herself with, and at this time began to hide food, leaving the crusts of sandwiches and apple cores under her bed, chocolate wrappers behind the radiator, sneaking upstairs with chips to eat alone.

We could smell the vinegar all over the house while she scourged them in the bed.

Her proximity to the aforementioned teabag was not to be sniffed at, as she was engaged in full scale war with Tom over her point blank refusal to consume any of same.

It became a battle of wills.

"You are not getting down from this table till you drink it" he would say, opening the paper.

"No way" she responded.

"Did you put butter on this radio?" said Tom lowering the Papal Peeper and gazing in disbelief at the dials that said **Hilversum Budapest** and **Prague** and which were covered with oily swirls.

NO she shouted.

I had watched her do it.

Long after everyone else had gone she was still sitting sulkily at the table plotting murderously to ring the cruelty man and tell on us. There could not have been a worse treated child in all of Ireland to her mind, and she stared at the cold milky tea in loathing

- "Drink a sup of it, hun" I would whisper. "You need a hot drink for your chest."

The night before her Communion, I had to kneel down with a measuring tape to take in her dress AGAIN.

"That one is no bigger than a God's cow" I mumbled through a mouthful of pins.

She was well used to standing or being turned or pulled this way and that as no amount of her huffing and sighing was going to stop me dressmaking or entering her into **Make & Model** competitions where she wore primrose yellow cotton dresses with a ring of daisys on the collar and armholes. Tom and I went to the Fancy Dress Ball when we were engaged, dressed as **Miss Wexford** and **Billy Bunter**.

Tom won first prize as **Miss Wexford**.

On that night he was supposed to be calling the bingo in the C.Y.M.S. but had let them know he was not well. News filtered back via a passing reveler, and one of the lads announced that the compere was after winning Miss Wexford in the Parish Hall Fancy Dress to hooting and cheering. I thought it was a great idea and very pertinent to send the child to the same fancy dress in a black plastic bag as **Article 42**. Of course it was won by an angelic Shirley Temple lookalike with sausage ringlets and a cloud of netting and lace who had a hand written sign around her neck saying "I'm forever blowing bubbles" and also a bubble kit and dispenser which she used to charm the crowd and the judges, blowing a soft ring of multicoloured orbs all over the table.

Her ladyship and her black plastic sack crinkled their way away and hid up the back, only emerging looking all gommy when she was awarded a foil wrapped gift as most topical entrant. All of the women were wearing coats inside, Poplin Mac's, Gaberdines, Tweeds, topped off with a headscarf to preserve either their set or their modesty.

I look like I was dragged through a hedge backwards says one to another as she tied and re-tied the scarf.

"I'm a holy show I'm like the wreck of the Hesperus without a screed of make-up on me" says another.

"They're giving it to lash tonight" says her friend folding her plump arms contentedly in anticipation of a night beside the fire watching a pitcher with a woman in it.

-   "Oh, Lort hun, I couldn't watch a pitcher without a woman in it".

By the time Tom and the scourge had their Mexican stand off by the greasy radio, neither giving an inch, the sky would be the colour of the cold tea in the blue striped mug.

She has not drunk tea OR milk from that day to this.

A Nun had placed her name in **The Far East** pen pal corner and so it came to pass that our letter box became as expectant as a Corinthians. She was writing to children all over the world, as well as Waterford, Dublin, and Meath and recording her daily thoughts and what she watched on TV in a hardbacked linen canary yellow diary.

"My Mother is a house wife" being the stock response from Carnesore to Korea, her Australian pal wrote endless reams on tissue thin paper about her pets and animals in Adelaide, her French pal about her life in Paris, her broken English delightful and hilarious by turns. She also had an admirer from Ballivor who entreated her regularly for a photograph or a sketch of her hair. She described herself in every letter as being small, with brown hair and green eyes. He wrote for years until a woman appeared on the scene who not being much of a writer - read him the Riot Act instead - whereupon Goodbye was all he wrote. Her Korean pal sent dolls and souvenirs and intricate ink sketches, her brother promptly responding to one of their more spectacular rows by bashing in the pale painted cheeks of the coiffured girl in national dress with the drum around her neck.

He also threw darts at her posters, mostly of Leif Garret and John Travolta.

It was around this time - as she devoured every book that came her way, moving from Enid Blyton through Richmal Crompton and then lashing straight into Edna O Brien and Christy O Connor – **The Country Girls** and **Down all the days** (part of the stash of banned books that lay under my side of the mattress that she had excavated rooting) I only caught her out when she started turning down the pages of where she had read to before she put them back. She had read **The Girl with Green eyes** and **The Love Object** before she hit double digits. She constructed an elaborate colour coded diary/aide de memoir system that hung on the back of her bedroom door. It had a series of dots, asterisks and squiggles that judged and calibrated her moods and whether it was a good or bad day by the size of the black circles. One would have needed the Enigma Machine to de-code it and it appears she often had problems herself. She spent an inordinate amount of time alone, reading or alternately throwing herself sulkily around the room in a fit of temper or crushing ennui. She became convinced she was massive and that she should get a job as a fat lady in a circus. It began when we were at the Strawberry Fair and a passing famer complimented me on my first born by commenting

    – "She's a fine lump of a child, Missus" and she bent her head against the glass of the car
        window and cried all the way home.

Little Mrs Up and Down was used to being told there was always either an arse or an elbow on her, and that she would rise a row in a barrack of soldiers.

She could never bite her tongue or let the hare sit.

  Plaster would fall from the ceiling, and paint from the door frames as she slammed and bashed around the house and ran up 3 flights of stairs to hurl herself on the bed. Herself and Tom would go toe to toe about the least little thing and I would beg them to consider the neighbours when the shouting started.

Neither would give an inch or the last word.

"You two are lick alike" I remarked and sighed as I washed up and dried them out of it.

He who washes up does the pots.

He who pays the piper calls the tune.

"As long as you're under my roof, you'll do as you're told, and less of your lip" Tom shouted up the stairs while I intoned "anything for a peaceful life" under my breath.

Spring 2012 - Year 7

I recently described how this disease impacts on family as being like a pilot over Heathrow waiting to land –

"in a holding pattern of grief" –

I am alternately numb or outraged.

Nothing makes me really laugh, but thankfully nothing makes me really cry.

Feel have detached from life and am viewing it as a partisan observer.

The Witness.

Siobhán has had a good week and has had her eyes open.

Thank Christ.

I am not exactly jumping up and down.

No matter how much I love you, and your company, there are times lately where I would rather eat my own foot than engage. If you see me in various cafes with my grey rooted head bent over a book then for the love of all that is good and holy walk on by.

I hope to return to normal service asap or as soon as I

a/ get a grip -

b/ stop taking the tablets

c/ get a kick in the swiss.

People when they ask about Mam always say the same thing -

"*Do She know ya hun?*"

The tiny things we take for granted like drinking, eating, scratching your own nose, cleaning your teeth are all a distant memory.

Siobhán is now slumped on an air cushion, swollen with meds and no movement, with no speech, spoon fed, in a nappy, with one tooth left as the rest rotted away.

Know me?

I like to think she has an awareness that the women moving and lifting her are her daughters. I like to think she knows the one burning the incense and singing is Me, and the one massaging her feet and cutting her toenails is my Sister.

I like to think she knows that the man feeding and wiping her chin is her beloved husband of 50 years. I like to think this as it keeps me from hurling myself over the bridge.

Once upon a time when I was heartsick and sore and generally feeling out of sorts with the world, and most especially my SELF - my Mother handed me a piece of paper. The title on it was "***How to find Peace***".

At the time being possessed of no more clarity than I was "*peace*" I stuffed it into one of a thousand places where I keep things.

They all end up in a multitude of scraps of paper, notes, beer mats, fag packets and hotel napkins - all scrawled with notes and telephone numbers - and which are thus transported from home to home and country to country, dwelling in the bottom of rucksacks, suitcases, satchels and handbags.

When I moved in to this tiny house, I rescued it from the place it had lain undiscovered and unread for years. I use the term unread loosely as there was a cigarette burn through the "e" of Peace.

My higher self may have read it.

I could not.

It has been propped on a mirrored shelf with photos of Siobhán, and other priceless things - a beautiful print of a naked woman wrapped in a golden silk shawl my aunt had above her bed, a silver cigarette case and holder, a miniscule wind-up ghost, a pair of tiny leather hand stitched dolls shoes I bought in Spain, a lock of my Mothers hair in a glass bowl.

I often wonder how Siobhán dealt with the enormity of her first born, the drama, the hysteria, the mania. How far removed she was from the bawling, cackling, wild eyed child she had birthed. A woman who believed that you held your head high and quietly, and did your crying at home behind closed doors.

Tonight, I read the page.

I share with you here the message.

"*There is such a thing as peace.*

It may be felt and known. My hearts desire and prayer for you is that you may be able to say I have peace. This peace is a calm, intelligent sense of friendship with the energy of the Universe. He that feels it, feels no barrier, no separation between himself and the Creator. Such a man can see death waiting for him, and yet not be greatly moved. He can go down into the cold river, close his eyes on all that he has, and has known on earth, launch forth into a world unknown, and yet feel peace.

It is the want of this very peace that makes many in the world unhappy. Millions have everything that is thought to be able to bring pleasure, and yet are never satisfied. Their hearts are always aching. There is a constant sense of emptiness within. They have no peace.

He that knows peace from within can lie down in the silent grave, and yet feel calm. Such a man can think of Eternity and not be greatly moved. He can see in his minds eye the assembled masses of the world, the open books, the listening angels, and an all seeing presence and finally know the peace that passeth all understanding. "

Dad had his eye "*procedure*" on Tuesday morning - (eyelid lifted and stitched) - and has been sitting at home since like the "*Phantom of the Opera*" - with a massive white bandage obscuring half his face.

We have ascertained the amount of fuel/food in the house, and I have been ferrying toasted sandwiches, mince pies, apple tarts and daily copies of *The Times* to his armchair. He is esconsced watching the snooker with the remote and his mobile beside his landline and the panic button.

He was asked the other day (as he has been for the last 4 years) what clothes will be left out for Siobhán on Christmas Day.

"The girls will do that" says he.

He was also asked would he like to have dinner there himself. Then he was asked if Siobhán would be taken out.

-    "OUT - How?" says he.

We used to take her out.

Well, mostly my sister and I.

Against his wishes and without his permission, I have pulled and dragged her out of chairs and beds and carried her to cars and taxis and taken her *OUT*.

To fields - to beaches - to water.

We caused consternation once on a manic beach that looked like Coney Island on the 4th July as I pulled this lady up through the dunes wearing a pyjamas, a nappy and an ankle tag.

This was when she was in the hospital and while they thought we were sitting on the bench outside eating *Icebergers* and watching the world.

It was a pleasure to drag my Mother through the soft sand, to see her stand at the waters edge as the foam drenched her slippers, my sister and I on either side holding her,

the Trinity of us reflected in the late evening sun.

Little Thomasina would have had a canary.

He has always been a follower of rules, the antithesis of his eldest child who is an inveterate breaker of same.

He does not like to "rock the boat" - it is my favourite pastime, apparently

Siobhán, when she would see me slumped in an armchair huffing and sighing that I was "bored" would respond –

"*Be active, be alive, get some air into your lungs, do a few physical jerks, shake the cobwebs off yourself*".

I have always loved water, and being near it, as has she.

Being from an inland town where their only water was *The Barrow* Siobhán spent many a happy hour with her siblings mucking about on the river.

There are fat green strawberries growing on the window sill in the baking sun. The dry heat from the radiator underneath has made the clay as fine and powdery as sand. I use the stale water from the untouched water jug to drench the parched leaves. The room is full today. There is a proliferation of bodies and bags nestled together on the bed. Half cups of tea and melted biscuits are dotted around the floor.

It is a pilgrimage.

My Handsome Uncle is having treatment for cancer but it is never referred to, rarely if ever mentioned, as if to do so would give creedance to the unnamed. He leans forward on the bed with the cup balanced on his knee, steadied by his large hand.

His suit is hanging from him.

He is the historian, the keeper of the archive, the holder of the information gleaned from narrative, recall and the still youthful faces in grainy sepia photographs. He has documented and collected the memories of his family for generations. His wife has put another dark rinse in her cropped hair and her white roots have turned burnt umber along the scalp and at the temples.

The sallow face at the door is lined and creased like a soft brown paper bag that has been folded and refolded many times. *Handsome* tells a story of them as children on bicycles out on the Barrow path on a summers evening.

Rounding a corner at the rivers edge cycling three abreast they had collided with an elderly gentleman taking a refined constitutional.

"We took the two shins off him with the pedals"

In an apolexy of pain and indignation he had taken to his heels and with coat tails flying beat a path across the railway tracks to their family home where he had literally danced up the path and stood hopping and cursing at the front door. He complained bitterly and at length and with such profanity that a very timid ladylike neighbour had been forced to pop her head out the top window next door and enquire

-   *Excuse me, Mrs Dooley, who's doing all the "fucking" out here?*

My sister and I exchange a look over our Mothers head.

We are looking at a deep indentation at the base of her thumb.

"This is new."

-Its called a *snuff* spot for obvious reasons.

Her voice tails off.

She is tired today.

Tired of treading water and wondering how many more surprises are in store for us.

We can do without surprises now.

We work as a double act, one holding the glass and one wiping the liquid that seeps out the side of Siobháns lips. There is jazz on the radio and candles burning in the window sill. The sky has darkened and is swollen and tumescent with the promise of rain. Clouds are scudding across the almost full moon and a single star is shining like a satellite.

It's wrong to wish on space hardware

In the dining room the red faced kitchen assistant pushes the old priest closer to the table so that his shaking hands can find the buttered bread.

"*Fawder, you're nearly in the far field*" she exclaims as she removes the cling film from the slices of ham and tomato.

At the assisted feeds table the women in their bibs wait to be fed their bowls of mush. The first time I wheeled her in there wearing the giant blue bib I had to be taken out by the fountain to have a cigarette and a cry. I feel more and more like **Randall P. McMurphy** and fear that one day I may actually charter a bus and take the whole damn lot of them *OUT* fishing or drinking, or both.

A wheelchair accessible bus has been booked for Christmas Morning despite the fact that I have been informed the Stephen Hawking chair will not fit through the doors but I replied "I don't care if it's like "*Weekend at Bernie's*" I will do it or die trying"

As she has said of me more than once –

"*That one would rise a row in a barrack of Soldiers.*"

Wexford 1979

*T*he Brother and her ladyship had their moments too. They had bedrooms on the third floor and would often be caught gatching around or messing on the landing when they should have been saying their prayers or in bed fast asleep. It was only when they could hear their Da take the stairs 3 at a time in his haste to get up and box their ears that the brother would relax his half nelson stranglehold on her - his tongue stuck out in concentration - and retreat to his man cave where he listened to Radio Luxembourg under the cheesey pong of his quilt. It was from this activity that he learned that it **WAS** in fact New Years Eve and not the night before (as they had been assured by their suspiciously fragrant parents as we left for a night out) and they listened to the countdown in wide eyed disbelief. I left her ladyship in charge of both siblings and she would be in an agony of delight at having the armchair and the fire to herself whilst consuming biscuits. Barty would arrive down as soon as he heard the front door softly click and assume his position in the other chair and demand the remote, the biscuits or both.

"You're as safe as a house on fire" I said while she gave me the hairy eyeball and a quivering lip. After she had checked to see the baby was fast asleep on her back and not smothered to death by the layers of foxford blankets, she would stand at my wardrobe inhaling the soft folds of the dresses and skirts , and imagining nightmare scenarios where we perished in fire or flood and she had to take over the running of the house.

According to her baby sister, she was an outrageous older sibling and spent days and nights tormenting her with a flat face doll named Roberta, locking her in wardrobes wherein she developed a lifelong phobia of enclosed spaces, and teaching our Maltese Terrier Midge how to become rabid by playing a game she invented called "Calm the Tiger" where she teased him to the point of madness where he was almost foaming at the mouth in temper and then tried to placate him with hugs and petting. Never was a pet more loved.

Or teased.

Midge thought he was a cat and had as many lives.

He was a small white ball of fluff with button black eyes, a pedigree show dog that we never showed. Keeping his hair out of his face (with a tiny bow) and keeping the tangles out of his *fur were a full time job, and one that was destined to be undertaken by me alone, despite their reassurances to the contrary when he was first mooted. In the bath, he whimpered and howled looking like a drowned rat or a gremlin as he tried to claw his way up the porcelain, his hair flattened on his walnut head and his eyes looking sideways like a terrified horse as his nails tried and failed to find purchase. I excelled at wrapping him up like a parcel in a towel that was supposed to be the Dog Towel, but which in reality was the closest to her hand. Then I handed over the reluctant pet to be towel dried of "the heavy wet "on a lap and then blowdried with a pale pink Pifco hair dryer,*

*They always swore they would look after whatever pet they were angling for, but never did. They had a Gerbil called Herbie she bought in Colman Doyles who ran around and around in a **Dunnes** box, emitting high pitched shrieks and filling up his bedding with pellets of poo. He died casually one afternoon and Tom wrapped him tightly in a plastic bag and laid him on top of the bin, where she found him by accident and got hysterical, as per.*

Match her better she would be saying her prayers.

September 2013 - Year 8

Mam is on an anti-biotic along with Alzheimers, Osteoporosis and Parkinsons meds. A lovely Night Nurse had a chat with me and said Siobhán is not inclined to take it in the morning.

(It is crushed in porridge)

I said Siobhán is a night owl like myself and to throw the rule book in the bin and think outside the box.

How would you like to be woken at half six to eat manky porridge with chalky grains in it? I asked.

She also explained how many times she is turned during the night and what the general nursing practices are.

She re-assured me about things I was unaware of not being worried about.

And then told me that one morning about a month ago she went in to open the curtains and said "Good Morning, Siobhán" always to silence but on *this* morning as she reached for the curtain a voice from the bed said –

"What the hell are you doing?"

I was unaware that tears were rolling down my face. To her credit, she did not bolt for the door, or fob me off with bullshit and platitudes but calmly and rationally let me vent. I explained that I had been numb but hearing that she had spoken was beautiful.

And even sadder that I cannot remember what her voice was like.

She told me to keep writing and talking about this as it may bring some help to some craythur who is reading it. I had described to someone once how this disease is like a Christmas Tree with all the lights winking out - one by one - and how sometimes there is a power surge and there is a moment of lucidity, clarity, or recall.

It is the one moment that we are all waiting for.

The Nurse puts the keys of the locker back in her pocket and says -

"It is the Miracle your Da is waiting for"

I put my head down on Siobháns shoulder and sobbed to know she is *still* inside, and listening.

She has the patience of a saint. The only form of communication left is non-verbal.

It is a gentle plucking of the blanket around her legs with the thumb and first 2 fingers of her right hand.

I watch for this the way a twitcher would wait for a rare bird.

I scan her closed eyelids to see if there is a flicker of the tiniest of muscles to indicate if there is anything I can do for her.

If there is an itch I could scratch for instance.

Or a position I could haul her into that would be a tad more comfortable.

I hold her hand gently and ask her to press mine to indicate an answer to various yes/no questions.

I wait for the softest of gentle pressings but I wait in vain.

As I kiss her goodbye I tell her I am going to write her story, and all the other things I said I would write.

This woman has been keeping everything I ever wrote since I was a small child. The gift she keeps giving me is the bagfuls and folders full of stuff that my Dad drops over to me on a weekly basis.

"Here's more of your stuff that Mam kept" he will say while I take it away to put in the pile of *"Mustsortsoonstuff"* trying to swallow the lump in my throat.

I put on my best *"Carla"* accent as I was leaving and I swear she smiled.

August 2011 - Year 6

Tonight as I sat in her darkened room, lit only with fairy lights and candles, rubbing Siobhán's hand where she had a ring cut off today, I reminded her of an episode of my childhood. It is all I can do to prompt the vast recall of memory that entwines us.

And so I talk of old times, and times past and they come blushing in, tippytoeing like a ballerina on point, afraid to break the hush.

The soundtrack of my Mother's life now is her daughter's voice.

The room she lives in is silent.

Apart from the steady thrum of machinery into her electric air bed and the faint voices permanently calling from the halls

For tea,

For a nurse,

For Bridie.

One evening in late summer I sat by the open window listening to the water trickling down the fountain in the garden and heard the plaintive sounds of singing coming from the sun room.

One elderly man had begun to softly sing a snatch of a song, one no doubt he had often sung in happier times and his chorus was picked up, first tentatively and then surer - the gentle voices rising and dipping in a faint reedy choir. The Palestrina Boys Choir is made up of young boys with high soprano voices - young adolescents their voices thin and high with an average age of 9 -12.

The combined age of the people singing here was over the thousand mark.

Enclosed nuns singing the *Magnificat* quietly as they observe their perpetual adoration on red velvet kneelers could not have sung sweeter.

Monks chanting *"Om mahne pehme hung"* draped in their saffron robes could not have been more connected.

There was a magic about those voices and the recall of the familiar words brought comfort.

Like a Muzzein being called from a rooftop spire across waves of misty heat

I looked wistfully at the dictaphone on the air cushion and cursed the fact I had not more cassettes.

When I was a small child I visited my Nana Dooley in Carlow and always slept in the same double bed as my Mam - she was caring for her own Mother at the time. All of the children - siblings and cousins - were as familiar with the geography of this room as I - Her own Mam sleeping in the other double bed across the chimney breast where all I could see of her was a bump in the blankets and the small hills of her feet.

She and I went to bed at the same time.

Margaret Dooley nee Kennedy from Gowran was a gentle woman exhausted from birthing a dozen children and the ridiculous amount of grandchildren that would be perched at any one time in the house.She was quiet and always in a good mood, and had a silent sideways laugh. Her bed was at the back window overlooking her roses and knowing who was downstairs *"Toping"* by the rattle of the latch. Me, at the front window, overlooking the houses and children allowed out still to play "Heck-the-beds", and in the gap at the corner of the crescent - the railway tracks that all night had a syncopated che /che che/ che soundtrack as they carried people and goods to Naas, Newbridge, Kildare Town, Leixlip, Maynooth and on into Dublin.

There was always the sound of a solitary dog howling like a coyote.

The room I lay in smelt of carbolic soap, and *Dettol*, and sometimes the commode. Lying in the dark- staring at the framed picture of the Sacred Heart permanently displaying his injury lit by a tiny flame - listening to the voices of the adults downstairs was anathaema to me. I wanted to be down there in the fog of smoke and laughter, drinking club orange and eating all the chocolate rings out of the tins of *USA Assorted*

Or maybe given a pound after bouncing on a drunken Uncles lap and asked to sing a *yella belly* song for them.

I wanted my Mam more.

Of course I played to the gallery, and it was only on very rare occasions that I would open the door to the stairs and sing from behind it.

One morning as she dressed hurriedly in the dim room I sat up and whispered

- Where are you going?
- Whisht - says she rolling up her tights
- I am running down to first mass in the Cathedal, I won't be long.
  I flung the covers off me and began to dress
- I'm coming.

Despite her protestations I accompanied her through the quiet grey Sunday morning streets, with the curtains closed the length of the Crescent, down the Staplestown Road and into the massive Cathedral.

There too, the choir of old women with purple perms was faintly heard - balanced high on their forbidding platform - and the sound of the organist and the combined voices made me turn to face them despite the disapproving glances of the pensioners in their black mantillas

On our way home Siobhán took me into *McDarby's* and bought the biggest cornet with a flake they sold. It had pink ice cream that tasted like medicine.

- This little madam had no breakfast and I'm afraid she might take a weakness on me" she explained.

I reminded her of this tonight and she listened carefully, her head bent to one side like a robin on a Christmas card.

It is all she can do. She is my confessor, my best pal, my Mother.

My voice has *ALWAYS* been the soundtrack of her life.

January 2014 - Year 9

Another Comedy of Errors played out tonight with yours truly as warm-up, stand-up, support, headliner and fat lady singing.

Did I mention we killed a phantom dog?

It was blowing a hooley with that lovely fine sleet that soaks you right through. I am giving it loads in the car and trying to manoevure the shopping, bunches of carnations , Tuc crackers, a block of cheese and chives and a chocolate orange around the front seat while attempting to smoke, fasten my seat belt, open the window and put on my coat.

When this driver and I get together on a Wednesday we have a pissing contest about who had the worst week, and there is a litany of complaints, medications and war stories swapped.

I was in full flow of a diatribe about how every call I took this week was from someone

A/ depressed

B/ more depressed

C/ At the end of their tether

and a panorama of people who had a pain in their head, chest, stomach, legs or arse.

And some with all 5

(Take a bow, Thomasina)

Out on the Newtown road just as the lighting goes from sodium orange to deepest pitch a flash of white bolted from a gate.

"Jesus h Christ" I shouted as she slammed on the brakes and I head butted the dash –

"We've druv over an effin' dog" -

In her excitement the driver turned off the engine and left us in what the Dulux colour chart would call "Country Black" (which is fine if you are a goth OR a jobbing vampire but not in heavy traffic on the **N25**).

"In the name of God and all his angels will you turn on the lights and the hazards before we are rear-ended and killed" I screeched.

I flung open the door in the gale and was tiptoeing back down the road to find the pooch in a tangle of matted fur, collar and Burberry coat.

Nada.

I bent down gingerly and tried to see if it was "under" the engine or wrapped around a wheel.

Nada.

The driver was rooting in the glove and produces a tiny torch.

Oh. My. God.

"I'll look then will I? I enquired while she was speedily closing the window.

I lay down on the road.

Did I mention I got my hair done today?

I looked under the car.

Nada.

I did lose the cheese knife though.

On the way back at the exact same spot a car was parked with its hazards on and its doors open.

"Ha, do you suppose they have a clock work dog on a string? Like the way people used to put fivers on catgut? "I asked

She laughed so much a cyclist had to swerve into a ditch.

I left Siobhán with red cheeks from a Cappuccino with Baileys in it and red ears from my nonsense.

December 2013 - Year 8

There is a smell of baking in the Home tonight and a hand written sign that says what date it is.

"*8 days till Christmas*" is written in brackets underneath it.

Because I have been out there so long and so frequently I am as invisible as the pictures on the walls.

I come and go.

I come and go.

I come and go.

It occurred to me one night recently that I have been there longer than most of the staff and the original line up of Nurses/Carers has changed dramatically over the past 4 years. They come and go too.

Because I am the witness, the silent watcher, I see the new people as they arrive.

The anxious, worn out, stressed faces of the families in the porch mirror ours when we were the *Newbies*.

On the night that Siobhán was admitted - (after exactly 7 months in Hospital - amid a fraught hilarious transfer that could have come straight from *Carry on, Doctor*) I was whitefaced with exhaustion and relief when I realised I could close the bedroom door, and that this room was Siobháns new "*home*".

When an angel in white ascertained that I had not eaten all day, she brought me in some cheddar, home- made brown bread and butter, a tiny pot of strong coffee and biscuits.

This simple supper and act of kindness slayed me and I dissolved into sobbing, as much for the humanity as for the realisation that Siobhán was *never* coming home again.

I watch the new residents now when they arrive.

In the early days they are full of chat and laughter.

Through some fog or shroud of memory they carry their handbags, and take strolls in the courtyard in pairs. They reminisce about old times, compare backgrounds, talk about their children, think they are on holiday and wonder who they should pay for the tea. And when the taxi is coming.

This is *Hotel California* though, and though they may check out, they can never leave.

I remember every room and its occupant. I can hear their voices in the back of my mind "*Have you a dog*?" one will ask anyone who passes all day.

Walking the length of the corridor to get a vase I will pass each numbered door and remember all of them and all that they said.

Sometimes it feels like "*The Overlook Motel*" and I feel I will open a door and see a barman from Portland, Maine or Portland, Oregon settin' em up.

It gets quieter the longer they stay.

An image of Siobhán looking fabulous in a new outfit with hair and make up done standing pitifully at the glass door watching me leave kills me. This disease has so changed her, even the contours of her face have altered and she looks different completely from the woman she was.

It is more shocking for visitors, I see it incrementally.

It gets much quieter, so that my voice seems unnaturally bright and breezy as they sit quietly, all staring at the over loud TV or out the window.

"There's a woman in a box in that big room down there" says T to me last week.

"I think she's dead, imagine?" she laughed.

I steer her back up the hall and put on a CD of Pavarotti to distract her and she tells me it's an "*alright place, but there could be more entertainment, I don't know that I'd come back next year*".

"Up ahead in the distance, I saw a shimmering light,
my head grew heavy and my sight grew dim,
thought I'd stop for the night,
there she stood in the doorway, I heard a mission bell,
and I was thinking to myself this could be heaven or this could be hell,
then she lit up a candle and she showed me the way,
there were voices in the corridor,
I thought I heard them say ...."
Hotel California – The Eagles

The Scourge - Summer 1972

I had grown up watching my older cooler cousin playing Bob Dylan and Leonard Cohen on her bedroom stereo and burning incense in a Buddha holder on the window sill, while she and her denim clad boyfriend reclined on the camberwick bedspread. I was not allowed entry and had to sit outside stripping the dressing up dolls that I begged her sister for. They lived in a biscuit tin on top of a wardrobe in a tangle of arms and legs but had about fifty thousand outfits that the older girls, my aunt, and my Nana made for them. It was like an old refrain when I arrived in my Aunt Rosies house.

"Please can I have the dressing up dolls and a curry with sultanas, Thanks very much. "
Siobhán was not in the habit of making curries and she preferred to make chicken casseroles so it was a rare treat indeed to get the spicy curry for tea that my Dad would never have condoned.
"I'd be killed if I ate that, it'll repeat on me all night. "
I imagined the curry repeating Indian mantras and impenetrable Sanskrit and keeping the whole house awake talking the whole night long. At a party they held for my cousin's birthday I took a sharp corner on the jacks landing and fell head first down the bottom flight of stairs, then lay catching my breath listening to the screams from the pass the parcel game in the front room and gingerly got to my shaking legs. My arm and neck were sore but I never mentioned a bar of it, instead re-joining the party, albeit in agony -but only crying when I was collected and safely in my Fathers car. I ended up in A&E having my fractured collar bone strapped.

- Why in the name of God did you not tell us you had hurt yourself says my Aunt.
I could not explain that I did not want any fuss or to draw any undue attention on myself in case I was accused of making a mountain out of a molehill and was prepared to suffer for the dolls and curry.
And there was the tiny matter of never disclosing to others what I had been up to or witnessed. Once on a cloudy Sunday afternoon where we had forfeited our Sunday Drive due to inclement weather, Siobhán began to assemble the Pedigree Pram and its hooding and wet weather covers that she clicked on and advised us to shake ourselves, and get the corns off our backsides and get a belt of that fresh air. One of her favourite pastimes was advising us to be active, be alive due to the popularity of said activity which also had its own advert and jingle. It was unfortunate that a baker's dozen of boxes sponsored by HB Ice Cream donated these t-shirts all over the school. Despite the Logo meaning Hazelbrook Farm, I was instantly christened Heavy Belly. I donned my new anorak with furry hood on appro from Johnnie Hores and followed along behind as Paddy Last, reluctantly dragging a stick along Harveys Field wall. Siobhán was leading the posse with baby Nicola in the pram and Little Thomasina had Barty by the hand in case he should break for the border, or the other side of the street, or both. I made up the rear with my stick and in the distance spotted a well dressed bandy legged man wearing a flat cap, pushing a giant Silver Cross pram. The bandy legged thing threw me from the off, as he looked like Charlie Chaplin in The Tramp, a pram instead of a cane. I stopped to watch him and he saluted the foursome when he drew level with them. I was overawed that I would get a look at a baby and maybe a mind of it and as he drew level with the slowcoach, he doffed his cap in an exaggerated manner and smiled. Stopping, he looked over his shoulder quickly, and then lazily drew back the knee length black coat - smiling all the time – and exposed himself to me.
I went hot and cold.

I could not understand where the baby was and did not realize for a split second the enormity of his actions. I watched as he let the coat slip back to veil the monstrous pink protruberence and carry on walking bandy legged up the road.

I ran to the family group and felt sure that Siobhán would have read my mind, and Realised that her oldest child had been scarred by an event out of her control. I felt bold and sullied and contaminated and that on some level it must have been my fault.

"Am I ugly, Mam"? I enquired.

Siobhán looked down into the impossible eyes of her first born and if she saw some small thing, something unsettling, some sea change in a nameless horror, then she did not say a word.

Neither did I.

Winter 2010 - Year 5

I appear to be running into exhaustion.

But the reality of what the dentist said to me today has made itself clear.

I broke a tooth away from its roots from grinding my teeth in nightmares.

The dentist calls his assistant and partner to come and look at the X-ray.

They stand in a ring and exclaim they have never seen the like.

He takes out the tooth, and then a week later, its neighbour, which had collapsed without support.

The Dentist said this was most likely stress related.

Stress indeed.

It also can't be normal to obsess about sleep, and focus so much on getting it.

Neither can it be normal to be as exhausted and stressed when on paper I lead a charmed life, having coffee and pistachio shortbread and reading a Kindle. The messages, e mails, texts and calls silenced and unreturned on my pc and phone add another layer to the layer of guilt. But I feel I am retreating and battening down the hatches.

Lighting the fire at lunchtime, closing the curtains early to keep the world out - whiling away misty afternoons with game shows and despair.

The canvas lies unopened, the paints hardening on their tray, the screen is blank, the printer silent.

I long for Springs green shoots, for brighter evenings, for the tulips to peep out of the mayonnaise bucket in the yard

My Brother in Law – the Quiet Leitrim Man, remarked once about the changing of the season as the vernal greens of his mountain started shyly showing slender stems

"T'is lovely to be on this side of it looking into it"

Siobhán has been a little more responsive and aware and has had her eyes open a few times lately.

Her gaze is fixed on a spot above her bed on the right hand corner.

I thought at first it was on a photo of us as a family, when my sister was a new born baby in the dark room bunched up in the window to let in the light and I named us all out to her

But when I lay my head down beside her to follow her line of vision it isn't.

Who knows who or what she sees?
Who knows what she is looking into?

Christmas 2012 - Year 7

"Well you are simply the living end" says the Nurse on duty tonight.
She is eyeballing the crisps, chocolate, Baileys and 7 -Up lined up to be fed to Siobhán, in a row on the arm of Stephen Hawkings chair.
"Well it *IS* Christmas " I respond.
Then I show her how I do it. She is impressed.
Tonight it has been my job to "*dress*" my Mother for Christmas. For the 4th year I have selected an outfit, accessorised it and hung it on hangers on the wardrobe door. The carers start asking Dad around Halloween each year what she will be wearing.
"Oh, the girls do that" says he.
It is girl singular.
I do the dressing, she does the cooking.
I do entertaining and watering of plants, she does driving and medical appointments.
I do perfume, she cuts toenails.
We are truly the Martha & Mary of sisters.
Actually, we always have been.
"*Michelle, you are supposed to clean FIRST before you start dressing up things*" said my Mother years ago as she watched in disbelief while I moved the fluff around the window sills to fit lovely things on them.
As a teenager I was known to paint an entire room in pink or black emulsion – (mood depandant) without moving anything. And when I say entire I include the windows, skirting boards, and posters. It looked like Mr Bean had done it, and I also only painted up as far as I could reach. A man always did the top bits and the "*cuttin' in*". I was like a bull in a gap.
Now I like to call this behaviour "spontanaeity".
The nurse asks whether I am on Turkey watch tomorrow.
- "*No, my house is too tiny and too mental*"
- "*Oh, you're in a flat are you*?"
I think she thinks I am a student. I reassure her that it is an actual house, with an attic and an oil tank but that my sister is the boss of all that.
I tell her I am 47 years old.
"*Jesus Divine Christ*" she says and whistles
She tells me that Little Thomasina had nothing but the height of praise for us both today.
The best daughters in all of Ireland apparently.
In reality we are two tired, middle aged women but to him we are *still* the girls.
Tomorrow it is me who will oversee the dressing, moving, lifting, wheeling, and installing by the fireside in her youngest child's house of Siobhán. The quiet Leitrim man may have to be on standby with a drill as I will take the doors down if I have to.

Carne Beach 1977

Halcyon haydays of heat, greening fields and peeling parks, basking in bee filled boreens at Ballask, horses hooves clopping up and down and down and up on deserted roads, blonde children under black suede hats astride their shining backs, laughter and screams from the swings, tractors drawing silage, the smell of the greasy chips , the click of the balls as the denim clad boys broke for pool, Status Quo on the jukebox, the silence of the house at the waters edge , the tide guzzling lumps out of damp sand, loamy land and seaweed and new potatoes , the voices of the men calling to each other at the pier, floating the sounds clear and clean across the still water, as they lifted lobster pots in the sunset.

Down, down, deeper and down.

We got homemade brown bread from the house that sold cylinders of gas, and apple tarts if we had enough money or visitors.

Or both.

They ran wild with the young fellas and all got jobs picking fruit or potatoes for farmers. It was back breaking work in the heat of the summer as they dragged their buckets across to be weighed on the trailer.

Carne people are a breed apart.

"Marra, Tom" they would salute with a solitary finger, a wave of a cap.

"That's a hash owl win today"

"By Jazus and them spuds will be brave and big when the pattern is on"

The sea crashed to shore outside the front door, lapped on grass lickily greedily, weatherbeaten paths, broken sceachs and soft cool sand enveloping dimpled knees as the tide came in full, and the seagulls flew to Wales on the topdeck of the ferry and we fell asleep like **The Family at Kilmory** listening to the slap and shush of the tides, hearing the lonesome sound of the curlew, lit by the loom of the lighthouse at Tuskar.

There was a smell of warm damp earth, melting tar and sun cream, sand in the bedrooms, towels stiffening in hedges and a red galvanized fire bucket found in a wardrobe was filled with powdery white sand and small green apple cores, shredded twisted papers.

They spent the long hot days tricking around the roads on the backs of tractors, and being roared at in the drills for "pegging schpuds" and generally misbehaving. My youngest still remembers that she nearly had to break the farmers arm to get him to pay her. After repeated visits to the back door he eventually relented and paid her in change.

The Scourge stood up against me till I relented and gave her £30 to go and stay with the Girl Guides in the Carne Holiday Centre, which was only a field away. She could not be restrained from sleeping in bunk beds in a dormitory with all the gang, and danced herself sick in the disco hall, and waved at me in the garden from the front seat of the bus on her daytrip with the Guides to the Hurdy Gurdy's in Tramore. She was too tiny to carry the flag in the Patricks Day Parade so she pushed Edel in her chair instead.

Once upon a time I stayed in Tramore with a gang of girls when I too was young.

 In Keegans Lounge we commandeered an entire horsehoe leather couch, where all the Uncles and Aunts could sit together and tell yarns and sip their pints. The men starting on Guinness and moving to half ones as a chaser toward the end of the night, and the women on glasses of cold Budweiser or Heineken which was called "Lagger" moving on to vodka and lemonade at the end of their night. The children were left with a free hand apart from amassing at the table miraculously when another round was being bought. Then they were straight back into whatever devilment was available. They tried to play pool and look cool when the country boys were staring, in their uniform of white shirts and denim jeans, comb ridges in their damp hair. The Country Boys also wore denim waistcoats over their leather jackets and every one of them had a motorbike of some description parked outside the lounge. No-one wanted to be caught dead on the back of a Honda 50 and the owner could leave the keys in the ignition till he staggered out to get a baked potato from the one armed man in his van or sick in a hedge.

There was a whore of a session in the lounge, and a fat man with a casio organ sang and sang till the sweat ran down the jowls of his face into the creases of his neck then down the small of his back. You could smell the wall of heat and armpits and smoke when you opened the lounge door. In the summer the place was packed to the rafters, scented with **Old spice** and **Charlie** and you couldn't have squeezed one more in if you tried, people waltzing around the tiny space in front of the raised stage and shouting for more at the end of the night, swaying bleary eyed stocious, singing the wrong words to the National Anthem, which closed every gig. In the winter, the place was a wasteland with people only opening the door to use the other toilets if the crowd playing darts were blocking the door, curse a God.

"Jesus, that draught would shave ye."

Tom had the table in the kinks telling yarns about his brother Mance who was 5 years gone to heaven, stories of him as a small boy on a homemade trolley car that they built, having joined a very disorderly mutinous crowd of other small boys in pestering a berserk retired Sailor named French for pram wheels to make it roadworthy, and lethal. They flew down John's Road Hill, straight through the crossroads, and down Georges Street, Mance with his feet stuck out at ten to three tearing his brand new shoes to flitters using them as brakes the whole way down the steep streets, in case they went through the plate glass window of the chemist shop at the bottom. When Tom saw the state of the shoes he said "you're going to be killed" and began to cry himself.

"Why was he called Mance instead of Richard?" asks Keyhole Kate as she stubbed out a Gold Bond in a giant yellow ashtray that nearly dented the table when it was slapped down by a busy glass collector with wet hands.

"Born in 1929, the Centenary of the Emancipation" says Tom whose middle name is O'Connell, after The Liberator, and the Avenue he was born in.

"Good thing you weren't born in Bastardstown" says The Scourge.

We drove home at night from the pub when Tom had been drinking.

This was an accepted social norm at the time, and people who could not put one foot in front of another were led to their cars and had their keys handed to them. Lads who had been asleep face down on bar counters were woken up for last orders. In all my life I have never seen my husband drunk, just occasionally merry, or nervous as a nesting hen when he had to make the speech at his daughters wedding. He was always a careful drinker and knew his limits. He was not afraid of giving offence and refusing one for the road, or a livener, or a stiffener, or whatever they called it.

"I said I didn't want it and I DON'T want it" he would say, placing a beer mat on the top and leaving it sitting on the table the same way her ladyship would leave the cold tea.

His in laws were not so careful and he was livid one day on driving home from town to Carne to find his 3 children M.I.A.

"They went off in the back of a flatbed truck, he said he was taking them for a cornet" I say placidly sitting in the evening shade waiting for the crabs to cook.

Tom knew where to look and as he drove away into the baking sunset he loosened his tie, his jacket flung across the empty passenger seat, his shape framed in the sunlight of the pub door as he arrived to retrieve them, high as kites on minerals and sugar, as the 2 men behind them laid into a feed of pints. I doubt they even noticed they were gone.

"Get it into you Cynthia, let it up, you'll be grand"

"Sure, the craythurs were parched" was a great excuse and years later in the Bullring I gave a shaking man a tenner to go in to the pub.

"All I need is me entry fee" says he "and I'll be on the pigs back!"

Another evening a man called to the door and asked me for the loan of a pound to get over his birthday.

I grew up in a house with 8 brothers, all of whom were fond of porter, and who loved the camaraderie of socialising, heading out early and coming in late, or with a few bottles in brown paper bags to prolong the session, and they sat in a ring around the fireplace, on the padded sides of armchairs or hard kitchen chairs carried up the steps, as they were throwing heavy coats in a pile on the Super Ser, telling yarns, singing or calling for songs. "Tom Mahon of Wexford for a song" - When he had exceeded his quota and the smoke was cutting the eyes out of him (he had thrown his cigarettes in the fire the night his brother died of lung cancer) he would head upstairs, to the room that his children were in, top to toe in beds filled with random cousins, and wait for me.

"Come day, go day, wishing me heart it was Sunday,
Hmmm hmmmm hmmmm hmmm
Drinking buttermilk all the week, Whiskey on a Sunday"

Little Christmas - Year 7

It all went off rather swimmingly in the end.

Despite the fact I left the house trailing ribbons and a tin of biscuits wrapped in 4 and a half yards of giftwrap - still attached to the roll - which I had to get my nephew to fix.

-    "Pull the paper off and tear the sellotape with your teeth".

He also had to pull up the straps on my Doc Martens (Kelly green) in the car to affix them to my tiny feet.

We rocked up to the driveway to see the wheelchair accessible bus parked and ready with its doors open. Inside Siobhán is being wheeled up from Mass and there is a sprint to the bedroom where I helped the carers get her ready for the off.

A part of me is amazed that my "*normal*" family are entrusting the care of this precious person to me. One of the nurses seems positively bemused that it is the hippy who is doing this. We left in a convoy - My Father in his car, my sister and nephew in hers and Siobhán and I in the bus. My sister has taken the precaution of drawing a map to her house on the back of a gift token.

She has lived there for 15 years.

I protest.

You have called me from too many lanes and fields trying to direct people up here Michelle, she informs me sagely and leaves to make the annual gravy.

I would swear on a stack of Bibles that Siobhán knew we were off on an adventure.

From the crowd around her in the room, checking things and placing an air cushion in the chair, to the speed of knots I took off down the hall at. She was alert and awake in the bus. To the shocked delight of the other passengers, I pretend to take a photo of the builder's cleavage of the driver as he buckles and harnesses the wheelchairs to the floor. A seamless transfer and we end up in the driveway at the mountain home where a small crowd await our arrival in the sunshine.

I wheeled her around and showed her the house, the tree, her son.......... things she has not seen in a while.

I fed her a baby dinner in the corner by the fire (which has canvases of a disappointed horse and James Joyce on either side, gifts that are still wet as I finished painting them in the car) and then wheeled her in to the top of the table for the main event.

I gave her an inch of Guinness in sips as we ate.

February 2012 - Year 7

There have been 2 words that summarise my existence -

"*Behave*" and "*Perform*".

They are not mutually exclusive. It would have been very cool if someone had used a smidge of reverse psychology on me decades ago and saved all that palaver.

It exhausts me now just to think of it.

Basically, I am incapable of either admonishment to order.

And quite frequently I have been known to confuse the two.

"Behave" is the word whispered out of one side of thin lips.

Usually on encountering other adults, entering people's homes, being brought on drives, going on school tours.

It was of course meant to offset the behaviour that it in fact encouraged.

This included - behaving outrageously for any/all adults and morphing into an Irish Shirley Temple singing, dancing and reciting for a £1 note.

- Opening every door and press in anyones house, rooting in drawers and saying "Can I've these?" with wide eyes.
- causing numerous fights in a moving vehicle, insisting we stop because of car sickness and then crying for ice-cream/chips.
- eating the packed lunch before the bus left town, buying pachouli oil in The Dandelion Market, and learning how to steal flip flops from the second boldest girl in the school.

"What'll we do if we're caught" says I in an agony of indecision and excitement.

"Leg it" says she

I watched in admiration and shock as she ran the length of the street with 2 left flip flops which were about as much use as tits on a fish.

A pair of flat flops.

Perform is the other word that works in inverse proportion to the command.

If I am wheeled out to entertain with a fanfare of "Oh, she's some funny lads" I will clam up faster than the Clammiest Clam from Clammytown.

Not a peep.

Usually to be found skulking amongst books and rooting in other peoples things saying "Can I've these?" with tired eyes, or sulking at the back door smoking.

I offer all of this to explain why Siobhán is gone to the pineapple chunk in her Surita hoist as pissed as a newt.

It may have been the dash of Baileys in her coffee at 3pm as we watched "*To kill a Mockingbird*".

It may have been the Hennessy while I was singing *Raglan Road* at the top of my voice with Luke Kelly.

It may have been the sherry trifle while Declan Sinnott and Christy Moore played "*Joxer goes to Stuttgart*" to a hysterical Glaswegian crowd in a mammoth gig.

"I lived there then, member?" I roared above the noise. (I like to think she nodded.)

All over the rest of the building Residents, Carers, and Relations were attending mass , singing hymns, exchanging gifts, listening to the choir, sitting round the old joanna at a knees-up.

But, wearing gloss and perfume, Siobhán is at a whore of a session in her own little space.

The jury is out on whether I behaved or performed.

Wexford - 1980

Her routine at this time was to get called at 8, ignore me, get called again at half, and turn over, and then have me banging on the stairs with a brush handle shouting it's five to nine, whereupon she would leap from the bed into uniform, clean her teeth, and run out of the house with her hair unbrushed and skid to a halt in the first class of the day. That's of course if she went. She used to manufacture ailments and maladies if she had a test, and would spend the night before planting the thoughts of illness with a series of fake coughs, sighs, and asking for her forehead to be felt. Then, she would repair to the pineapple chunk with a book and play a blinder next day as the dying swan. When I stopped calling and came up, she would murmur "I never closed me eyes" and I would suppress a smile and say "On your own head be it" and go back down to make toast and marmalade.

In an effort to control her wildness I volunteered her as a Child of Mary in the Legion of same and produced the ancient threadbare cloak I wore in Carlow when I was one myself.

She refused the cloak but jumped at the chance to join the legion as she could operate the stall outside the church that sold the rosaries and missals and miraculous medals. Indeed, it was miraculous that they gave over the running of the shuttered shop to a gang of teenagers.

She was shunted out the door for first mass on a Sunday to sell leaflets, prayer books, rosary beads and indulgences in the wooden hut outside Bride St Church

Her first dance with a chap was overseen by a nun with a meg in the rooms over the Parish Hall.

She had made herself sick with excitement at various Christmas parties as a child when there were boys present and had to be led from the throng with her fringe plastered to her head from acting the maggot.

It was in the spirit of reward that the powers that be held a Christmas Party for the "volunteers" and invited the craythurs of boarders down from the college to be the dance partners.

They sat mournfully around the table of curled up egg and onion sandwiches and **Peek Freans** *biscuits sipping club orange from a bottle with a straw, as the boarders fell on the food in a clatter of elbows and crumbs.*

Never before in the field of human conflict has so much been eaten by so few so fast.

"And now for the dancing" says the octogenarian nun putting an LP onto the turntable while they pushed the chairs back against the wall.

After much blushing and huffing a chap comes over to her

"Will ye dance" says he belting his trenchcoat

"I will" says she belting out to the "floor" - (2ft x 2 ft of space) where he manfully moved her from side to side in his arms like someone trying to gauge the heft of a sack of spuds.

The song the nun played was neither religious nor Irish.

It was "Goodbye Stranger" by **Supertramp**.

She can never hear the opening bars now without being transported back to that tiny room, the girls, the nun, the boys, the smell of their damp coats and heads, the reek of the onions in the heat from the gas fire where the steam rose from the priests soutane as he chaperoned.

She always had a knack for asking outrageous questions usually when there was an audience, or I was trying to portion a chicken to feed 5.

"How do babies get out of stomachs?" says she as I am spooning stuffing onto plates.

"I know how they get in there - I saw two dogs doing a bold thing in Dunnes by the blouses"

I caught her playing a game with her sister whom she had pressganged with threats to play the woman in labour with a number of cushions under her jumper and she played the Gynaecologist who lifted them all out.

"Lie back down, Mrs Mahon, there's another one here behind that one.

She thought she was an actual Gynaecologist herself.

I walked into the bedroom to tuck in the small one and found her standing to attention on her bed in her blue pyjamas while the other one was cocked in the window doing the same. They were having a minutes silence for Elvis.

The King is dead, long live the King

Little Christmas 2013 - Year 8

Tomorrow the annual Christmas party will be held for residents in my Mothers nursing home. It will be my 5th year in attendance.

The place will be packed to the rafters.

All morning there will be a frenzy to get things prepared and get lunches over and done with. The kitchen staff will be purple by noon.

Trays of cold meat, salads, and homemade brown bread with smoked salmon on, beetroot salad, followed by fruit flans with cream, pavlova, christmas cake , mince pies, the works. They throw up a great spread

My sister has never attended.

I doubt my brother even knows there *IS* one

My Father - Little Thomasina - did the first year with me but bowed out gracefully without an encore. He has had me primed and ready for weeks.

"Don't forget Mams party on the 6th sure you won't?" he will mention in his twice daily call to remind me.

As if.

I have become so innured to the repetition that at times I resemble a little Dutch weather doll - out and in and in and out, rain or shine.

Don't get me wrong. I cannot even now, think of anywhere else on the planet that I would be..............*should* be.

I tell my sister tonight what it entails.

"It will be like mission control at N.A.S.A. over there tomorrow" - says I nodding in the vague direction of the kitchen, as I crush an ice-cream with glistening shards of melting chocolate. "You couldn't get your foot sideways in the door to get a spoon there will be bedlam and nowhere to park, there will be tall country men carrying chairs all over the gaff with their shirts stuck to them. There will be a crowd unseen since the days of the moving statues at the mass beforehand, and a queue longer than Lourdes at the door of walking aids and wheelchairs. There will be a clatter of hysterical red faced over -heated children running wild in the halls like a re-make of *Lord of the Flies*, and elbows will be drawn at the stack of plates and cutlery."

By a miracle I have sanitised my hands with the antiseptic foam at the door so I push the triangle of melted chocolate into Siobháns mouth and lick my fingers.

I am wearing a pair of my deceased Aunts slippers.She has been dead for 9 years. Name of God. Actually, they are black embroidered with the words **Angel** in gold. I am either being coolly ironic or completely self absorbed.

While my sister rests her aching back drinking a strawberry smoothie and looking at my texts

-   *"This phone would drive me MENTAL!!!"* she shouts –

I fill her in on the mass thing, the choir thing, the speech thing, and she looks suitably aghast.

"I know, right?"

"We won't be there though will we Siobhán?" I ask the small woman in the massive chair.

"We will be in here having the crack and with only the tree lighting listening to jazz and eating ice-cream" I say rubbing her hand.

I lean in to kiss her goodnight and whisper

"No matter what she says I am your favourite child and always have been".

As I retrieve my coat from the bed my sister leans in for her own kiss and I hear her whisper

"No matter what SHE said .... before I open the door.

Wexford 1987

*T*here has always been great consternation in our house, as to whom is the favourite. Child, that is.

Tom and I have a 50/50 split depending on what they actually want at any given time, dinner or a lift.

I would like to settle an argument here once and for all.

Her ladyship is the favourite as she is my first born child and that's a no-brainer.

The brother is the favourite because he is the one and only son, and that bond is sacred.

The child is the favourite as she is the baby, and the pet.

Her ladyship was a complete scourge as a child, and then only got worse.

She bought her Da a packet of putty for Christmas and was livid when he laughed.

She hit me across the hand with a print of a Heidi House she bought in a bargain bin for 49p when I pretended to pull it off her. She rooted everywhere she had no business and dismantled a pack of sanitary towels on the carpet to see both what they were made of, and what they were for. She excavated the backs and tops of wardrobes she clearly had no ability to reach, and hauled out the Santa Claus presents we had secreted there, finding and opening boxes of Plaster Caster and Wizards, Hair- dressing Heads ,Miss World Dolls Monopoly,Jigsaws and train sets,Meccanno, Lego, Tiny Tears, Cameras, Clothes, Teddy's, Annuals, Selection Boxes, Tins of Biscuits, Bottles of Minerals, and red mesh stockings filled with crackers and surprises and lucky bags. She read every book in the house including the ones that were banned and had language she should not have seen. She named the little orange seller on the stairs Conchita and re-named herself Cassandra. She had to have a tooth pulled by a butcher of a dentist who knelt on her chest when she jerked and swallowed the anaesthetic and she felt the whole thing. I brought her into Woolheads and bought her a Barbie in a navy nylon swimsuit to make her stop crying. When Ollie took us to the town baths in Ferrybank she was skipping in the water when she slammed her foot down on a broken bottle and had to be carried to town to have her heel stitched. She went face first over the handles of a bike in the church yard and came home like something from a horror film, hysterical from the taste of blood.

When they were sick at night with the eggy belches they would come to our bedroom and crawl up under the blankets to have a tummy rubbed, and then kneeling by the bucket, have their backs rubbed as I told them to -

"Let it up, let it up, you'll be right as rain"

November 2010 Year 5

By accident I opened a file on my phone that has a photo of her taken on Christmas Day last year.

I almost dropped it.

The difference is shocking.I would hazard a guess that anyone visiting her after a long time would walk on by. Unbelievably, and almost impossibly, out of a strangers face shines my Mothers eyes.

As the illness progresses and dental hygiene starts to slip, and then become untenable due to the clamping of the mouth the teeth begin to disappear.

On a nightmarish trip to the dentist where I had to pry her mouth open, the dentist informs that she has only one tooth left.

One?

The rest she says *have rotted away, been re-absorbed and eliminated.*

Right.

The shape of my Mothers jawline has altered.

There are times when I walk in when I will glimpse my Grandfather or any one of a parade of Uncles - all gone - but not my smiling blonde Mother.

Her eyes have also changed. When they are open one is fixed and staring, the other gazing off to the left. It is not a sight for the faint hearted. I watch sadly as my tiny niece gives her a Hollywood style air kiss and am amazed at the honesty of children. Unfortunately these small children will never remember their *Nana Vaun* "well"

Inside Siobhán, lying barely under her skin is the essence of her.

Scratch the surface and she is there, present and aware and patient.

There are times she must just want me to shut up, to stop singing or giving a running commentary, to stop "*wooling the head off her*" with the hairbrush, to turn down the music, or blow out the candles.

There are symbiotic moments of perfect clarity and understanding between us where I sit in silence massaging her hands and opening the curled fingers.

She communicates with me best in the silence.

It is in the silence, and the space it allows, that all things arise and have their being.

She is simply *being* when I am *being* simple.

Sometimes I will spot her for a nano second - in the tilt of her head - in an involuntary sigh - or a half smile that plays around her lips when I am being completely outrageous. Other times it is like she has come back for a fleeting visit. These times are hard to witness and as a family we find them disconcerting.

Her eyes will open, first a tad, then halfway, then wide, then round like she has been surprised, or shocked or both. It is like when the electricity supply is flickering, and then gives a power surge momentarily before it shuts down.

On this night I thank the silence for leaving her to let me love and learn from her still. Thankfully for all of us and the children, I well remember *Nana Vaun*.

Wexford 1979/81

I couldn't let the two oldest ones sit with each other at mass because they would outdo each other in a laughing competition, their shoulders shaking and the pew rocking while they were in the kinks.

They had graduated from sitting as a family in their woolen hats and crochet bonnets, to going to a later one, and when being called on Sunday mornings would shout down they were going to half twelve or evening. They had not yet graduated to pretending they were going and standing around the railings outside talking shite, calling in at the end to collect the missalette that would prove their whereabouts when they threw it casually beside the steeping peas, and opened the oven door to steal a piece of crispy skin from the roasting chicken.

Who said Mass? asked Tom as he mashed the spuds.

Father Such & Such they would reply having conferred or confirmed.

"What was the sermon about" says I whipping butterscotch Angel Delight to pour over the tinned peaches and the block of HB.

She has a head of snarled hair now that her cousin said was another colour entirely when she sat her down and actually brushed it, despite the yelping. She has hair that is as fine as a baby's and tangles as soon as it is looked it, staying straight only when it is wet, and then curling into ringlets, dreadlocks and frizz. It looks like a home perm when it is short, and despite the seeming bulkiness of it, can be harnessed by a single clip. It has also been thin enough on her scalp to look like she has had a bald spot since she was a child.

On the radio they were playing **Sultans of Swing** and Tom was trying to watch the news about the hostages in Iran. It was the 61st day of the siege and dead men were hanging from cranes.

"Turn down that Godforsaken din" he shouted. "I can't hear me ears"

He was also prone to banging on the banisters when the roaring upstairs became untenable.

"Name of God if I get up to yee! Stop all them Andermartins will yez"

She began to call her Father **Mr Minto** after a hearing specialist and he was the butt of many a joke about deafness which he took in good part.

Little did we know.

In Carne a procession of concerned individuals, activists, hairy arsed hippies and Hari Krishna had amassed in a huge melting pot of dissent. Someone was intent on building a Nuclear Power Station, but the people came out and said NO. She pinned an **Atomkraft, Nein Danke!** badge to her lapel and was brought over to see what was occurring with the rest of the family.

There were tents everywhere, and music, and food, and mud and drugs.

"Jesus Christ" said Tom as he shepherded us back to the wet mired field we had been charged to park in. She was mortified to be a teenager at a rally as big as this, and one that would be the Irish equivalent of **Woodstock** with her Ma and Da.

By the time it dawned on her that she was sitting her Inter Cert in a few months she barely had all the necessary books, losing them, or leaving them in her locker, or spending the money on something else more important, like chocolate.

The teachers were beginning to despair of her as despite getting a brilliant report and grades had taken to doing the bare minimum of homework in the class preceding the one before, knitting a lemon and lime tea cosy in the maths class, which she found to be indecipherable. They lost her after the first few months and it was thanks to a man who taught her enough theorems that she scraped a pass. For some reason, he also advised that a useful cure for depression was the washing of one's hair, sage advice she has taken since, unlike the bloody X & Y. Once, when a teacher had spent a good 40 minutes drawing symbols all over the board in a cloud of chalk dust and frustration, she turned around and said –

"Now girls, is that clear"

"CRYSTAL" she shouted while swinging on the backs of the chair legs.

The teacher banged the duster off the desk and pointed at the door.

    – *Leave NOW!*

She was spending more and more time loitering outside the classroom door, or being summoned to the Principals office for a dressing down of epic proportions. Far from having a marked affect on her behavior, it in fact worsened.

She was caught impersonating the teacher, her accent, her mannerisms, her tics and proceeded to give the class a sex education lesson which began with her drawing a giant penis on the board and ended with the Principal catching her red handed and red faced when she came to check up on the source of the screaming. She had been forging my signatures on her own notes for years, to get herself out of any and all misdemeanours. She was always too sick for P.E. or had no kit and excused her disappearance or no shows from all classes with a series of headaches, migraines, periods, colds, chest infections, viruses and mini plagues that were localised to one house in town. She was suspended for jumping across desks singing, or hiding on Sr Spit in a wardrobe with the wet gaberdines where she got bored after half an hour and jumped out to re-join the class, in her innocence believing the elderly Nun would never notice.

As if.

The more they gave her down the banks the worse she got.

She would beg and cry to be allowed out to the Ceili in the CBS to dance The Walls of Limerick and the Siege of Ennis with a red faced Brother Casey marshalling the dancers, musicians and miscreants. The boys danced in lines in their fair isle jumpers and the girls all horsed around the floor in a ring or undulating waves, swapping partners and holding hands that were too sweaty, too clammy or just right depending on who one had the fortune or otherwise to be paired with.

"Assume your proper positions please" says the cinema usherette brusquely, shining the torch into their startled red faces while they tried to pull up or down clothes in a lather of embarassment and frustration.

She extended her own curfew which was to be home before the dancing had even finished.

11pm and that is it! said Tom in a voice that brooked no argument

She wailed and howled.

The roars of her and the bawls of him.

She could not go traipsing around the streets with a gang of excited teenagers in pursuit of a shift or a fish supper with the thought that she would be killed indoors.

"There'll be mucking furders if I'm late again" she told the boy with the cold tongue as they kissed on the freezing bench beside the phone box she was a martry to tapping. It was her first French kiss and your man was energetically trying to insert his face into her mouth. It felt like a cold ice pop and she detangled from under his Parka with some considerable relief. The solitary squad car slowed for a look before the Guard pulled over into the barracks. He had the misfortune to be sent out one night you wouldn't put a spade out in to discover the reason for the screaming alarm from the county clinic and found herself and the country boy engrossed in a clinch so passionate it had made the shrieking bells go un-noticed.

He had taken her name and address though.

    – *I know your Father, says he.*

He was to hear more of her in the coming months.

Her brother was to marry his daughter.

"Céilí my arse" said Tom as he held up her black stilettos for inspection. Not only had she tried to pretend she was Irish dancing in them but had screeched to a halt in the silent square on the back

of a motorbike where she tapped the leathered visored figure on the back as a signal to get gone. I watched her from the window, glancing across at Tom in the bed waiting for the soft click of the door, so he could stop reading prayers and memory cards and put out the light. I got in beside him and began putting on cold cream and reading a course called **You CAN remember** by Dr Bruno Furst. He has never closed his eyes till his family were home and to this day she rings him still to let him know.

The heels on her shoes had burnt down to two tiny stumps from having her feet on the roasting exhaust as she sped home through the glistening country roads.

The Country Boy was a man she met in Carne. She spent a lot of time tapping the payphone around the corner and knew the number of every pub in the County. She fought off all the shouting from Tom and all the quiet advice from me and fell harder in love with him the more ructions there was, saving to buy him a digital watch with a gold plated face.

She was now back in Carne, not as the townie, but as the girlfriend of one of the boys. She stole a motorbike for the craic from outside the Lobster Pot while the owner was inside downing pints and rode 5 miles up the road in first gear, passing the open mouthed crowd outside **Butlers** drinking cider in the sunshine waiting for **Route 66** to sing Black Magic Woman, and crashed it spectacularly in Allenstown while they gave chase in a Reno A Heen playing Kid Creole and the Coconuts on the radio.

"Oh, Annie, I'm NOT your daddy"

She appeared on winters nights like an apparition through the fog, smiling in quiet bars with only locals playing darts for Turkeys, and **Match of The Day** on the Telly in the corner. We failed to qualify for the World Cup again, this time only losing out on goal difference.

An old drunk in a suit you could make soup on would try to make a grab at her on the way to the toilet.

"Haw, Haw, I'll getcha, I'll getcha so I will."

"You wouldn't catch cowld, Jemmy "said the barman topping the pints.

"I'm some man for one man!"

"It takes a worried man to sing a worried song" sang Jemmy as she extricated herself from his grasp and went to the ladies with the other women.

She was supposed to be at home studying but was after telling lies as quick as a horse could trot to get a window of opportunity to sneak out.

And now here she was going to an engagement party in a caravan.

As the time ticked down nearer and nearer to her curfew she frantically did the math , factoring in the wet roads, the amount of pints consumed by the driver, the perishing cold, the warm caravan, the vodka that she had drunk neat having been assured there would be no smell of drink off her, and the general mayhem she would cause - and feeling that she may as well be hung for a sheep as a lamb, laid down on the babies bunk and curled up in a ball.

It may have been a mistake not to telephone somebody.

Anybody.

But in the grey morning, she took a crawsick look around her and realised that this would have to be her life now as she could NEVER go home again.

A man who sits up half the night reading prayers and memory cards would never condone this kind of carry on, and with the stoic acceptance of a fait accompli, she realised she would have to lay in the childs bed that she had made. She had a similar experience once as a child, where she had taken silver coins from the **Gourmet Viola** ceramic dish where Tom kept change, to buy macaroons and toffee tuffy's and when he had a surprise audit, sat crying on the stairs, composing the speech in her head she would say to the judge before he sent her to Borstal of how she would stay on in the house and work as a scullery maid to pay off her debts in community service.

It was the same skewed thinking that had her undone now.

They talked of trying to get up the country to get the ferry from Larne to Stranrare and from there riding to Gretna Green to get married.

It was an ambitious plan for two hungover, penniless, virginal teenagers and the farthest they got was New Ross where they ate **Tayto** at the side of the road like a latter day Bonnie & Clyde and reconsidered.

Unbelieveably, they ended up back in the caravan again that night. She had so shut out the possibility that there could be a reconciliation at home that she also blanked out the fear and panic she had caused us and how frantic we were.

Tom was up to high doh.

We had the Guards at the door with their hats on their heads.

We drove the length and breadth of the county, calling to the country mans homeplace and speaking to his embarrassed and bewildered mother who could shed no light on the situation, standing in the porch of the vested cottage, wringing her apron with red hands.

Birds nesting in whispering trees, a line of limp washing in the field behind her.

Drop me here she shouted over the noise of the engine, tapping him on the shoulder as they pulled up outside the shop that all the schools of the town converged at on their lunch break. It was the last tapping of shoulders or phones she was to do for a while.

- OH MY GOD says her best friend walking out the door with a curly wurly.
- You are so DEAD. They think you ARE dead. There is mass being said for you above in the school hall"

     she announced and carried on chewing, her eyes wide with the delight and the scandal.

We were at the Mass.

And when we went home she was there.

Sitting on a trunk in the kitchen staring defiantly at us coming home big when she was feeling small.

Tom, who was ravaged, walked across to her with tears in his eyes and a look of disbelief on his face, slapped her once across her own cheeky face. Then he had to sit down to cry. Her siblings were looking on in a combination of awe and anger, a crowd of rubber necker's in the hallway who had chinesed whispered the news that the wild one was back, the dog trying to jump up on top of her in excitement.

"Never mind hun never mind, sure isn't she home now and that's all that matters" said Nellie as she put her arms around him. The Principal and a Priest called over in the afternoon and I knew she could hear our hushed voices downstairs rising and falling as she lay curled up in her quilt, listening to the tyres of the cars and buses as they sheeeshed and shooshed through the rainy grey streets and closed her eyes.

I was worried sick she might be pregnant but she was intact.

I burst into her room where she was lying on the bed reading a new magazine called **Kerrang,** a picture of a rock star in a schoolboy's uniform on the front.

Confronted, she admitted tearfully that nothing had actually happened, and I thanked St Anthony and the Little Flower as I passed the boys room blasting "Don't fear the reaper" on his transistor radio and went down the 3 flights of stairs to make tea.

It wouldn't have surprised me one iota if she had got herself into trouble as she always loved babies, and once when I asked what would she be when she was big, she said "a Mother".

March 2010 - Year 5

Fortunately I made a collage of Siobhán for her birthday a number of years ago.

It was a collection of family photographs that I had copies made of and then butchered with a scissors to get only her from the various shots. I mounted them on board, laminated it and gave it to her.

It hung proudly in the living room at home.

Now, It hangs directly in her line of vision from the Stephen Hawking chair she lives in.

There are many and varied shots of her, as a young bride, a new mother, at weddings, pregnant, on holiday in Carne, Clare or Lake Garda, asleep in the back of my Dads camper van, swimming, sight- seeing, walking, sitting, her silver wedding anniversary - (the night her son and daughter walked in the door shouting "Surprise!" from Germany via London) -holding Grandchildren, drinking a pint of stout, holding her pet terrier Chloe on her lap, straight haired and curly.

In all of them she is essentially herself.

There is no posing, no artifice, just honesty and a quiet ladylike disposition that negates my oft used adage - "Trot Mare, trot foal" –

In one of the images she has been captured in a moment that my sister and I discussed the other night.

She is hanging curtains.

Siobhán always had a "great pair of hands" and could turn them to pretty much anything. Apprenticed to sisters who were seamstresses after she left St.Leos' in Carlow town, she served her time there and then in Wexford was one of a host of green tweed clad assistants in **Corrys** with Cornelius de Groot. This is a woman who knew her way around a needle and thread -and could run up a pair of curtains, hem your school skirt, take up, down and in your levi's and fix your "project" for domestic science while cooking bacon and cabbage, and apple tart.

She also loved to paint and could always see faces or animals in wallpaper patterns or cloud formations.

Once when a wall was being stripped to be dry lined she drew children and faces and dogs on the scraps of paper left behind. I think my Dad became suspicious even then. I like to think she was just spontaneously creating and not that the lights had begun to wink out one by one.

I have steadily rifled and filched from her hot press for years. I am a magpie when it comes to cute unusual things. Which may explain the eclectic state of this house and the depletion of her blanket box. We have had a thing about going upstairs at home. It was horrific and traumatic to go into her wardrobe and take her things out to a nursing home.

I did it.

Even when the ceiling in my old bedroom collapsed and Dad turned down the ear shattering volume on the TV and up his hearing aids she did not venture upstairs.

"I thought it was thunder" says he

*"Member Mam always had pins in her mouth, and I used to beg her to fix things saying I'd ate it first?"*I asked. She laughed. I believe in the energy of old things, and love keeping things that hold memories. We stop and look up at the collage of her, hanging the curtains in the living room and smile.

November 2010 - Year 5

I am the best supporting actress in a real life Benjamin Button re-make.

Whether I am nominated for an award or overlooked is up for dissecting by a jury of my peers. I will have to call on all my powers of method, detachment, awareness and eternity to pull off this role. The show must go on. All of life a stage and every man must play a part. Lights, camera, action.

I hope I don't fluff a cue.

And speaking of fluffers, we're gonna need a smaller sock.

Cue the music I'm ready for my close-up.

The chain appears to be have been steeped in a corrosive acid of fear and doubt and is weakening but who would have thought the blackest sheep, the weakest link, the craziest broad would step forward, seize the mike, and squinting into the spotlight begin falteringly - and then with confidence - to sing a warriors song.

January 2012 - Year 7

There was not a peep out of Siobháns room last night. She was sleeping heavily and I was wrecked.com.My sister and I made an appointment to see Siobháns Geriatrician back in 2008. Basically, we needed to sit across a desk and ask her what the crack was. We sat as 2 sisters and listened as 2 sisters about 2 other sisters and the implications this may bode for us down the line.

"What's the dealio with vitamin b? Ditto aluminium pots, salmon and broccoli, fish oils, coconut oil, crosswords?" I ask in my usual forthright way.

(THC from Marijuana I did *not* vocalise.)

"Is there something we should be doing or more importantly - Not doing?" While her answer did not include the words "tilting" or "windmills" it may as well have. We may as well be pissing in the wind.

"It's not genetic, it's completely random." says she.

"It can affect members of a family or not."

She made it sound a little like lightning with flashes hitting the ground sporadically. This is actually a lot like good news in my humble opinion and I may have as much chance of inheriting this illness as winning the actual lottery.

I left the room only once last night to get a glass and met a resident in the hall.

"*They're doing B&B in that house down there*" she says pointing at her own room.

"*They have no-one in tonight though and there are cushions fired everyway, but they have a photo of MY Grandparents on the wall!*"

I stood looking at the photo of the couple in their Georgian finery and imagined the photographer under his black cloth and the smell of the powder as they stared into the future from over a century ago. They are only a memory too but one she has retained. It gives me hope which is all we ever have since Pandora opened that infernal box.

Tempus Fugit.

September 2013 - Year 8

My Father has always called my Mother "Mam". Since I was a small child he has referred and spoken to and of her as Mam or Mammy.

"Get up and help your Mammy in the name of God tonight"

"Ask your Mam"

"Ring Mam when you get to Dublin/London/Stuttgart/Spain"

And the last one - "Mam is waiting on you" said in a plaintive tone as her illness manifested and the ground started to slip.

She called him Dad or Tom, mostly Tom.

And usually with two syllables.

"To- om " as she called gently up the stairs while he was teaching himself (nearing 70 years old) to play the fiddle at the top of the house. He only recently sold the upright piano in the living room - oddly enough back to the family he bought it from. He has a warchest of music, CDs, vinyl, speakers, amps, and players too. He has a better sound system than I do. He plays anything he hears instantly by ear which is bizarre as he is mutt and jeff and wears a spectacular pair of hearing aids to his constant mortification which surely belie the "*Hidden Hearing*" banner they were mis-sold under.

He is 83 years old.

While my father was painstakingly teasing out the chords upstairs, (*Kurt Vonnegut's advice to writers is "pity the reader"* - in this instance it should be *"pity the neighbour"*) Siobhán was downstairs getting some down time. As I was living in the above mentioned places and many others I cannot for sure be exact with my recall of the 2 hours every night after tea that she was alone.

Tea at 5.30 pm - Tv turned on for the Angeles - Six News, a quick doze by the fire while "**Nationwide**" is on -

"*I'm WATCHING that*" - with one eye open if you dared to flick to the **Simpsons**, and then a stretch and off upstairs.

Siobhán would be sewing, or hemming curtains, or baking cakes, or making stuffing, or ironing.

Ironing in the alcove of the press under the stairs listening to the drama of the British Soaps play out as she sprayed steam on the shirts.

In the end she resorted to banging on the bannisters to call him down - for the News at 9, his supper, his daughter on the phone. I think the vibrations travelled up the 3 flights of stairs where he was ploughing through jigs and reels and folk tunes.

His music has been his saving grace.

A little boy of 9 when war broke out - in a house of 5 children - where money for lessons was nonexistent, finally has a world of music at his fingertips, and literally now that he has high speed broadband on his laptop.

Ahem.

Apart from a few years in the 80's when I called him "Mr Minto" after the hearing aid guy, I have always called him Little Thomasina and am aware that it is the feminine. So does everyone else by now.

Our conversations sometimes revolve around his hearing.

"Turn them UP for chrissakes"

"STOP coughing so loud, Jeeee zus"

"Are the batteries working?"

We have indeed become a spoof of an Alan Bennett farce.

Last night when I had finished sighing on the phone he said

"Mam was trying to say something today"

I amost fell over.

"She was trying I think, and I said to her "What are you saying eh? and she laughed."

My heart sinks.

I think maybe if I had been there I would have understood, or heard, or coaxed something from her.

Something.

Not the third secret of Fatima or The 4 last things, just a word.

"You know when she blinks she is saying I love you right?" I ask.

"Yis" says he.

"And she squeezes your hand fair hard too."

"Especially the left" I tell him.

It is only when he has hung up that I realise he did not need to hear to listen, and that whatever Siobhán was saying was for his ears only, broken and all as they are.

Carne 1982

We watched her like hawks from then on. Under surveillance of an epic proportion which made her feel like a butterfly trapped in a jam jar, she began to write. She turned to a diary to vent, and began to submit shorts to magazines like Young Ireland and Irelands Own and had a ridiculous letter published in the paper ranting about recession and poverty and unemployment. The Careers Guidance Teacher had taken off her glasses and massaged the bridge of her nose in her cramped office as she tried to explain a points system and the finer details of the Central Applications Office forms and deadlines. When she stopped messing about talking about the circus, she told her she wanted to write. She advised her to get a secretarial qualification. Then she advised her right back that she wanted to go to the College of Commerce in Rathmines to study Journalism and they rooted out the forms.

She won the **Bord Iascaigh Mhara Award** for the best fish pie in the town, piping half a stone of buttery mash on top of a concoction of fish in sauce, topped with a single sprig of parsley and a lemon fan. Other than that she tried to keep her head down. There was only the tiny matter of a Oiuja board in the 2nd Year toilets and some whisperings about a Séance, but it was all smoke and mirrors. Her reports advised that she was holding her own in the exams but was still a loose cannon in the school. We removed her from the streets of town filled with the smell of baking bread from Kellys , with all the lads hanging out at the record counter in Woolworths, fecking jelly babies off the **Pick N Mix** when the woman with the buck teeth was looking at the weighing scales for the price of cinder toffee.

She got herself a summer job in a chipper at the beach.

The caravan park had a shop with a takeaway on the back of it and as it is widely documented people at a beach will eat a Nuns arse through a convent gate so the place was up the walls from sun up to sun down. She liked to mess at the back door with Ned, the man driving the tractor that delivered the food from farm to fork. It wasn't so much fun at the counter with the nation standing shouting their orders and the sweat pouring off them with the heat of the fryers and hot pans. There was always a queue, and at first she was intimidated and content to stay cooking and wrapping behind the counter but then was dragged out and found her forté. When the sun went down a wave of burnt shaking people staggered over the dunes, hobbled across the stones with their sandals gone for a Burton on the evening tide, shrieking for chips and cold drinks before they collapsed in a heap in the name a Goddle Mighty. Most of them were Dubs and had a slang we had never heard before. A one and one, a single, a dunphy, and she took orders, kept the queue from becoming mutinous with a stream of patter, skidded around in an inch of grease wrapping parcels and prising pound notes out of tiny sandy disembodied fists as they reached up to the counter.

- Me Ma says lave them opened!

All the talk in the kitchen was of the beach party in St Margarets.

"You'll surely be there" says the boss woman.

"I'm under house arrest since my last performance" says she.

The Uncles and Aunts were down from all over the country and so we went that night as a family group and she saw the crowd toping in the lounge, readying themselves for the nights entertainment to come. She found out all the details and promised she would be there later or die trying, ominously. When we went home she had to try and stifle the screams of frustration in her pillow as Tom and I made tea and chatted. Eventually, when we had all emptied our cans, there was silence and she gingerly tested the small window of the twin bunked bedroom she shared with her sister. She threw her clothes out the window in a plastic bag, tiptoeing around like some demented thief in a jewel heist.

So far so great. Nicola was sleeping like a baby and she balanced on the edge of the bunk and threw one leg out the window and realised the gap was small and the drop was big. It was as she was steeling herself to haul the other leg over and sit astride the frame that Nicola woke up and stared at her.

She stared back.

She had only one option open.

"Go back to sleep, you're dreaming" she said in a calm voice.

Nicola maintained eye contact for about 5 seconds and then her eyelids closed and she turned over. She dropped with a clatter onto the wooden decking and crouched like an assassin. When she knew she could stand on her ankle, she got up and began rooting for the bag of clothes which were in a bush.

- I see it, but I don't believe it – intoned a deep voice from within a cloud of smoke.

Crunchie the Sailor was having a fag and contemplating the night sky and had watched the whole scene unfold from the back step.

- Shush, will you – she hissed – or the whole house will be up.

She took off at a trot down the road with her clothes in the bag and was planning where to change on the beach when a speeding car coming from **The Bakehouse** hit her. She flew up in the air and landed awkwardly on the stones outside the very chipper she had slaved in all day. The driver slammed on the brakes and ran over, his passengers propping her head up on coats and asking "Where in the name of Christ is the nearest payphone"

"She came out of nowhere "he said over and over, shaking his head.

"I'm a nurse" says the woman.

She felt over her and under her and her hand came away black in the moonlight.

There was gravel embedded in her back. Her shoe was gone, and she could hardly move.

"We may drive her to A & E, the very least she will be is in shock" says the Nurse.

"Shock my eye, bring me to the party" – says she horizontally

And so it came to pass that she was driven by 4 strangers to the appointed rendezvous on the beach which transpired to be a few Reno A-Heens with their lights on and the cassettes playing - Nicole singing a little peace – "we are fezzers on the breeze, sing with me my zong of peace" and the other cars had Smokey singing about where the fuck was Alice, and Sylvias Mother was telling them not be calling here again as she was Happy marrying a man down from Galvestown way. There were a few rugs but as it was pitch most people sat on the bonnets or roof of their own vehicle, or in a ring of damp sand if they were gee eyed. The occupants of the car, feeling awful, hung round for a few cans to monitor the go of her. The country boy was gone home stocious as he had been out all day. She was the only one at the party wearing a nightdress and picked lumps and shards of road chippings from under her skin at the water's edge as the sun rose. She wrapped the lemon nightdress in rocks and flung it out to sea and watched it bobbing on the waves, wondering whether the Dyfed Powys Police might instigate a murder inquiry on that evidence alone and then limped home at 8am to wake her entire sleeping family by calling them lazy stop outs and announcing that she had been on an early walk down the beach. Tom's hair was standing on end and he arched an eyebrow and re-tied the cord at the fork of his pyjamas as he shuffled back to bed. She went to bed herself and could not be roused with promises of lunch, Pitch & Putt or a swim in **The Great Southern** Pool. One leg was twice the size of another, and when I glanced across and saw the little and large limb I coughed and stifled a small scream.

- "What in the name of God have you done to yourself "–

She told me she fell between the rocks down at the pier and I bought it.

Until I had to venture into the queue for chips and the boss woman told me -

- "Mrs Mahon, that daughter of yours was knocked down last night on her way to a party.
   She should be taking a case against them, we found her shoe on the roof"

October 2011 - Year 6

Lately I have come to notice that the inner monologue that runs in my head is my Mother's voice.

As I hastily mop the fluff and coal dust from one side of the living room to the other - wet of head and wearing my coat to run out the door - I hear her say — *"Give it a lick and a promise."*

When I am washing up my solitary plate and glass, a single fork, I hear her say *"Dry them out of it"*.

If a knife falls on the floor I hear her say *"Oh, here's a visitor"*.

All day long the old words return, or maybe just re-appear.

They have not been far.

Some have been sunning themselves like lizards on rocks - some have been hiding underneath them. They awake now like sleeping snakes and coil their sluggish drowsy selves around me so that I am encircled and consumed by them.

These words of memory rupture like fragile soap bubbles all around me and inspire the story behind the words, which leads to the words becoming something other than the sum of their parts.

"She's a real "Mary Hick "in that get up."

If she could only see me in the fur coat with hood I bought for one euro yesterday.

"I can't find a thing in this ship of a house" flung over a muffled shoulder from the depths of the coat press under the stairs.

"Would you be interested in this?" as she tried to buy me clothing/crockery/books.

"Oh, he's on the usual aul Cant, I see" about a politician on the evening news.

"You'd give last to nobody" when I came reeling in the door at stupid o clock from some outrageous affair.

Icky Ocky Horses Cocky

And her stoic, silent presence outside the bathroom door (when she heard me sobbing loudly in the shower after the premature ending of yet another doomed love affair) - observing only *"What's for you won't pass you"*.

For a woman who was reared to be as cool as the proverbial cucumber - quiet, refined, softly spoken and oath free, it must have been a baptism of fire to produce a daughter who screamed her way into the world and immediately began behaving as if she was a minor deity with the temperament of a hysterical Italian housewife - think Sophia Loren having a tantrum topped off with Cleopatra in a strop, and Marilyn Monroe having a breakdown — all wrapped up in a precocious tiny child.

"She's no bigger than a Gods cow"

"That one is knee high to a daisy" said as she took up another 4" on my white dress the night before my communion.

I remember still the smell of coffee and cigars in **The Talbot Hotel**, where we went for Holy Communion dinner. In my excitement, and with my white purse stuffed and bulging with notes, I stood on tippytoes to shout up to the woman behind the glass display case which was filled with Waterford Glass, Belleek china, and Newbridge Cutlery —

"How much is the bottle of Jemmy? It's for my Dad."

She has always been patient and methodical, unassuming, gentle, loyal, a keeper of secrets, reliable, punctual, and content in the essence of herself. The Gods must have laughed long and hard to send her a baby that was the complete antithesis of all of the above and then some.

She wraps her words of love around me, and reminds me of my life.

Sitting in her room on Wednesday night, the TV on low in the background, I caught a glimpse of a fat man being weighed.

He was poignant as he described how his weight gain, subsequent marriage breakdown, and sheer loneliness in an apartment where he was a "Weekend Dad" led him to stand on the balcony to hear the sound of traffic on the overpass and the cawing of crows for company. And of course his weight ballooned as he sat comfort eating and unconsciously watching TV

I contemplated my own stomach as he spoke.

It is the size of a full term pregnancy now and I almost hold it like such. I find at times I will have been cupping it, or absentmindedly stroking it, loving the fat squashy softness of it, the sheer size of it.

As my Uncle Ollie would have said when teased about his paunch - "It cost a lot of money to put that there!"

Or as Siobhán would have said (if she could) - *"That jersey would fit Finn McCool"* or *"She's as big as a Bishop"*

It is my last hurrah as a pregnant wanna -be. That ship has sailed and unless there is a star in the east and a trio of moderately clever men found wandering with gifts it ain't happening. The Universe has decided that the only thing I will give birth to will be a Novel. I made a snap decision and pressed the bell.

The tea girl pops her head in.

"You rang?"

"Yeah where the Nurses at?"

She locates and returns with a pair.

Their eyebrows are up.

"Everything's grand, I just need you to tell me what I actually weigh now. And I need someone to write it down, and an audience."

They laugh and we set off merrily down the hall.

In the room filled with Zimmer frames, sticks, crutches, walkers and wheelchairs is the chair the elderly infirm patients are weighed in. I sit down. It is in kilos.

"Just multiply by 2.2" I tell the teagirl who is writing on a bandage wrapper, plucking this information from the ether.

I will draw a veil over the actual amount. It caused much amusement to all and sundry.

Put another way I appear to be as wide as I am long.

This simply cannot stand.

And either can I carrying this extra load.

This self- indulgent /self sabotage/seratonin dependancy must cease now and forthwith. The next day filled with plans to hibernate at a 5* detox retreat - emerging in summer unrecogniseable - are shattered on meeting a friend. She walks a Buddhist path , works as a psychologist and shaved her head and took a nuns veil until (in her own words) "the lure of men and red wine proved too much " - and on hearing me bemoan my stomach smiled and said "*Sure, aren't you beautiful? You're taking up more space in the world.*"

January 2014 - Year 9

The big sky is charcoal. Skeletal trees and a distant purple mountain shrouded in bulging black clouds sits placidly observing.   The people carrier with the tyre chains on it inches slowly down the glasslike lane. The windows are fogged with condensation. I am in the back with the children. We slide to a skewways stop. At the glass doors with its tinkling wind chimes we read a hand written sign.
Closed due to winter vomiting bug. Please ring bell.
The nurse with the dark hair comes finally as we freeze.   She shouts through the glass. We pass the bottles and bags in through the top of the open window and drive slowly away.

Day 2.

Still on *Lockdown* for *Containment*
I asked the Nurse who answered my call to put the phone to Siobháns ear so as I could tell her why I was not there. I prefaced my opening remarks by informing her that it was "the Scourge" calling. It feels bizarre not to be there and I have unaccustomed time on my hands which I am filling (literally) with wool and needles to knit a jumper for a male by Wednesday.
We are all anxiously awaiting the outcome where it gets sewn together, no more than the wearer who is fortifying himself in a local hostelry with pints of plain in trepidation.
I have been approached by an artist who has worked with Alzheimer patients and their carers to do a piece on Siobhán, using my words, Siobháns sketches from the 40's and family photos.
Don't even get me started on the photos.
Well, first of all I had to breast Little Thomasina to get them for me.
"They could be anywhere by now, I moved them when we got the work done " - he announces.
-   "You know where they are so get them, I have to do things on the minute for you, and no, there is no reply from the email I sent in German to the guy on eBay about the Hohner Accordion"
-   "I didn't give my permission" he huffs.
-   "Good, as I didn't ask" I blowed.
We always huff and blow like this.
Long story short he left out a wicker bag of albums today.
I had let myself in and smelt the familiar smell of home in the warm hall.
The house is as tidy as a new pin. He has washed his soup bowl and mug and the fire is set and ready for his return. I sit in my Mothers armchair to quickly scan the photos before I meet the Artist.

They are jaw dropping.

A picture paints a thousand words.

I left the house clutching a small precious few to replicate and walked into him on the street.

He is off to buy himself another cap.

"I lost the other one yesterday playing for the old folks".

He is 84.

It is no wonder he did not want to find the images or look at them and be reminded of a life.

Day 4 of the lockdown. -

And now I am stitching together the matching hat for the jumper I finished and wondering how in the name of God is Siobhán.

She never leaves my mind, and judging by the state of the rest of the family, theirs either.

This strong woman this tiny warrior, this legend.

I imagine her world to be a more silent place these last 5 days. There has been no trickacting around with the radio to find the Lyric Concert, or Jazz, or John Creedon. "I love the sound of Val Joyces voice, it's so soothing" said she one day turning the dial through the white noise to see where was he gone. He had been moved from the afternoon to late night. The soundtrack of my childhood is the radio – *Liam Nolan, Valerie McGovern, Let's Go with the Glenabbey Show, Mike Murphy, Gaybo, Night Bus and Knock at the Door, the Angelus, the sea area forecast –*

"from Rossan Point to Carlingford Lough, to Carnesore Point, Loop Head and the Irish Sea" – wind, weather visibility .... the stations all broadcasting up and down the dial depending on where you are tuned in –

The soundtrack in my home is always the radio, sometimes I even leave a small silver transistor on in the attic as company for the house. I like to listen to the voices and the music and the Doc on One, making my own mental images, as like a great book, radio feeds the imagination.

In my Mothers room, the radio may be unplugged to keep the electric air in the mattress circulating. The Yankee Candle will be unlit, the plants parching over the dry heat from the radiator on the window sill. The chocolate in the drawers lying uneaten and unwrapped in its' glistening purpleness.

There will have been no saucers full of bashed up Magnums, no knitting strewn on the bed, no fur coat hanging on the door. No one to manoevure the Greek head scratcher, or spray the Christmas perfumes on her neck and wrists.

The neck of the Baileys bottle will crust over and flake off.

She is on silent retreat.

As are we.

Maybe in some grand Universal plan we are all supposed to take time out this week

I continue to send her wellness, joy and peace and can almost visualise her bowed head in stillness, in awareness, and in thanks.

Day 5 of the lockdown... it's been a long week.

Day 8 of the lockdown.

If it has been tough on my sister and I, then one can only hazard a guess as to how much Little Thomasina has been missing his daily visits.

You could set a clock by him.

It is his life now, and his routine, and the people he meets there are his touchstone and yardstick.

Apart from a brief stint when he was in hospital himself - he has not missed a day since Mam was diagnosed and hospitalised.

We knew as a family that something was up with Siobhán long before a geriatrician sat us down in her office and confirmed our worst fears.

She lost her purse a lot.

She called *Hewhomustnotbenamed* Owen.

She lost her keys and couldn't remember how to cook.

She had to be reminded to do the simplest of things.

Her mood changed and this normal placid, laid back gentle women became moody and ornery.

My brother remarking one day that he liked the new "*feisty*" Siobhán - I was too busy coming to terms with the enormity of what was happening to do more than roll my eyes and sigh.

In every family who are faced with this disease there seems to be a level of refusal to acknowledge, to believe, to confirm the awful nameless beast lurking in the dark, lying behind the door listening to the whispered conversations, rubbing its greasy paws and cackling.

Nowhere to run - nowhere to hide.

We become culpable in our complicity.

Little Thomasina must have been aware of so much more for so much longer and my heart breaks to think of what he endured alone. "Don't tell Tom" being remarked more than once when new keys were cut, or a purse replenished. Or a saucepan had the arse burnt out of it cooking vegetables with no water.

"*Don't tell Tom*" was a mantra for a considerable time with us and all the time he knew so much more than we thought.

In a vain attempt to tilt at windmills he tried to double bluff the Universe and believed that as long as Siobhán was showered and dressed with her make-up on sitting beside him in the car then everything was tickety boo.

He made excuses, turned down invitations, left gatherings early, (once even leaving a family wedding before the meal was served) and yet lay alone and sleepless at night praying to a God who wasn't listening.

He took over in the house, cooking cleaning, laundry, shopping and generally behaving like a hero. One day I walked in and watched the pair of them folding sheets.

He was exasperated that she could not follow the instructions to walk to him, and meet in the middle.

On another morning I let myself in and walked into their bedroom where I found him on his knees - his white head bent - as he put on her socks, while she sat patiently on the bed like a vague child.

These moments like to replay themselves on the video screen running in my head when my ego is in a battle for control with my id.

Today they are playing in HighDef, 3d, surround sound as he tells me is having soup for lunch and then will just *potter* around.

His routine has been thrown a curve ball out of left field and despite his best efforts and no snow to stop him driving he has been locked out from his best friend.

I stopped working for the man to care for her and brought her everywhere with me - even into pubs for a mineral, sitting in the window looking out at the people walking the town - and would get an alarm call from him every morning with the plaintive refrain of -"Mam's waiting on you".

One morning I got a call that was different.

- "Mam's had a stroke" he sobbed.

I ran to their house with my breath in my fist and my face the colour of a boiled shite.

She had slumped sideways at the kitchen table and he called an ambulance.

It was a TIA (a trans- ischaemic attack) where the veins and arteries to the brain close only momentarily and then recover with no lingering affects in speech or movement.

She was admitted and sedated.

Little Thomasina was exhausted and emotionally wrung out. I told him to get some rest and to take advantage of the break for a day or two.

Next day on her chart I saw **LTC** written in marker across the bottom and knew it meant Long Term Care. She was wearing an ankle tag that would close the doors if she tried to walk up the hall.

She has only been home to their house once in a wheelchair since.

I wheeled her down the hall explaining we are *Home* and watching for the smallest of responses to the familiar room, but there is none. And consequently no reaction when the wheelchair is wheeled back out to the waiting car and we do the lift on three and bolster her in the back with cushions and my arm.

And I watch my Fathers face as we drive up the street, taking her away in the dusk.

I know as sure as eggs that her spirit essence would walk to him and meet him in the middle in a heartbeat.

I know that I also would walk through walls to get in and give her one quick hug.

I know that this too will pass.

Day 9 of the lockout.

Little Thomasina rings in the am to inform me he is making Shepherds Pie and that there is a plate with my name all over it. My sister has also agreed to attend.

I am late as per and she is dishing up when I burst through the door with my coat tails flying. For a change my hair is not wet as I thought I would get a good run at the day and had my shower at midnight.

It seems bizarre to sit as a trinity at this tiny kitchen table (which has been pushed back in against the wall) and to not have Siobhán sitting in her usual spot.

As a child the kitchen was always the centre of our home. On one wall a picture of a Pope, a Sacred Heart with a tiny red lamp, and between calendars (plural) a motto that loomed down on the moody hormonal teenagers in gold thread on a red velvet background that proclaimed

"Christat is the Head of this house,
the unseen guest at every meal,
the silent listener to every conversation" -

to much derision and bawdy remarks from my brother and I.

When I wasn't almost being expelled (again) or running away on the back of a motorbike , or having a hysterical prima-donna style breakdown amid much screaming and slamming of doors, and while my attention was otherwise engaged , my brother took up the baton and ran with it.

Which may explain why he was found drunk as a lord in his bedroom aged 16.

(He and his friends purloined a bottle of vodka from a drinks cabinet before they went to a Céilí - Needless to say he did *not* end up dancing around the school hall that night.)

He had been led astray early in life by his big sister whose general nosiness caused mayhem. I like to think it was the writer in me who was so forthright with random strangers. And as for the wide wide eyed child looking on - my baby sister decided then and there that she would NEVER be bold or "as wild as a March hare".Siobhán was a familiar constant presence in that kitchen. Cooking, washing up, preparing, serving, baking, sewing and at times referring to it (when she couldn't find something) as "*being fed-up with this ship of a house*" and being a stay at home Mother and Wife.

If the house was a ship, then she was the anchor, the calm harbour and haven after our stints on stormy seas, and we flung ourselves like flotsam and jetsam onto the decks of her patience. Today I ask can I have a root upstairs.

"*No, in me own time*" says he.

LISTEN I shout but my sister cuts me off.

She explains calmly and rationally what exactly I need but I am taking the stairs 3 at a time. Upstairs I pillage and plunder the bags, boxes and cases like a thief on speed, unearthing what to strangers would be tattered paper but to me is a treasure trove.

Downstairs by the fire I spread my haul out all over the carpet.

Little Thomasina is confronted with memories.

My sister is laughing at some of the funnier drawings and sketches of mine that Siobhán has kept. She makes a clever remark about a "tweed arse" and he interrupts.

"*Be careful what you say or she'll put it up on her Blob*"

Ha, I'm putting THAT on my blob, I laugh.

There was another thing on the wall in that kitchen. Just an old small tile framed and hanging on a ribbon. It has been hanging there all the days of my life. The words on it I share with you now.

To one who bears the sweetest name,
And adds a lustre to the same,
who shares my joys,
who cheers when sad,
the greatest friend I ever had,
Long life to her,for there's no other,

can take the place,
of my dear Mother

Day 10 of the lockout.

Newsflash
Little Thomasina is sitting beside Siobhán. (((^ - ^)))

Wexford 1982

*W*hile she had been blazing a trail of boldness, the brother was catching up behind her. He had discovered pool and beer and was busy ignoring curfews himself and catching the eyes of the local ladies in Carne, one who was so infatuated she ran away with his smelly runners, which were not allowed in the house and reposed nightly on the decking, covered with the silver trails of the slugs who had crawled away to die horribly. I was gone to Carlow to mind my ailing Mother, and take the pressure off Ollie, who was playing a blinder nursing her. My father had gone a bit senile and he was in a bed with railings around it, banging and roaring, he was washed and shaved from the bed and was helped to a commode by the men. She took advantage of my absence to tell Tom some bare faced lies about a sleepover in a friend's house, and ended up by accident spending the night in Our Lady's Island public toilets, watching a rat run around the floor and waiting for it to get light enough to walk home.
She met the Ford Fiesta on the road with them all travelling to first mass in Tacumshane.
Where are you after being? says Tom dreading the response.
The fittings for her grad dress were interminable and she was like an anti-christ in the dressmakers house. She could not invite the Country Boy and so decided to ask no-one and attend on her own and have a great laugh. Her friends protested and said they knew of a lad that had his own suit and could be pressed into service at the 11ᵗʰ hour. Karma was revisiting as she had behaved outrageously and unforgivably the year before, having been asked to a boys graduation, a boy without a partner or a clue, and she entered the foyér of the hotel on his arm, to much hilarity from the assembled masses.
"Oh, God, did you see her? She opened the door for HIM!"
She ran off to a different party at the end of it, abandoning him to his own devices. His Mother turned up at our door at 7 am looking for him.
The lad with his own suit arrived on time bearing chocolates and a rose, albeit wearing a navy velvet jacket and a pants, and the deal was explained to him. She would vanish like Cinderella at the stroke of midnight and there were to be no questions asked and so she disappeared down the country lanes wearing a leather jacket over the yards of white satin, and a helmet on her perfect ringleted head.
She took a summer job in a Hardware Emporium which was known the length and breadth of the county as somewhere to buy anything from a needle to an anchor. The owner was a larger than life character who was known for his personality and patter along with his trademark flat cap.
Hiya kid, he would shout on the opening of the tinkling shop door.

Seeya Kid, he would shout as they were leaving.

If I haven't got it, I'll get it, he would shout as they marched around the shop.

*She became immune to the heckling and teasing from the builders and painters in blue dungarees who idled around, leaning on counters, picking their teeth with a match and giving her the eye. They called her Sally O Brien, after the way she might look at you. She told me stories of long stands and tartan paint and sky hooks and send the fool further written on the bottom of a docket book in tiny pencilled letters – **S.T.F.F.***

She boiled a Piranha to death, inadvertently making chowder when the heating element fell into his tank as she was feeding him.

Isn't that an awful dose said Tom when he came in from work with his suit stuck to him in the hot evening and then saw his silent Aunt sitting in a fireside armchair for the night.

The pub smelt of channel blocks and soup and had a line of ashtrays bigger than bin lids and nosebleed high stools that hugged the counter. The barman in his gleaming white shirt and tie would be picking horses from the paper, listening to Larry Gogan on the radio.

*God forbid we should get an **ANCO** trainee, highly visible by the red tie which signified that he was only an apprentice and had not served his time as a fully fledged barman. He was always the most easily spotted, his shirt hanging out of his waistcoat, his pants halfway down his arse, a ring of sweat under each oxter while he made a complete balls up of your round and couldn't tot in his head. Neither could he whip cream for an Irish Coffee or stud a lemon with cloves for a hot whiskey. He also actually looked for the people when the phone at the end of the counter rang, instead of laughing and putting it down, or saying, you've just missed him. Back then, there was no such thing as barmaids, and only men, young and old, carried on the tradition of confessor and bouncer. In **Dirty Nellies** in Shannon, the pint of stout was so creamy Tom said he would drink it off the sawdust.*

We had gone on holiday not by mistake, but by accident. Again.

Lockout Ends 2014 - Year 9

It is a pure pleasure to walk through the doors. To see them all in the sunroom grouped around the TV, to smell the familiar smell of the house.

If familiarity breeds contempt then I am like a castaway who has found survivors and absence has definitely made the heart grow fonder. I feel I could waltz even the most ornery of them down the hall.

Outside Siobháns door I am engaged in salutations to nurses and so the dramatic gesture I may or may not have envisaged whereby I fling wide the door and stand gazing at her, drinking in the sights and sounds and smells to document later becomes a moot point as the door is already open.

I perceive her almost in stages.

As the nurse is talking I am watching like a hawk, taking in her posture, her clothing, herself. She hears my voice and there is a barely perceptible reaction, a micro -movement, a slight stiffening of the muscles in the neck, the tiniest nod of the head.

She knows the **Scourge** is in the building.

In the conference call on speaker from her room last night my sister tells me all that they are doing and what has been given, as fluid intake is being measured.

"Never mind all that palava, I will be gatching tomorrow night and getting Siobhán drunk as a lord" says I.

Even the girl in the garage shop knows about Siobhán as she helps me pick out ice-cream and soft drinks telling me what is on offer and wrapping them in the foil lined bags from the deli counter. She too, is joining the ranks of the people who have never met this woman but who have a window into her life from reading about her on a facebook page.

Tonight as I picked the chocolate off the crunchie blast and placed it into her mouth, I leaned my cheek to hers so I could feel the popping. She is surprised by the popping and the noise it makes.

As am I.

I laugh out loud and continue to narrate the story so far. *"Well, look at the head on your one, the brazen hussy. That's what you get for standing in your pelt wrapped in a towel at the top of the stairs, me lady"* says I and Siobhán smiles.

"Massood is after firing the samosas in the bin".

Siobhán looks well.

Her clothes are matching and she has a rather fetching scarf around her neck. I check her temperature and rub her feet. I wonder how many millimetres of lucozade are in the small whiskey glass and decide 100.

One could be forgiven for misconstruing that I am, in fact, a TV addict and that I actually watch the soaps.

Nothing could be further from the truth.

The TV - when it does go on - is late at night in this house.

It is my wind-down after all other avenues have been explored and I manage to catch things on BBC4 about planets, or history or architecture.

It is enough.

I left Siobhán wrapped and rubbed, cuddled, kissed and cosseted - and with hiccups.

The Scourge has left the building.

June 2011 - Year 6

Tonight there is a new piece of "equipment" hanging on the bathroom door. It resembles a parachute with canvas straps and colour coded buckles. It is to raise Siobhán from her Stephen Hawking chair into a *Surita Hoist*, to assist with swinging her body to a commode. There are now so many things in the bathroom I can barely fit my hips in to warm the cloth I use to wipe her face.

I run the flannel under the scorching taps for a hand scalding minute to gently wipe her face and rub her eyes. The woman staring back at me from the mirror is barely recognisable as Me.

I remember once reading a lovely line from *"Eat, Pray, Love"* which talked about how we often mistake our image in mirrors,or quick glances in shop windows where we spot ourselves rushing by and in that moment try to salute our mirror selves, or smile and begin to say hello until we realise, and awkwardly stop.

Gilbert's line was *"Never forget that in an unguarded moment, you recognised yourself as "friend".*

It is in this vein that I try to smile at the woman in the mirror while I check my face for signs of ageing, puffy circles, crows feet, or that downturned mouth thing.

Apart from more Chins than a Chinese phone book, I appear to be escaping quite well. I just look exhausted despite sleeping for about 9 hours yesterday.

Maybe I will just age by looking like I have been up all night for about a year.

There's no wrinkles in a balloon.

Siobháns own face is remarkable in that she does not have a single line in it. In fact, as the pockets of her brain become slowly coated with the plaque that is shutting them down - she appears to have even erased the frown lines on her forehead and between her eyes.

I was such a *"divilskin"* as a youngster that her face has every right to resemble a cracked desert creek.

Doctors with clipboards would walk around wards in the hospital looking for her.

I watched this happen numerous times and would follow them out saying

- "Are you looking for Siobhán?"

They could not reconcile the date of birth on the chart with the face in the bed.

The lifts in the hospital are mirrored too.

I would ask the ward sister to disable the electronic tag on her ankle that would close the doors in our faces at our approach. I was always making a break for the border - and would take her up to outside, to sun, to air, to noise and children and humanity in all its shapes and forms and watch the hatch, match and dispatch play out in the car park.

We would sit around the back at the stores entrance outside while I read to the silent figure in the chair with the massive sunhat, our twin selves reflected in the late evening sun on the parched yellow grass.

One evening as the lift doors glided open and our twin selves were mirrored back to us, Siobhán opened her eyes wide in pleased surprise and smiled at us both.

She tried to speak and I smiled and said "Well, here's the women"

I watched as her eyes clouded and a look of shock and then understanding dawned on her as she heard my voice come from the woman in the mirror, and the awful, shocking realisation dawning that the other woman was *HER*.

I give silent thanks now that she does not recognise that woman, or any woman anymore. Mostly on the evenings when I have to stuff my fist into my mouth to stop from screaming aloud. I give thanks that she is unaware of the enormity of what we witness. I give thanks that she is a warrior and that she is still in my mirror as I reflect on her life.

February 2013 Year 8

For ages I have been contemplating the nature of family, love and loss, trying in some vain way to dissect the fabric of the essence of bonds, nostalgia and memory.

I have been navel gazing, soul baring and shedding - both layers and tears.

I have become the unwilling expert in illness, caring, and information about intervention and fair deals.

I am learning how to walk the walk, how to behave and cope, as on that level I am but a pup.

Siobhán had a baby Jameson tonight while Joni Mitchell sang from the radio -

"*I could drink a case of you and still be on my feet*"

When I was small she used to say "*that one was vaccinated with a gramophone needle*" as my ability to hold forth on various and disparate topics since I could form sentences, was legendary. My first words were not "Mama" or "Dada".

As they were househunting with me strapped in a harness as a precocious toddler in the car they heard a voice coming from the back seat where I said - "*dat lubby house oba dey*". Siobhán remarked that I had "*put the heart crossways in her*".

Today I have talked myself up hill and down dale and into a cocked hat.

I should be exhausted but am high on nervous tension, emotion and adrenaline.

It all started this am when M arrived to pick me up.

At 7 am I was dithering in the kitchen about footwear when she honked the horn.

Could I do "*Double-Inn Citaay*" in heels?

The *Mini Slippertons* called but I refused their flat fur lined pleas and zipped on my boots. I am wearing a dress that a country woman might have worn in the 50's. Navy with a pink flower. It made me look like a pregnant toddler and I teamed that with tights, boot socks, and a military style trench coat with silver buttons and topped it all off with a soft leather Trilby tipped at a rakish angle.

I am going to a funeral.

So of course it seems perfectly rational to bring my work bag with diary, notebook, and dictaphone.

It all went swimmingly till Avoca.

After a caffeine break M insists that I google the city and buses so as I know where I am going, and more importantly how to get back. She pulls up at the bus stop and shouts "Go, Go, GO" as if I am singlehandedly storming the beaches at Normandy or jumping out of an aeroplane door at 10,000 feet.

I skid through the rush hour traffic in the rain and leap aboard the bus as the door is closing.

"City Centre please" I say and eyeing the notice about exact fares only, hurl the contents of my purse into the dish till a ticket comes out.

I turn around and face the *ENTIRE* bus and have to sit mortified in the bucket chair facing them. Their eyes are boring into me and I feel like shouting "*I'm up from the country you know*" as they stare, but refrain and spend the journey into the city pretending to be mesmerised by the view through the steamed up window.

Of course I get off (out of sheer politeness) 5 stops too early and have to walk around the gaff reading place names like a tourist. I almost began speaking with a German accent for the craic.I reeled around the streets in the rain for a while and then decided to shit or get off the pot. Throwing myself on the mercy and at the feet of various strangers, I walked to another bus stop at the other side of the city.

The name of the road where the church is located   - is on the sign.

Hurrah!

I have made a new friend. She has white hair and a long black coat. She is a widow who downsized and she knows exactly where I am going. Her name is Dolly

The name of the lady whose funeral I am trying to attend *is* Dolly.

Oh, yeee of little faith.

We drive for miles. She goes up to tell the driver where exactly I am getting off. It is the very last stop. I am alone on the bus bar the driver. He shows me the short cut and says he will pray for Dolly. I meet a man walking a Japanese poodle through the estate. He tells me his life story and leads me to the church.

I am early.

Joy of joys there is a coffee shop beside it. I repair to the toilets to fix my boat race. And then casually sit with my Americano reading. After half an hour I glance idly at the menu and read the address printed on the bottom.

Sweet Merciful Christ, I am at the wrong church!

After the cashier stopped laughing she tells me I will need a cab. The pale woman at the table across says I will *never* get there, as she sighs into her tea. The funeral directors outside smoking by the empty hearse - when they stop laughing- announce it is Mrs *Byrnes* funeral.

"NO", I need Dolly " I pant and start running blindly (down the *right* road accidentally) until the men fixing the road at the lights tell me to go around "**The Kestrel**" and then down and left and right and straight and left. I run holding my hat on and don't stop till I skid into the back of the *REAL* church.

I am in a lather.

People are staring again.

I kneel in Mount Jerome as the strains of the music prefaced the slow sliding of the curtains for the very last time, and took the proffered tissue from the woman beside me and said goodbye to Dolly in a very small voice.

Now I can visualise a chorus line of angels highkicking in burlesque outfits singing

"*Well, HELLO Dolly! it's so nice to have you back where you belong!*"

I told all of this (and more) to Siobhán on my visit tonight and then sang "*Amazing Grace*".

I think I may be overtired.

Kerry - Summer 1975

Tom would never usually give us a heads up about holidays so what started out as drives ended up with us staying in those far flung B&B's , where we would have to be outfitted in chain stores, as only the rudiments of underwear and tattered clothing were actually placed in the boot, with the bait and rods. Once after driving for hours around Kerry, he had enquired from everyone in the entire County about where we could stay. The shopkeeper sent us to the publican who sent us to the post master who rang his brother and we managed to let a house for a week in Beaufort.

"Isn't this desh?" I said as I ran excitedly back to the car to retrieve our belongings.

Her ladyship was contrary with the heat in the back seat and gave me a look that told me she was not amused by my usage of colloquial slang, and that I was **not** being cool.

If there was a wake she'd want to be the corpse.

The house in Beaufort was a great base to tour the area as we did not have to be subjected to the whims and vagaries of various landladies who would offer a list of instructions as long as your arm along with the keys.

First we would do a recce from the garden and read the signs about **Bord Failte** registration and hot/cold running water and tea/coffee available in all rooms.

They would try and make themselves smaller in the porch by bending their knees as per warnings from Tom as sometimes children under a certain age were a reduced rate, and we would as often as not, share a family room which had a massive bed, bunks and a cot. There would be nylon bedspreads, flouncy pillows and valances, a carpeted bathroom with an avocado suite and sink, place mats on the breakfastroom tables of a hunt in Lancashire with a master and beagles and lace covers over the milk jugs. The landlady would enquire the night before if you wanted full Irish which was a fry, or continental which was concentrated orange juice and a hard bread roll. She would enquire what part of the country you were from and try to work out who she knew there. Tom would go through every single person he knew in the world with the same surname and would try and place her. She would send us to her cousin's pub where there was a trad session on every night of the week for the tourists. We would try not to flush the toilets late at night and wake up the entire house.

We went to Muckross and Glenbeigh and Rossbeigh and did the Ring of Kerry hanging off the sides of two giant horses while the children jeered and laughed from a pony and trap. They fell around in the back of the trap, shouting and being secretly raging that they did not have a horse to hang off themselves. We went to castles and cities and churches. We went to museums and beaches and cliffs. We wore our plastic coats when it lashed and brought Aran cardigans and umbrellas even on the most moderate of days.

When he had exhausted the country side and everywhere that was not the North, due to the propensity of being bombed to death or being shot with a rubber bullet in what we casually referred to as the troubles as if it was no more than a minor spat and not a civil war, Tom took the enormous step of taking us abroad. We did not follow Steptoe and Son to Spain - we went on a daytrip to Fishguard. It did not stop her being hysterical with excitement from the moment the ship pulled away from the quay wall. Due to subterfuge she still did not even know if we were bound for France or Wales but all she knew was we were sailing away. The smell of diesel and petrol from the car decks permeated the smell of the sea and the various people leaning greenly over the side, and I watched in delicious horror as a woman got a belt of sick from another passenger as the wind blew it from one face to another. We barely had time in Fishguard to turn around before the ship sailed again for Rosslare, but it was enough time for her to kiss the Welsh ground on the pretext of doing up her sandal, as if she were the pope or a visiting monarch. I could marvel at the red postboxes and the Cadburys machines on the platform and the sterling coins. I watched enviously as the London train idled in the station and thought how glamorous it would be to board it, and arrive into the city I knew only from reading about. It was a place I imagined through a pea soup fog, and that I would live down a cobble stoned lane beside an olde curiousity shop, buying my clothes from Carnaby Street and would meet Edna O Brien in a smoky nightclub and talk to her about small things, one country girl to another.

The last child was now old enough to go to Secondary School and arrived as a nervous 1st year while her ladyship was creating havoc in her 6th. At her admission Familiarisation, a teacher heard her answer her surname and enquired tentatively if she was any relation. On her affirmative response, her card was duly marked and they came down on her like a ton of bricks when she happened to be standing near a fire alarm that apparently spontaneously broke its own thin glass and set off the shrieking bells in the entire school. Nicola has never been a bold child, and watched in a combination of horror, awe and admiration as both of her siblings not only did not toe the line but literally tore the arse out of it. Perhaps as a direct result of their behavior she felt she had to be a good girl and make amends to parents who were already stressed to the bejesus trying to cope with the demands of their unruly teenagers, and she felt in some way responsible for easing their burden by behaving. I spent my days alternately shopping or cooking for my brood, and then cleaning up after them. No sooner would one meal be over than the preparation for the next would begin. She would run in from school at lunchtime tearing past me in the steamed up kitchen to stand precariously on the seat in the corner near the radio which she would turn up to full blast and start singing along with.

"Angie baby, you're a special lady, living in a world of maaaaaaaaake believe, well, maybe"

- What are you doing up there, Shell?
- Heat rises and I'm perished.
- Would you like an egg, Shell?
- No, I'll just have the egg, thanks.

God help her, sure she thought she was hilarious.

A cat never bred a rabbit.

February 2013 - Year 8

Well, there was a right hooley out in the home today. They are known to throw up a fine spread when there are celebrations to celebrate and what better reason to throw a party than a birthday.

While all the festivities were in full swing I breasted the teamaid Leanne for a sanger and a sausage as I had dined solely on a biscuit for the entire day.

It is only when I get a headache that I realise I have not eaten and am wondering if it is too late to luncheon at midnight.

I poured a baby Jameson at 6.04 pm and I left the glass back down on the table at 9.49 with an inch still in it.

The going was steady. A fair number of drops of the craythur trickled down onto the towel, and a fair number of drops trickled down into the creases on her craw, but the majority of the drops hit their intended target and made Siobhán cough.

I laughed out loud.

"Well, that's hit the spot eh Mrs........" says I and then explain the story of the Magdalene women to her.

When Siobhán is listening she really *listens*.

She is curled up to one side of the massive chair and I am as close to her as it allows me to get, my knees pressed sideways into its metal panels, my head bent under the headrest so I can watch the micro movements on her face.

I relate the stories of the day to her in language and images she can understand. I like to mention Carlow and Gowran, Killeshin and The Hill - Burrin Street,Tullow Street, Staplestown Road, Graigcullen and The Crescent.

I talk about the Dooleys.

"*Hang down your head, Tom Dooley*" I will sing and watch as a muscle twitches under her eye.

Her fathers name was Tom Dooley, although not he, the eponymous rebel of the song.

"Siobhán, member the time Ollie took us up the hill in banger of a Morris Minor....."

"Siobhán, member the time Paddy Matthis flashed at me" -

Years ago in Ireland we did not have paedophiles, we had *quare fellas*. A quare fella was any oul fella who was a bit soft in the head and who walked about either foostering with - or displaying himself. Your Nana would warn you to stay away from "quare fellas, and the Booshey Man" .These lads were harmless and gormless at the same time. A lot of them ended up in *The County Home in their latter years*. A distant relation of Siobháns was a resident in a County Home, in her 60's she wore a pink pinafore and her blonde pudding bowl haircut was combed to one side like a child. She spent her visits swinging on the iron gate and over and over again pinched her thumb and index finger together and licked them repeating - "Not a Talla, Not a Talla" grinning. Little did we know at the time that all the real foostering and abuse Nana didn't know about, was happening behind the very gates of the institutions that were supposed to be protecting and educating the innocent.

Two hours in to the drink and my arms ache from leaning over. I become all Roald Dahl and try to make her hold the glass. I watched some home movie footage of Dahl try to re-educate his wife after a massive stroke. At times bordering on torture - as he manipulated her limbs and made her try again, and again, and again - it is a seminal piece of archive. I am aware that she will not suddenly say "here's mud in your eye" and drain the glass and slam it down.

I am aware that her own birthday on this Tues 19th will be a much quieter affair with no party food and only her family to mark the 5th birthday she will have had here.

I am also aware that I can only narrate this tale, document this progression, photograph and film this, from a space that is of me, but not me.

It is as if I step outside of myself to type this.

In that vein I am way more *DOOLEY* than Mahon.

February 19th 2014 - Year 9 - 80th Birthday

The re-inforcements arrive just as the smoke from the candles is wisping its way out of the room. My sister, nephew and I join Little Thomasina and Keyhole Kate to stand around the Stephen Hawking Chair.

The lady herself seems blissfully unaware of all the fuss.

"Ah, you missed it" says Dad.

One of the staff comes back in and takes a photo of us grouped around the chair holding hands. It is one of those photos that I particularly loathe - the tiny figure looking so much worse on celluloid than in actuality, where the essence lingers. On film the enormity of the ravages of the disease are glaringly obvious.

In the parallel universe that runs in tandem with ours, the world of chiaroscuro, of stills and film capture a moment and preserve it for posterity. I take some video footage of gifts being opened and know that I will watch it aghast late at night and compare it to other footage from a few months ago in disbelief.

There is always *muckin' furders* about who does what when we all get together. Each of us has our own way of doing things and freaks out to see the other do things the "*wrong*" way. (In other words not OUR way)

Simmering tempers run high. Words are exchanged. Tantrums are had and fags are smoked at the door.

Then I came back.

My father is manhandling a yellow rose tree into the space behind the chair at the window which the carers will curse to high heaven as they move it out of the way every day. I move us all down the hall to a cooler room where we can make coffee and sit at an actual table.

Little Thomasina is furious.

"They'll be bringing her tea" he fumes.

"Let them" says I.

He is a creature of habit and a stickler for rules.

I am his polar opposite.

Although we are "*lick alike*" at the same time

The nurses ask me if they have the right Date of Birth on the chart as it seems impossible that this woman, with her unlined face, is the age that makes her.

I like to think I have inherited her genetics and have the same skin, although mine appears to have not been overly strained by a skin care routine that consists of pints, fags, and never removing make up, moisturising or using soap.

I take a look back in at the tiny vulnerability of her, at the cards ranged around the room, and the outpouring of love and tenderness to mark the day of her birth and feel lost.

At home last night I am ornery and out of sorts.

I can't write, I can't think, and at times I forget to breathe.

I have the fear.

March 2013 - Year 8

As humans we tend to spend a lot of time in our heads -
or frantically trying to be elsewhere,
or striving to achieve,
or do, or have, or be, other than we are.
Despite years of study and an awareness of the frailty, the fragility, the temporal nature of things, I am as guilty of this as anyone else. The last few days have been ones of solitude and introspection. The sky looks like a fat mans face in need of a shave, whiskers of steely cloud, streaks of stubble of charcoal, con trails and seagulls shrieking over the attic glass.
A whistling under the crumbling wooden window frame of the unrelenting wind.
The dark grey oppressive clouds have matched my mood.
A sneaky wind came and brewed a storm around our door a decade ago.
It began slowly, tickling, prodding, forcing us to notice, nipping around ankles, stealing around shoulders, banging windows that sad faces looked out of, forcing doors open or slamming them shut, till we were blown away.
It rustled up dry leaves and memories like pages flicking in a manuscript and blew words and memories around us like snuff at a wake. It confronted and confounded us. It laid us low with body blows and sadness and bewilderment. It shaped and moulded us like soft sloppy cement splashed into a late evening mixer where with sand and water and time, it blew a clean channel through the wide open spaces of our hearts, and carved its name on the minds of those who love this woman, and we have emerged from the pummelling, polished and shining like emeralds at the other hand
When I forget to be "aware" I will find that I have been sitting hunched forward, straining to hear, forgetting to exhale. When I catch myself unawares (literally) I will go through a mental checklist and tick off my worry list. I try to remind myself to stay present and aware and awake and in the NOW.
When do we remember the past but in the now?
When do we worry about the future but in the now?
Now is all we ever have.
Part of this mulling and thinking and wishing led me to mentally narrate all of the things that I had been concerned about and in an agony of self sabotage and maudlin reminiscing I wished the following.
I wished that -
I had been more aware of Siobhán when she was well -
that I had remembered more of what she said or thought or felt -
that I had paid attention to her advice -
or remembered the last thing she said to me —
or , God help me, what her voice sounded like -
that I had sat and conversed with her about her hopes and dreams, her favourite things, the minutae of her life -
that I had not been so busy and distracted and filled with a sense of my own importance -
that I had not been so hysterical and dramatic and unreliable and spent so many years

lurching from one emotional crisis to the next, hurtling through jobs, homes, countries and men like a pinball in a giant machine -

that I had spent more time with her -

that I had taken her on the Spanish Sojurns I took alone -

that I was a better daughter ....

Now is all we ever have.

Now, today, this moment, I am breathing in and out.

I am aware that I am carrying the essence of myself within this battered body, this baleful heap that I schlepp around in, that needs to be fed and watered and washed and have its hair and toenails cut and put to bed.

It is the greatest thing I will ever own.

I need to be easier with it, to love and respect it, to lighten up on how much abuse I give it and hurl at it.

I am a living breathing human female.

My legs walk the me named Michelle around - her arms carry and hold, her brain works, her ears hear, her heart despite all its bruising still beats, her soul is reflected in eyes that are jaded but hopeful.

I remember as a small child walking home from my Nana's house down Johns Road to the Square. It was Christmas and there was a frosty fog on the darkening streets, the lamps lit in every window, and I hurried in my coat and bonnet past Traynors in the icy dark. A blind man is tap tap tapping his way with a cane up Johns Gate Street. I know he is blind as not only does he have black glasses and a white stick, but he has a partially sighted wife who links him by the elbow. Tonight he is alone, and I walk on the opposite path watching in amazement as he negotiates the broken pavement and holds on to the walls, the stick held out in front like a beacon, the bells ringing in Rowe Street Church calling him in for evening Mass. I hung back to watch him, and to listen quietly to the other sound I can hear, under the bells. It is the blind man softly whistling. The blind man is whistling, I think. And then I realise what it is.

The blind man is whistling "Joy to the World"

June 1983

I ran across a churchyard after 11 mass in the Cathedral in Carlow because I spotted a lad I had gone to school with back in the day, who was the Editor of **The Nationalist** — I caught up with him and smoothing down my hair asked him had he any jobs for a girl who could write. He told me to tell her to send stuff or ring him, neither of which she bothered to do. Ollie was livid.

"Disgracing yourself running after that lad "says Ollie as he rolled up his shirt sleeves to lather his hands with carbolic soap before mashing the parsnips.

Instead she wrote a fawning letter to a Gynaecologist asking him did he need anybody to be his P.A./Receptionist as she could type and answer phones and was good with people and babies. He wrote a charming letter back explaining that he did not need anybody and wished her well and hoped she would find something suitable in the near future. She wrote him an even more charming letter back , heaping him with praise and thanks, and wishing every seed and breed of him all the best for now and ever more, and calling down blessings on his curly head.

He gave her a job.

She became the face at the door and the voice on the phone trilling good afternoon and asking women if they were pregnant or not.

Would your appointment be for Ante Natal or Gynae?

"Wha?"

Are you pregnant or not?

She spent the mornings dancing around the hallway with the radio blaring,

"LAST Christmas, I gave you my heart, but the very next day you gave it away………" straightening up the magazines in the waiting room while singing at full throat into the sweeping brush and calling people from the phone which was supposed to be for incoming calls only. One day while she was smoking the butt of a cigar from his ashtray and harmonizing at top volume with Joni Mitchells "River" his tiny wife came in and caught her. She was shuddering having chanced upon photographs of surgery where a pensioner had cysts the size of a small child removed from her womb. She also read every single chart, and all the letters back and forth between specialists and fellow surgeons, and every note on every file until she felt she was an actual Gynaecologist herself.

Again.

I had to attend him myself before my hysterectomy and would advise her to turn up the radio and take her small ear hole away from the keyhole as quick as she liked.

If she knew the woman well, and had bonded with her, she would enquire what she had.

- A baby – was his response invariably.

I watched her placate a waiting room full of hormonal women when they saw him run out the door to the labour ward.

"Aw, Christ almighty, I've my children/Mother-in Law/dogs in the car" they would wail and she would prophetically intone "it could be YOU!" years before the lottery. She mopped up ruptured haemotoamas from the bathroom floor, took semen samples in pill bottles wrapped in hankies from mortified men at the door, and conducted a long distance telephone romance with a lad in London town.

He held a large bottle of macardles in the small of her back as they danced to Phyllis Nelson urging them to "Move Closer" and would collect her from the house in a Datsun Sunny 120Y that he had souped up, Tom, reading his prayers, already dreading and anticipating the roars of the engine idling when he dropped her back. He took her to the Red Bar in Whites and made her sing while he played his guitar, and brought home random musicians and cans to his front room for sessions while his parents remonstrated from the bedroom by banging their shoes on the floor.

When he moved to London, she told us she was going on a weekend shopping trip with the girls and we gave her money and a list of things from Argos but she legged it off to visit him instead, navigating alone from one side of the teeming city to the other.

The Swan was the kind of pub that was packed all day, and there was always something dodgy going on, somebody fiddling a raffle or running off with the spot prize or the pot man. It was filled with old Irish men in wrinkled suits and stained collars. She was paraded as someone from the old country and bought round after round while they told her they had been 40 odd years in

England and could not go home.

"Sure, there's nothin' left for me now, all my people are dead and gone" said the Mayo man with the Charlton Athletic Baseball Cap as he drank a bottle of Gold Label to steady his calloused hands.

-   I'd only go home now to ask the time and come back - said he wiping the sides of his mouth.

The men that built London, forgotten and faded as dust motes in slanted bars, in high rises with tin openers, cassette tape of Irish ballads, empty bottles of Whyte & McKay lined up like dead men around the bottom of the stinking bin.

– I just called to say I love you by Stevie Wonder was playing loudly on a radio when she woke and it was as surprising to her when she slept through the alarm and the banging door and arrived out to a roomful of people at lunchtime with a hairstyle like Patti Smith dragged through a ditch backways.

-   The first 6 months are the worst- said the old men in The Swan that night as the girls sailed home without her. She watched the hands of the bar clock ticking inexorably towards anchors aweigh and pondered the reaction in the quiet kitchen at home when there was no daughter to pick up from the early morning ferry.

-   We were watching the clock hands too, with excitement, and in anticipation, and secret delight that we would never voice.

After 48 hours of mayhem Tom's sister called the number she had been given on the back of an envelope in the boutique and told her ladyship in no uncertain terms to get herself on the next sailing and cop on.

-   I have NO more money to give you – She fumed to the obese bus driver on the Slatterys Coach as she placed the life size teddy she had won in the raffle on the seat beside her as the bus left Kensington.
-   You can put him in the hold.
-   He won't fit with the bags - he huffed and lurched back down the bus with his hips bouncing off every seat.

My first born child and her teddy sat estranged from the rest of the passengers and tiptoed around the motorway services, vowing never to consume a sandwich with cucumber in it again. She was very concerned with what she would say to her Father, who would be waiting to collect her at the Pier. The journey home was a different one than out, not least because she was travelling alone but also because the sea looked like soup someone had forgot to take off the boil.

Tom sat in the car on top of the cliff in his own black and white movie and watched the lacy foam waves breaking on the swollen grey ocean and worried. The irony of being on the top of the hill that every family came to sit at on Sunday afternoons watching ships was not lost on him and he bit his thumbnails, and picked his fingers as he watched for a ship himself.

It will be a miracle if she docks, he thought looking at the listing ship.

It will be twice the miracle if she is on it.

The ship rolled back and all aboard were flung around like the feathers from a burst pillow.

People were lying everywhere and anywhere, including wedged between the long steps of the stairs and they cried and heaved and prayed to their Redeemer to rescue them and please let them set foot

on dry land again one more time and they would never leave it. He spotted her arriving white faced into the Port dragging the giant bear and his stomach turned with delight and shock.
She decided that the best form of defence would be attack.

- *Well, if yee were the kind of people I could talk to, none of this would have happened she flounced as she flung open the car door.*

To his eternal credit, and her shame, Tom did not respond.
I was waiting in my blue dressing gown in the kitchen and I quietly went about the business of letting her know, not in words, but in the set of my shoulders, which were not stiff and angry but relaxed and open, that she was welcome home and in the bustle of the breakfast ritual, let her find her land legs again. I have always and ever been the quiet support, the buttress, the pleader of leniency, the stoic patient one, the polar opposite of my husband, and my daughter, and thus able to mediate between these two highly strung people I loved. It had occurred to me that she may not have come back at all, and would have stayed in the City of the Buckingham Palace, the Westminster Abbey, the Tin Pan Alley and the Covent Garden, and we would have lost her.

Winter 2012 – Year 7

I am sitting on a round table with white linen - waiting for coffee -today and I hear myself saying words to the woman beside me.

It appears that I actually know what I am talking about.

No-one was more surprised than myself.

It appears that I am telling the woman on my left how the woman on my right is being so strong.

"I think" says I, "that when there is a crossing like this, when the soul is just about to leave the body, there is a tiny chink, a hairs breadth of a crack , where the peace comes in .... like a draught.

"A miniscule breeze of ease, a sliver of eternal consciousness wending its way in, and winding its way around its closest soul, to offer strength and endurance and safe passage in stormy seas."

I know, right?

In my belief system there is no angry God with a beard floating about on a cloud judging and condemning to hell or purgatory.

Hell IS other people.

There are no winged cherubs toting harps.

There are no gates to be admitted by.

St Peter is not waving the longest print out on the planet.

In my belief system there is an eternity.

It is a consciousness of pure loving energy, it is an awesome presence that black holes are mere specks in, it is the Be all and End all, and we *ARE* it.

You ARE the thing you are praying to.

I believe as your eyes close here they open IN it.

"*Impossible is Nothing*" says my wristband - in memory of a life.

The day after my Grandmother died we three children arrived with my Father to my Mothers childhood home. I was curious to see how grief would have affected her, curious even then about how people cope with loss and devastation on a grand scale, and noticed that she seemed harried and not quite herself, greeting us at the front door (which was seldom used) in a distracted manner, missing my cheek as I stood on tiptoe for a kiss.

The smell of the laburnum hedge which we children all loved to shred much to my Uncle Oliver's consternation, was at its strongest in the late August heat and the trains that hurtled through the gardens at the back (and on whose tracks my "senile" Grandfather had been found wandering in his pyjamas) evoked a note of normality that was strangely absent from the house. The relations had assembled en masse and people from all over had called in - *Rossmore, Killeshin, The Hill, Castledermot, Pollerton, Tullow and Gowran*. A parade of characters and personalities and newsy neighbours had taken up residence in the front room and were holding court over ham sandwiches and whiskey. Over the smell of gas from the superser was an aroma of rashers frying and tea stewing, spent matches and scuts of cigarettes on saucers on the mantlepiece beside a picturesque blue ashtray that was enscribed "*En Fumant pensez au Moi*!" It would be years before I would know enough French to translate it.

"*God, an' I'm sorry for your loss, Missus*" said Blind Bill from Castledermot.

The house was full with children.

The cousins were running wild, daring each other to drain the dead men in the pantry and sneaking sips out of glasses and bottles. I am sure there were surreptitious pulls off fags happening out on the back step, especially with the English cousin with the long hair I had a secret crush on. My brother may or may not have been a willing participant - he has always been a bit of a Jack the Lad, and up to all sorts of mischief. Undertakers had been phoned and meat ordered and drink collected and now they were only waiting on the last daughter to arrive from England.

Maura Eilís Nash nee Dooley - whom I called "Emmee" after her initials - was a trend-setter and girl about town in London. Think **"Doctor in the House"** with Dirk Bogarde and you pretty much sum it up. She was a slender Irish Cailín with huge blue eyes married to a British Doctor, who had served in WW2 as chief medical officer in Her Majesty's Navy. They met when she nursed him in the Brompton before he moved to a Sanatorium to recover from TB.

Emmee skidded from arrivals at Dublin Airport into the back of her brother's car, applying her make-up on the way down, and insisted on being brought to the club for a stiffener before she could even contemplate viewing her Mother in Carpenters Funeral Home. What she did there is unbelievable for the time.

She took a photo.

In the days before camera phones, digital cameras, and all the other palava she took a photo of her Mother in the coffin.

There was probably even a flash.

"Well" says my Uncle in the kitchen – through his teeth as he lit a cigar - lifting his brandy balloon while shrugging his Cromby off his shoulders "you won't *believe* what your one did below at the wake"

There are nights when I am with Siobhán and I am taking photos of her while she is unaware or sleeping that this memory will come back. I will wonder if I am crossing some invisible line drawn in the sand, or worse, that I have gone so far beyond the line that I may as well keep ploughing on through the dunes to see what lies over the ridge of the next. Some nights the yellow room feels like a tomb in the cemetery of my soul.

I found that photo recently and saw for the first time the image that has been captured of a Mothers face in Eternity for Eternity. I will also feel a link down through the decades, an invisible gossamer thread that binds me to another Dooley woman, and *all* the Dooley women, a woman who sometimes at my shoulder I can hear whisper -

"Go on, tell it, tell it ALL!"

Write it down.

Remember this.

Winter 2011 Year 6

I am the woman who names things.

I also *have* as many names as there are days in a week, Michelle, Mee shell, Mitch, Shell, Shellakeypookey, Seashell and Shellshock.

Passwords are a bitch.

There are things I cannot name.

There are no nicknames and euphemisms for my visits.

I sat surreptitiously smoking in the residents smoking area tonight while the whole toilet thing played out in Siobháns room. Lit with only the neon green of the EXIT sign and the single red glow of my solitary Marlboro, I watched the rain beating down sideways on the glass and run into little funnels at the sill. I watched the long strip of road in the dark with the vast hulking mountain looming a deeper shade of indigo.

And I imagine the occupants in the speeding cars staring out the windows into the lit rooms I am sitting staring back from, and wondering if it's a hotel, the lines of little orange lights in the dark night.

The only sound sadder than a curlew is a motorbike changing gears on a lonely road.

I watched the sense of dread creep under the door and spread its groping tentacles around the skirting.

It will find you in the end, it always doesThis time I met it with a cold glare, and gazed down my exhaled smoke at the absolute cheek of it.

"Well, we meet again. Now, me boyo, you can scoot off back to whatever loathsome swamp you slithered in from and take all belong to you with you. Don't let the door hit you in the arse on your way out."

With a puff of air and a sigh it was gone.

Like all bullies, it needs to be named and shamed.

It cannot stand the light.

It only feeds on pain and finds joy indigestible.

I put out my cigarette and walked out with my head held high.

I continue blithely down the hall, waving absent- mindedly at the massed crowd in the Sunroom as they sat in a ring around the blaring TV and turned into her room. Her chair was empty, the bed stripped to its rubber mattress and the windows wide. My stomach turned.

I saw a blue uniform in the distance and called "Where is Siobhán?" with a tremor in my voice.

"In the Sunroom" she responds.

I walked back.

In the ring of bent white heads I struggle to spot her.

It is the chair that clinches it.

It is the biggest by far.

How can I have missed her?

I nod and smile at the hopeful faces and excuse and squeeze myself in till I am kneeling beside her.

"Look at you, chilling with your homies!" I tell her bent head.

I work on the premise that humans can hear every word said until the last breath leaves them. It explains why I am adamant not to allow, or participate in, talking above them. I also have become adept at policing conversations that should not mention trigger words.

I realise that I am in the way of a lady bearing down on the last seat left in the room, She is using her walking aid like a Diviner wielding dowsing rods. I manipulate the gargantuan chair out the door with the brakes still on.

"Coffee" says I and make a bee line for the hospitality room.

It has a table set for 4, kitchen appliances and a radio. It is also a room with a view. Beyond the green garden is a view of the Mountain, where her other daughter lives.

As I wait for the kettle to boil I am minded to think of all the times it was Siobhán doing the caring.

As a child on a scorching summer evening in our mobile home, I opened my parent's bedroom door to be confronted with the sight of Siobhán washing her own Mother who was half undressed, lying sideways across the bed.

"*Close the door please*".

It has always been Siobhán who deals (without drama or fuss or a shred of revulsion) with the caring, the cleaning, the minding.

It was my Mothers calm presence, acceptance and awareness that I recall now and how every little thing she did was without fanfare, hysteria or tantrum.

I only wish I could say the same.

I flick around the radio dial and remember putting butter on the one at home as a small child out of sheer devilment and find The Crab playing "*Come -all - Ye's*" while I add the milk.

It is then I remember the brace of chocolate and caramel magnums in my hand bag.

Hey brain, enough with the Cortisol already.

Michelin have been on the blower about using me as a mascot.

Michelin Mahon.

In a moment of madness I wrap mine in napkins and put it in the freezer drawer untouched.

Go me.

With every piece I break off and push into her lips I wipe the dark chocolate stains from her mouth and chin. She loves this ice-cream. So would I if I had to exist on a diet of semolina. I told a friend the other day that at the end of the visits I always can't quite believe that I am leaving her behind, that she and I are not going for a drink or coffee and cake and exhaling after the trauma of visiting someone disappeared. I miss calling her at night to see how things are, I miss her quiet advice and her husky voice, and just a million little things when only your Mam will do.

How could I have missed her?

How can I not?

The Scourge - Majorca 1985

I asked the Doctor's wife for time off to have holidays and she gave me a shrewd look.
Are you coming back this time?
I'm going to Majorca, says I.
It was to be my first time doing lots of things.
Getting on a plane, burning to a crisp and eating Iceberg lettuce. In Ireland we only ever had a huge dark green lettuce with a copper spade mark across one leaf, and on it we placed the following –
- A slice of ham (rolled)
- A slice of corned beef (rolled)
- An egg cut with an egg slicer with paprika shaken on it
- A spoonful of potato salad from a tin
- A scallion with frilled ends
- Half a tomato
- A slice of beetroot with a bit of black on one side

On the May bank holiday my cousin and I stood hitching outside **The Talbot Hotel** to blag a lift to Carne for the crack. Our families had left in convoy the night before and it did not raise an eyebrow that two young women would be out thumbing lifts. That was how we got around then. A hackney was only for going to Dublin for the big shop on the 8th of December, when every person in the town went to the City, and every country craythur that could put one foot under the other climbed out from under a rock, put twine around their trousers, and went to town.

The only 2 hackneys in the whole town were Syl Carley, and Walter Busher, one you rang to book a big car for a wedding or a funeral, the other you stood on the step in the rain at 3 am and rang the top bell and waited for his head to appear in the window. My Nana Mahon booked Syl once for the Christmas Shop and had her purse lifted by a **gurrier** in Dublin. She never forgave or forgot. The cars were smiling and waving and making those turn off gestures where they shrug their shoulders and smile ruefully as they blatantly lie. An open topped sports car came hurtling around the corner, its occupants 2 males in tennis whites, pulling in with a screech of brakes up the road. "I don't think much of yours" I laughed as we ran up alongside trying to keep our hair fluffed and without breaking an ankle in the heels. We were wearing geometric dresses and had our hair backcombed into Robert Smith bouffants a mile wide, with purple lipstick and eyeliner. It seemed like a perfectly reasonable idea to stop for a drink on the way, and thus to make dates to see them at the slow set in **Cedars** that night.

Katrina & the Waves were singing about walking on sunshine and I was in a frenzy on the floor when my tennis coach turned up and tapped me on the shoulder. I smile now to think of the fun we had that night, the laughing, the flirting, the way we danced to REO Speedwagon, swaying in his arms, knowing inherently that if I angled my neck an inch it would be kissed.

By the time it was boarding the plane time, I was in love and hysterical at the idea of being separated. Apart from bullying a friend of mine into knitting a jumper in a hurry with chessboard pink and white squares to wear in 40 degree heat, I played the single he had sent me in the post over and over.

"I'm gonna KEEP on lovin' YOU 'cos it's the ONLY thing I wanna DO …….."

It had a black and white photo of him inside the sleeve.

He is wearing his tennis whites and is pouting beautifully while pretending to serve a killer volley. I arranged to meet him on the day of the flight. Like all country people we got off the bus with our cases and marched into **McDonalds** for a burger at breakfast time. Then we went to meet my love and his wing man. Suffice to say a veil will be drawn over proceedings but that a lot of imbibing in various hostelries all day culminated in me singing on top of a piano in **Casper & Giumbini's** in Wicklow Street that night, watching as the barman placed the phone on the counter. Through a fog of drink I heard the wing man mutter and slur, over and over, into it that he was in fact in no fit state to say evening mass, and could one of the lads in the house take one for the team.

In the airport I did a bit of wallfalling, a bit of crying and a lot of messing about with a security guard and a hat. I have no idea how I was allowed on the plane. I spent the entire flight in the tiny stainless steel toilet poking tomato skin down the vacuum and leaning my tear stained face against the mirror while the stewardess banged on the door. A combination of alcohol poisoning and turbulence do not good bed fellows make.

There was a smell of Marlboro as soon as the door of the plane opened and the heat hit us like a wall. We never felt heat like it.

Which was true.

We gasped our way onto the coach and drove through the sleeping volcanic country side and I marveled at the sights, the villas, the whole glittering Island displaying herself like a debutante, teasing us with coquettish glimpses of impossible flowers and plants, orchids and succulents, flashes of blue, azure, aquamarine and tourqoise from the pools and the flickering sea. Our apartment was small and aptly named for the Bougainvilla that hung from every available inch. I laid all my stuff on the bed near the wall, unceremoniously claiming it.

I spent the first morning of my sun holiday nursing the hangover from hell and writing a 7 page letter home about the flight.

We explored and came up with the general consensus that the place was the size of Rosslare, with a couple of beach bars and a supermarket. It was on the 3rd day we realised the whole town was just around the next corner - the one we had stopped walking to because of the heat.

We were young Irish girls let loose on an island with sun, sea, and sangria and no-one to say "fasten up your craw" I will let you do the math. I met a Scottish postman who wore about 50 gold chains and gave me a string of spectacular love bites in a ring around my neck. I spent a lot of time alternately holding in my stomach in my togs and trying not to get thrown in the deep end of the pool. It used to come between me and my sleep and I would hyperventilate at the thoughts that one of the random gangs of marauding British teens would hurl me by wrist and ankle into the pool to screams and applause. I nearly drowned once as a child and never told anyone and so had never learned to swim.

I was persuaded though to go on the water slide. It took about half an hour to get to the top and they positioned me in the middle so as I could land on someone and the one behind would take up the slack by pulling me up by the hair. We practiced the manouevure of this many many times on the way up, as the man checked our wrist bands. The fatal flaw was my friend deciding to do it facing front down, and she tore the hips off herself on the seams the whole way down, and was in agony by the time she hit the water. So I sank like a stone and the thought that flashed through my mind as I plummeted past all the legs was – this is it and I became calm. A stunning Spaniard pulled me up by the straps and I lay flopping like a mackerel on the warm tiles gasping and heaving up lungfuls of blue water. As soon as I could breathe I said "Again!"

We had made friends with sisters who holidayed together a couple of times a year and were addicts for the sun, darkening till they looked Spanish themselves. They laid out all day come sun or shade, They were also addicted to Barry's Tea, Black Pudding, Rashers and Superquinn sausages and had a veritable feast of vacuum packed meats in their cases. They even brought butter and bread and YR sauce for the sangers. They had dressing gowns and took off their make-up and sat around wearing moisturiser and conditioning their beautiful hair like mermaids, and all they ever said all day every day was "Fuck off, no WAAAAAY" whether we were telling them the time or the third secret of Fatima.

One night after consuming my own height in vodka and coke from a barman with a gamy eye, I collapsed in a heap on the shining Spanish street tiles, and was revived by an ex pat in a wife beaters vest with a scouse perm and a t – bar chain, who used espresso and salt as an emetic and I woke in a foaming pool of various liquids, rubbing my eyes in disbelief. We bought dolls and lace and perfume and fags and fell around an ornament shop filled with Ladro and crystal like hysterical young bullocks before we were ousted. I bought my sister a model of a fat arsed puppet on a spring who would bounce around the ceilings when you pulled his legs. We lay around the pool all day talking about men and what we would eat that night. Or both. But as the bus idled at the terra cotta walls in the baking morning heat and the last stragglers ran aboard clutching souvenirs and love bites in equal measure, the driver admired his square blue chin in the mirror from behind his shades as he manoeuvred the coach around the tiny curves and we left the sun drenched slopes of one Island far behind and flew back to a mild green temperate Island that was gearing up to be part of a little bit of history by hosting Live Aid. I was barely off the plane before I was back in the pub with the girls watching Phil Collins on 2 big screens as Bob Geldof begged us for our fuckin' money.

I had a head like Holyhead after being out toping with a gang of reprobates the night before and all I needed was the crook of an eyebrow to go out for the curer.

Angie was a country girl, who had come to school on the bus with thick ribbed green knee socks and a pair of Nature Trek shoes. The country she is from is only a couple of miles from town but back in the day, the top of the hospital road may as well have been Alaska.

She drove a Renault 18 christened and forever more known as **They -heen.**

This afternoon though she had a different car, her sisters, a tiny fiat I had christened the beantin. The sister was gone off harebaiting around the roads and needed bigger wheels so we set off in *the beantin. I tried to repair the damage to my face in the small mirror over the visor and was painstakingly drawing on a Clara Bow pout in a scarlet lip pencil to keep the red lipstick on, when she started mucking about with the wheel, turning sharply to the left, straightening, and then turning sharply to the right until my face was a zig zag of angry red lines and I shouted at her to stop messing.*

"The Jazus steering is gone" she shouted back as she tried to keep the car on the road. We rounded a corner at speed and saw a family on the roadside verge, a toddler on a tricycle and in front of us a brick wall. She tried her best but the wheel spun uselessly between her hands and slamming her foot on the brake we headed for the wall.

This is it, I thought. I die by slamming headfirst into a wall. Who knew? And then we skidded to a stop an inch from it, our necks snapping back against the seats, our hearts in our mouths, and the people running up to wrench open the door to see the state of us.

- *Can you move? Don't move- says the man. Oh, the blood, you must be cut - he looks for the glass.*
- *It's my lipstick, I tell them faintly.*

In the bar of the hotel that afternoon, the medicinal brandy fell back out of my mouth in a series of splashes as the delayed shock kicked in. We met a nice couple of young men who entertained us all afternoon, and flirted with us and bought us drinks.

These lads are great gas altogether says I to Angie in the jacks as we got ready to follow their car to a house party. Not a bother on us to drive home. In the house I excused myself to go to the bathroom and noticed the following –

- *An **Alf** doll on the window sill that I promptly put in my handbag*
- *a Soutane behind the door that I promptly put on.*

After negotiating my way down the stairs kicking it out from me on every step like a Zigfeld Follies Showgirl, I arrived into the kitchen wearing it, much to the shock and consternation of the Priest who owned it. I watched him move a baby stroller across the kitchen with his foot and with an exchange of glances and a hurried goodbye myself and Angie legged it out the door in a hoop.

March 17th 2013 - Year 8

Siobhán is being fed when I walk in the door and her impossible blue eyes are open.
I rub her legs to say hello.
It is the closest I can get.
She has a shamrock badge sewed or stuck or both to her cardigan.
It breaks my heart.
My day has been exhausting.
I like to talk in bursts and then stop. I like to be able to walk away and be quiet. When I am in full flow, it is like someone turned on a volcano that spews forth endlessly, quips, incidents, stories, tall tales, things I have seen or heard, or eaten, or watched, things I have done in this and many other lifetimes.
If I love you I want to inhabit your skin, feel the insides of you, inhale the smell of you, see the world from behind your eyes.

But I also want to walk away and think about you quietly on my own where I can process the information and unwrap the essence of you, slowly, like chocolate, one square at a time.

I like to carry my happiness home to a safe space like a small white ball of baby wool that I detangle and thus process.

I like to sleep alone curled up in one corner of the mattress with only my thoughts, and the memories of you to keep me awake.

I don't do intimacy well.

Even as I lay bare the fabric of the presence of the self, I reserve a small crumb of that self, one I appear to want to only dissect with me, myself, and Id.

Who is listening to the constant chattering, the devils haircut in my mind, other than the true self?

When the traits of personality, voice, action and reflex are absent what can remain...............

Looking into my Mothers eyes on this St. Patricks Day, I realise.

Siobhán is as dependant and vulnerable as a baby.

She is spoonfed, washed, dressed, turned, hoisted, examined for marks, has enemas to evacuate her bowels and is elevated and bolstered on her air bed.

This baby is not going to roll out of the cot.

In this real life Benjamin Button this baby will not gurgle, or reach out a hand to clasp a finger, or smile a colicky grin.

I wait in the sunroom while the hoisting to the commode is carried out and watch the shadows on the candle lit curtain to let me know when I can go back in.

I sit amongst the women who a couple of months ago I could have had full scale conversations with. There is silence now, save for the rasping of chesty coughs.

They are beginning to disappear.

They are shadows of their "selves".

We are all shadow selves, wrapped up in ego, waiting for the self to appear and reclaim us.

In Siobháns room we sit silently beside each other in the dark, she and I. The only sound the guttering of the lit candle, its wick flickering and gusting in the crack of air from the open window.

We are our selves.

Our job and raison d'etre being purely the gentle rise and fall of our chests as we breathe in and out.

You don't wake up at night to breathe, so something, some awareness, some intuitive source within you carries on your breathing all by itself to let your self sleep and recover.

It watches over your unconscious self and loves it more than we can fathom of the term.

It is this self that is gazing out of my Mothers eyes. It is the very soul of her, gazing out the windows of honesty, of complete and utter dependence, with complete and utter serenity and love.

October 22nd 1985

She booked the Kincone Motor Lodge Motel for her 21st a full year before the actual date as it was always the fireworks night of the Opera Festival, We were up the walls with her tantrums and demands as she organized the DJ, the bouncers, the band, the invitations, and mustered the entire attendance to outfit themselves in fancy dress from Riff Raff Theatre Company who hired outrageous outfits for exactly that purpose. The legs were worn off me up and down to **The Star Bakery** adding yet another tier to a cake that would be photographed by a newspaper photographer, sliced, portioned and sent in small white boxes to aunts in England and cousins in Convents. By the time we were finished counting the RSVP's on the hall table and allowing for the fact that everyone would bring a half dozen or more along with themselves, and by the time we factored in the ones travelling and looking for beds, the cake looked like something **Walt Disney** might have constructed if he had smoked crack.

It needed to be transported in its own van.

She had a wardrobe malfunction at teatime and became hysterical.

After having a tantrum of epic proportions about her outfit, and giving herself and all around her a headache, she lay down for an hour to compose herself , while I calmly furnished her with a new outfit out of my black velvet ankle length dress, a blue satin headband and a borrowed cigarette holder and she went as a flapper girl from the 20s - her Cinderella rags/ballgown combi proving to be unmanageable and ridiculous.

It was also ridiculous to cling film the toilet seats so people would wet themselves, and to attack a woman's nipple with a cake tongs, who has not spoken to her from that day to this. At midnight the man appeared as if by magic to take our photo for the Papal Peeper. We held the silver knife and gurned into the flash, the massive cake eclipsing us, barely seeing the tops of our big hair behind it. I still remember the silk polka dot blouse I wore. 2 Waitresses wandered over like Mrs Overall and heroically steered the giant confection back into the kitchen to be portioned.

It was never seen again.

The manager spotted me looking anxiously into the double doors of the lit kitchen when a good half hour had passed. He looked concerned. "How in the name of Jazuz can you lose a cake that size in a hotel" said Tom as he lit a cigarette with a shaking hand. He had been traumatised by his sister Rosie lepping out at him wearing a fright mask and wig and his nerves weren't the better of it. Now he had to contend with a hysterical daughter to boot. The staff put out an apb for the missing cake and searched high and low, scouring the toilets, the bedrooms and the car park. What they were doing cleaning at a time like this was beyond me. The manager stood at the reception desk scratching his head and apologising and offering to throw up a few desserts in lieu.

The mystery of the disappearing cake became the stuff of myth and legend.

The double doors into the **Kincone** Kitchen assumed in Mahon family lore, the same curiosity value as the **Bermuda Triangle** and became the subject of much debate and hilarity every birthday she had thereafter.

Member the night your cake went missing though someone would shout in the chorus of Happy Birthdays and all would evolve into helpless laughter.

The use of the term missing was a misnomer however, as it somehow surmised that the giant white iceberg that could have sunk the Titanic had in fact grown tiny legs and moved slowly off of its own volition, inching its way down the grassy slope , sliding into the murky waters off the ballast bank, and sailing slowly away to the freedom of the open sea.

The truth was it was obviously fecked.

Who in their right mind would feck a cake at a party? God knows there was enough to eat, and most of the lads had been to **Turners** chipper before they came out, fortifying themselves for a night on the lash with rissoles and mushy peas. A Musician who had lost a leg in a motorbike accident hauled himself on crutches in the door one night when the queue was half way up the Kay, revellers and American tourists from the **Wavecrest** being enticed in with the smell of hot grease and vinegar - and he asked the chipper man if he had left his leg there the night before. Without a blink and without stopping the complicated business of turning golden pillows of cod in batter, in vats of boiling oil, he reached behind him and silently passed a wooden leg across the counter.

Open or wrapped someone shouted and we watched as he drove off unsteadily across the bridge, the leg tied precariously across the back seat. Could the cake have been strapped to the back of a motorbike? Was it stolen by travellers who hawked it from door to door with the continental quilts and floral carpets? Had someone shrieking for a sugar fix become entranced by the sheer size and scope of the concoction and spirited it away to overdose on marzipan and hundreds and thousands for evermore? Wouldn't that just give you the pip?

It would take us 19 years to find out.

The following year her brother opened his arm from wrist to elbow sliding on icy wet January tiles into a ceramic basin in the jacks and would spend half his party in A & E being stitched back together.

The child had her 21st party at home, safe in the bosom of her family, thankfully.

Anything for a quiet life is my motto.

March 13th 2013 - Year 8

The noise of the bells draws me out the door.

The sky is coalblack and scarlet at the same time. There is no-one on the street - no passers-by, no cars, no stray terrier.

I have just posted a jocular photo of Cardinals lighting cigarettes with a caption of "Smoke, you say" on twitter when they announce on the radio live from the Vatican that they have white smoke.

Now I know why the bells are pealing, and they are so appealing that I run across the street, through the car park where I stand sentry on Saturday, over the worn steps of the Transept and up the belfry stairs. I have left my hall door wide open and only have my phone in my hand, as per. I run up step after tiny step until my laboured wheezing, and the clipclop of my boots draws a brace of faces over the hand rail to peer down at me.

It was mooted a number of weeks ago for me to ring the Angeles at the Friary, but they were being a little misogynistic about it.

"You're too small" they said.

"You'll be dragged skywards" they said

"It will be too heavy for a woman to pull" they said.

Ahem.

The only thing I may be is tiny but what I lose in height I replace with girth so there was no way in Heaven a mere rope could lift me.

It is an all male enclave in the Bell Tower too.

Vincenzo, and the duo of Beary's are sweating like choc ices in the sun.

I am beside myself to get a go.

I am also beside them.

They laugh at me and in my general direction for a while and then they realize I am serious. I wonder if I will have to jokingly seize the rope from the man's hands and hit him with the knot in the face if he won't release his grip. They either take pity on me or realize that the lady is not for turning.

"Watch me" says Vincenzo.

I am determined to follow his advice as the last thing I want is to be hurtled skywards and traumatise the tiny Beary child looking on.

Did I mention I was wearing a dress?

"Feed it down, wait, pull hard, wait, let it go when you feel it pull"

Piece of cake.

It may in fact have been the myriad of cakes I have consumed that will keep me bolstered to the ground. It may have been a mistake to refuse the gloves. The man explains for 47 minutes why it is *imperative* I wear them or I will have no skin from knuckle to elbow.

I don the gloves.

"Are you right?"

My stomach gives a little twinge.

"As I'll ever be" I quip and take the rope.

I am lifted 3 feet into the air on the return. I come to the conclusion that it would be remiss of me to remove my gloved hand to smooth down my dress or I may in fact go higher like some monstrous child in a Willy Wonka movie.

"Habeus Papa" shouts Vincenzo as I get into my stride.

It dawns on me that I am ringing the massive bell.

People are listening to this all over the town, the ones glued to the tv sets live from St Peters Square, the ones watching The Simpsons, the ones listening to the radio, the ones driving home to light the fire with a Cd of Pearl Jam on, the dogs are barking and whining. I am part of telling the people that something has happened. I am following in a tradition that started here in 1265. I am but a link in a chain of men who have rung this bell.

In times of Invasion or Siege, when Cromwell laid waste to the Franciscan Friary, when people were be-headed and the streets according to history ran with blood, a Friar ran to this tower to ring this bell, in times of celebration a Friar walked through the walled gardens to this tower to ring this bell

-    I may in fact, be the first woman who has rung this bell.

Friar "*Tuc*" Biscuit.

I am still jumping up and down on the rope and trying to remember the view and the history and to keep my dress down all at one and the same time. I simply cannot stop. Over the din I see the hand waving to signify that my work here is done. I release the rope and drop back down to the platform rising a cloud of dust and pigeon shit as the last echo of the bell fades away on the breeze.

Only **Gerwhoonlytalkstomen** sees me walk away from his perch near the corner.

At home I call my Father to ask him has he heard the bells. He is wearing 2 massive hearing aids and cannot hear over the din of the crowd in St Peters Square.

He lives in St Peters Square too but he means the TV.

I live on the Street named for its Friary, so it is Francis Street.

The Pope, looking overwhelmed at the spectacle, but looking stronger than his 76 years, a Jesuit, a Philosopher, an Argentinian, bows his head and prays for guidance.

I am not ashamed to say I bowed my own. For the good of all and harm to none.

His Name is Francis.

April 2013 - Year 8

Matron comes barreling down the hall and breasts Little Thomasina.

Siobhán has been found in the bed holding contraband and when the nurses prise her fingers open, it is a cigarette lighter.

Mine.

I have no earthly clue how.

Thomasina gives me down the banks for a while but I am used to his goster. It rolls off like the proverbial off the proverbial's back. Last night I am perched at the kitchen door reading the sign that says "NO Residents are allowed to have flammables in their rooms" and asking the tea lady for the matches off the micro-wave to light a scented candle. She hands me a lighter. It is wrapped in a yellow post-it and sellotaped tightly.

It says "**Siobhán Mahon**" on it.

"T'is better to light a candle than curse the dark.

I decide to make Mam an Irish Coffee. I meet a blonde woman with crab salad and Pavlova in the hospitality room. She has just got off a ship so I trade her a seafarers tale to share her banquet, as there is no such thing as a free lunch.

It's 5am on a film set on a freezing night shoot at a harbour, I begin as I flick the kettle which is still warm. Myself and Patrick Bergin are perched on some coiled ropes wearing the entire railing of clothes from wardrobe - (Dead mens coats and flat caps from Oxfam) - in a vain, and somewhat fruitless attempt to stave off hypothermia, and he is truculent, to put it mildly.

I decide to divert him with tales of my sea faring life.

"That's Tuskar" I tell him, pointing out the lighthouse and talking about the loom of the light, and the men who lived on the rock for weeks at a time with tinned food and VHS Cassettes. I talk about lighthouses for a remarkable length actually, The Bailey & The Stack from the Dublin run, The Hook, and then how Cromwell coined the phrase "by hook or by crook" as in how he would capture and conquer those rebellious Irish men.

His eyes are glazing over.

Or else he is taking a turn.

Or maybe he is overcome with emotion. I had made the fatal mistake of asking him about the towels in *"Sleeping with the Enemy"* and he had turned Turk. Now in my guise as Production Assistant/Caterer/General Factotum/Fixer/Dogsbody/ and Raconteur, I waved my radio mike wildly in the direction of the approaching funnels of the ship on the horizon. I look at my phone for the time. It is off due to filming and the sound guys repeated entreaties to have them off and

"not on silent, people, I can hear the effin' things on my cans!"

"There's the Isle of Inismore coming in bang on time" says I.

"Echo, India, Delta, X-Ray".

Bergin turns his jaded eye on me and asks how I know.

In the hour or so it took me to tell him, I told him a story of what happened one morning when I had let a lad go for a smoko during his mop-out and he in his innocence had left me in charge of the buffer.

How hard can it be?

Very.

I was swinging it wildly trying not to take the shins off passing passengers and lumps out of the captains carver chairs when 2 Yanks came promenading up the aisle

"Oh, this is simply wunnerful, just wunnerful" says one blue rinsed broad to the other.

They are staring at the islands sailing slowly by.

The Giant Kerry Purser sighs with annoyance behind the desk.

I hear him mutter "Jaysus" under his breath.

"Oh, Sir, I say, sir, could you possibly tell us the name of these?" she trills calling all the way across the main square.

The Kerryman, with hands like shovels and a porn star moustache sighs and groans and puts on a fake smile. He calls into his colleague in the back office.

"What are the name of those foooking Islands, Eddie?"

Without glancing up from his paper and with his feet crossed on the desk he responds monosyllabically -

Skokum

Now, I know they are Skokum, I even know they are a bird sanctuary because I found out, but what the Kerryman shouts over is *"SCROTUM"*.

"Scrotum" says he to the women. *"Scrotum Island"*

"Wunnerful, simply wunnerful" the women chorus and march away.

Sweet Gentle Jesus.

There is no-one to tell.

Apart from Bergin who almost falls into the sea and wheezing says "Christ Almighty, have you got more stuff like that?"

"Buckets" says I. "Buckets".

I wipe the cream off my face and hands in a tea towel and leave her laughing.

Make em laugh, make em laugh......................

Make 'em laugh

Make 'em laugh

Don't you know everyone wants to laugh?

(Ha ha!)

My dad said "Be an actor, my son

But be a comical one

They'll be standing in lines
For those old honky tonk monkeyshines"
Donald O'Connor - Singing in the Rain.

Wexford 1987

She got engaged to a London Chef who left her waiting 6 months to hear the punchline of a joke.

And so it came to pass that the pair of them were sat down in the front room - listening to Tom giving the lecture to the man who had asked for his daughters hand in marriage - about love being a lifelong commitment and that they had better take the whole thing seriously and not be messing around.

From the kitchen waiting on the kettle to boil, I knew by the go of her she was messing around.

When we were going to the Vintners Ball Tom took his Tuxedo with the satin lapels out of the wardrobe and held it at arms length. "There's some stench of hippy stuff off this" says he leaning in for another smell. She had worn it to the Tourist Office Disco reeking of Pachouli oil, with her hair in cornrows of Rasta beads, topped off with a parka with a target on the back and badges all over the front, one of which said **Legalise it** despite the fact that she had not yet started smoking.

"Who are you supposed to be hun?" says the man on the door.

"Forgive me, I'm very confused" she answered with a swing of her beads and went off to sail around the Crescent on a home made raft as one of the Scooper Murphys asked a woman up for the slow set.

"Lay Lady Lay, lay across my big brass bed"

They had 2 engagement parties, at opposite ends of the town, with 2 separate crowds, which involved a lot of toping of champagne out of flutes and a warchest of his & her towels for their "bottom drawer".

The inlaws and outlaws sized each other up over the trays of sandwiches and a noble call went around the flocked walls for the best of order and Danny Boy.

The following night she sang Fever with a jazz band on a high stool in a club while her new fiancé went back pot walloping. One of the mermaids from Santa Ponsa came down from Dublin with her boyfriend -who bore an uncanny resemblance to Barry McGuigan -to drink champagne out of her stiletto.

She returned the favour by drinking champagne out of his grey loafer while he squirmed in his white sock and the barmen queued for his autograph.

My blue eyed boy and only son had emigrated to Germany in search of work or prospects. He got a job as a short order cook on an American Airforce base outside Stuttgart called Pattonville, after the General. He spent a considerable amount of time frying things and being told heavy on the miracle and hold the mayo and the rest of his time drinking the head off himself in **Bier Gartens.**

"Yee should come over there - it's great craic" says he to his sister — "and there is the world of work" wiping the froth off his mouth when he visited.

They believed him.

One minute she is tricking around in the Doctors with a phone book and a desk and the next she is on a plane to Stuttgart, having received a small piece of Lladro from the Doctors wife for 5 years of outrageous service, and the Nicky Rackard **History of Wexford** in **The Crown Bar** at a German wake.

She was distraught with homesickness.

She didn't draw a breath that didn't evoke memories of the small grey town with the train tracks and mussel dredgers, the misty fog, the sound of seagulls, the narrow tumbling streets, the smell of the sea, the people left behind. My heart was broken now that two of my children were in a different country. They called their Aunt's house across the road, from payphones in roasting city streets with the actual time they would call back at. We would be sitting waiting on the slope of the kitchen for the old cream rotary phone in the hall to ring on the stroke of six, with the Angeles.

"That **Dinkelacker** tastes like horses piss" says the brother.

She got a job in a kitchen shaving cheeses as the breakfast chef. German people eat about a thousand different slices of childrens meat and plastic cheese for their breakfast, allegedly. They also smoke everywhere and a woman in a Prada suit will ask a homeless wino for a fag. The highlight of their week would be getting a lift to Plóchingen to collect the parcel from home, where I had wrapped the Papal Peeper around a turnip and bars of chocolate, and letters from home with a photo of myself and Tom with the little dotie terrier Chloe in his arms, which she has carried with her from that day to this.

Joxer was coming to Stuttgart too.

And suddenly the homesickness became a distant memory as an influx of Paddy's arrived in the city, looking for porter ,women craic, beds and tickets to the game, in that order.

Ireland beat England 1 – 0 in the European Championships and all over the Irish countryside the natives were singing - who put the ball in the English net - Houghton.

She learned to curse in German, Turkish and Urdu making beds in the Hauptbahnhóf.

She sent reams of letters home, detailing her life and the people and places she had seen. They made me laugh, and also gave me an insight into the country, as I longed to travel. From when she sent a 7 page letter home describing the plane journey to Majorca which was posted from the hotel on the first morning, I had been keeping her stuff, and placing it with cards, and essays, cutting out little snippets of writing she had done, a poem to The Irelands Own that won her a £1, a letter to the Editor of the local paper bemoaning the lot of the emigrant and a Catch 22 situation about unemployement. I put all these and the random doodles and cartoons into bags and boxes, and on more than one occasion, took out and looked at the little pencil sketch of herself and the London Chef as they are walking away.

"How can she possibly know what she looks like from behind" I wondered.

Being paid monthly was a shock to the system so they lived like Lords Bastards for a week and starved for 3. They ate Bratwurst and Sauerkraut and Leberkase with plastic cutlery standing up in an outside booth with the queues of middle eastern men in faded suits, and Turkish kebabs with lemon and salt, and filled their plates into towering pyramids of rice in the Marché. They fell on the meats and salads at Barbeques where they brought Baileys and Guinness to underpin their Irishness and as a treat ate McDonalds McRibs when they could beat their way through the throngs of Italian teenagers clogging up the steps.

On the morning of our Silver Wedding Anniversary in August of 1988, they called home as *arranged with the Aunt, from a crackly phone box, and then unknownst to us, took a train to the airport, flew to London, changed, flew to Dublin, took a bus to the city centre and alighted at the Gresham.*

She spoke in German to the bus driver as she dragged her case from the boot. It would be another decade before somebody had the foresight to invent wheels for luggage and exhausted from bickering and fighting around airport carousels, they went into the hotel for a cup of Tay.

"Jazuz, they should be lynched with the prices" says he as he unrolled a bill and his eyes to pay for it.

Tom was driving home along the quay, having had his usual game of snooker in the **CYMS,** *when he spotted the tall boy and the small girl hefting bags of duty free and manhandling cases up the Woodenworks.*

If I didn't know better, I'd swear a hole in a pot that's my children he thought while he slowed, glancing in the rear view mirror.

We were beyond delighted that they were home.

I'm not going back, she thought as she curled up in her old bedroom that night after the party.

He flew back alone.

November 2012 - Year 7

Tonight I bent my head over the chair and muttered *Christ* as I gave up.

50 tissues, a soaked blouse and an inch of hot chocolate gone from the glass.

I rinsed it in the bathroom sink and watched as the rivulets of chocolate stained water ran down the plughole, fading from caramel, to cream, to clear.

Siobhán is deeply asleep.

And has been in her bedclothes since I arrived. I arrange the step of the chair so the blood is not rushing to her feet if they are left hanging. I wrap her feet tidily in the soft patchwork fleece.

Tonight is bitter and a skinning wind makes me rue not bringing a coat.

Coats are for walking, clothes are for cars.

The tea trolley arrives and before she can open her mouth I say -

"Unless you have heroin on that trolley don't bother coming in".

She laughs.

They know me.

They ought to by now.

My sister is lying on the bed resting her back as the air mattress pushes against the resistance. She is watching me and says nothing.

We leave early.

Smother of Morrows 2012

It occurred to me today that I know more about Siobhán now than when I knew her.

When she was well, she was just Siobhán, or on rare occasions Mam, the calm hand on the rudder of my life, the understated presence in our house, the quiet voice in the bedlam. Now as I dissect her I feel I have come to inhabit her very skin. More and more of late, people are calling me Siobhán when they meet me, her old neighbours and friends, the nurses and carers, once I even called myself Siobhán on the phone.

We become intimate with the geography of a loved ones body, its curves and contours, its small secret spaces and places – the softness of the pale skin, the light other worldly heft of a limb. Things that would have been considered a bridge too far in their awfulness become as familiar as anything one repeats on a regular basis. One becomes innured, if not immune. I stare aghast and filled with admiration at the young man who presents at my Mothers door, smiling as he comes in. Of course I have to find out every single thing about him and how he came to be training for a job that frankly leaves me humbled and speechless on any given day.

He asks if Siobhán is my grandmother.

It is in this moment and in the dawning realization as I stare at the latest image of her on my new phone, and it comes to me that this illness has finally done to her what being the mother of a maniac could not, she has aged.

My life at the moment is consumed by her. If I am not in her physical presence I am in her presence still. Her face smiles up and out and over and down at me from a positive mélange of images of her. They are stuck on walls, peeping out of envelopes, saved & copied and edited and framed, and balanced precariously in an impossible Jenga tower on my printer. This cornucopia of a life, these notes on a memory, these ramblings about Dementia.

I am typing in a tiny dark space where the snapshots of multitudes of moments in her life, are frozen forever in time, in space and reality, out at the edges where worlds collide and the lines soften and blur.

In the small row boat at the horizon, as the luminescence of water and mist collide in a pale blue light, she waits patiently for me.

I type furiously sometimes.

It all comes pouring out in an endless stream of consciousness where my fingers fly across the keys and I wonder are there enough words in the world to get it down, to pin it to the page, to nail it.

Other nights I stare blankly at the white space.

It has taken on a life of its own, this story that refuses to be left alone and abandoned, untold, forgotten. The words too, have escaped from my head and out into the ether and they are touching and impacting on people I have never met, an artist is doing an installation of pieces of art that Siobhán painted when she was a small child. A producer wants a radio documentary about her illness and her life. A musician has written a song about her using my words. I have become the narrator, the custodian, the keeper of the archive.

When I was small if I looked sad or had a lip on me Siobhán would come over to cajole me back to good humour by tickling me and saying "Ah, would you look at the Mother of

Sorrows here" until I laughed. Tonight I returned the favour. But as I was stroking her cheek I inadvertently spoonered the saying and said – Smother of Morrows.

January 2014 - Year 9

It has always fascinated me what we leave behind
The lingering smell of baking in a warm kitchen at evening time that tickles every hopeful nose, the smell of gel and toothpaste from a steamy bathroom, the indentation of a head on a pillow, sleep rumpled sheets.
These memories of a life. The things that hold the energy of the owner. I never find it morbid, in fact the total opposite is true.
The flotsam and jetsam of a life.
I love unearthing treasures in the most unlikely places. The remnants of a day, a napkin pressed between the folded pages of a diary, a train ticket creased neatly into a purse.
All of these tiny things tell the story of Us.
In the rooms that house the people of no memory the very bricks hold the imprint of their story. The slates above them witness their confusion and tears, the agitation, the frustration. The halls ring with their calls and taps, a hand knocking, knocking softly on a closed kitchen door. The handbags open and gaping and the sticks tap tap tapping down the skirting boards. The bulbs in the garden spring up with the memories of all the hearses that have parked in front of these double doors.
Today I am in an abandoned derelict house with a camera and a tripod, shooting. The windows are gone, the house is open to the elements, shards of patterned wallpaper blowing in the breeze.
It is a woman who has left this place.
Her ornaments are on the mantelpiece, a line of poignant plastic pegs strung across the hearth of the fireplace, a bunch of rusted keys hanging on a cup hook, a sacred heart lamp, a plaster statue of the Virgin Mary, a Readers Digest dated 1956.
The wind whistling in through the open pantry would shave you. The vegetation is lush and encroaching steadily, vines and creepers and crawling things are taking back the bricks and all the memories of what happened in here, dragging them down through the wet wormy clay to the core of the collective consciousness.
Once upon a time a woman laid down in that back bedroom and thought about the long day she had put in. Up for first mass to read one of Paul's endless epistles to the Apostles, home to bake soda bread and tarts with her own apples, she watched the daffodils rear their impossible yellow heads while she waited for the postman to cycle by, digging beds for spring onions and lettuce and rhubarb, She listened to the hurling on the radio on a hot August Sunday while she got herself ready for the bingo bus. She drank sherry at Christmas and always gave coins to the Wren Boys.
She blessed herself nightly with Lourdes water from the font and said her decades and her "I confess" before sleeping the sleep of the just.
She is gone now.

On a shelf I find a tattered book with her signature on it and find that it is a play in 3 acts. "Would it be terrible if I took this home with me?" I ask he-who-must-be-obeyed-today-

He is trying to check the light and cue up a shot and he arches one devastatingly handsome eyebrow at me.

I put it in my bag.

I am the woman who remembers everything, and for everyone. I live surrounded by the energy of those who have gone before me, and I sleep in their house, surrounded by all the little things I find, or collect, or am given.

If Death is merely the closing of one door and the opening of another then I like to imagine sometimes that I have my foot wedged in the crack and that by retaining their memories after all else has gone, that I am connected to all that is and ever was and ever shall be. Amen.

Spring 2013 - Year 8

It may be because I live alone that I engage like someone on speed, then race home to the controlled madness that is my house, where I slump in a corner like a deflating, softening balloon the morning after a party. Cherrypicking multiple and various topics simultaneously, getting distracted by someone on the path who looks *weird*, forgetting what I am twittering about, wandering from story to story, a child playing hopscotch, breathlessly trotting out the punchline to an audience, that the more ornery I get the funnier they find me.

"*You should sell tickets*" they say.

"*You should do Stand-Up*" they say.

And the truth shall set you free.

This is how my drives to Siobhán are.

When I walk in the door I am still smiling from leaving the driver alternately amused and aghast. The grin is wiped off my puss when I open the door.

Siobhán looks tiny tonight.

Her hair - fading from her natural blonde into silver - is flopping across one eye, and she is slumped sideways awkwardly and deeply asleep. I throw the bunch of home-made flowers onto the bed - (one from every jar in my house so she has a combination of lillies, tulips, roses, sunflowers, chrysantheums and giant stalks with purple things on them) - and head back down the hall as I have just seen a vision in white.

A very tiny old lady is coming up the hall in her nightie with a halo of soft white fluff. She is pushing one of those tables on wheels they have in hospitals to fit over beds.

And moaning.

I steer her back down the hall to her room and ring the bell for the nurse. She is put back into bed while the nurse tells me fondly that she is a little unsettled tonight.

"She was making Siobháns bed last night" I tell her.

"Yes, she is very particular about beds and covers. She likes to go into the other residents and tuck them in and smooth their faces."

She thinks they are her children.

Tonight it is me who tucks her in. I don't even know her name. She reached up for a kiss and I bent and kissed her wrinkled forehead and she held on to my neck.
Tight.
I think she was giving me the hug that Siobhán cannot.
Back in our room I arrange the flowers in a vase and tell her what they are and what colours. She may see them if she opens her eyes soon. I tell her whats happening in my life and that I write about her and that people *read* it.
I kid her that she is a celebrity. I tell her tonight that I am meeting a radio producer tomorrow to discuss a "*hardhitting*" programme we are making about her. I'd say if she could she would do a jig as she is the quietest woman I know - or knew - and the polar opposite of her diva of a daughter whose every move is designed to court publicity, *it would appear*, despite wearing a t-shirt that says -
"***Introverted Socialite***".
Maybe what I thought was a curse may in fact turn out to be a blessing in disguise - as they always are.
Maybe a miracle will manifest. If wishes were horses then beggars would ride.
It may have been a compliment when someone who shall remain nameless said –
"*That one could talk underwater*".

Send in the Clowns

Isn't it rich?
Are we a pair?
Me here at last on the ground,
You in mid-air.
Send in the clowns.

Isn't it bliss?
Don't you approve?
One who keeps tearing around,
One who can't move.
Where are the clowns?
Send in the clowns.

Isn't it rich?
Isn't it queer?
Losing my timing this late
In my career?
And where are the clowns?
Quick, send in the clowns.
Don't bother - they're here.
(Lyrics copyright of Mr Stephen Sondheim)

I listened to the recording of the radio interview in the dark with a single candle lit in the window with the 2 most important women in my life, my sister Nicola, and Siobhán.

C'est la vie.

C'est la Guerre.

It was poignant in the dark room to hear my voice and the music playing and neither looking at the other, Nicola focusing on the wall and me foostering with the glass and a towel.

I exhaled as the strains of the strings in "*Meditation from Thies*" echoed away and asked her what she thought.

She swallows a lump in her throat.

"*That was very very good*" says she.

Of course Little Thomasina did not hear it either as he is out playing his violin with his orchestra and they are rehearsing for a benefit concert they will play next month. It was far more important that he keep up his routine, which has been a lifesaver for a man in his 80's who is missing his best friend all the time. The soundtrack of his life has always been my Mothers voice, and its absence is felt in his home as he sits alone at the empty family table, or glances across to her vacant armchair by the fire, or climbs the flight of stairs to his bed listening to the radio on quietly in the background, doing the Simplex in The Times, and thumbing through the collection of prayers and novenas he says nightly

He did not need a Meditation played for him tonight. His whole life is one and I don't tell him often enough that I am proud of him, and that his bravery humbles me, and how much he means to us and how much I love him. Their likes will not be seen again. My wish for all people is to be home safe of a night, with your fire lit and you can glance across the room to lock eyes with someone who loves you.

Wexford 1989

She wangled herself onto a **FÁS** course called How to start your own Business where she had to sit at a desk in a breeze block room with a heavy smell. It had the kind of carpet that tears the knees off you if you fall. I fell outside the Doctors on the Clifford Street steps once and arrived home with my knees bleeding and my tights in ribbons and she cried with the fright. Oscar Wilde once said that crying is the refuge of plain women but the ruin of pretty ones. She spent 8 hours a day watching a man in a suit tricking around with diagrams on a whiteboard for weeks on end. She even began to miss making a hundred beds in an hour, having been shown the trick of reversing the duvet cover by a woman in a Burka. She spent the days laughing and drawing caricatures of her colleagues, while instigating riots and smoke breaks.

The course instructor resorted to sending her a letter.

In it he detailed her various exploits and misdemeanours and how she was wrecking his head behaving like a scallywag. I think he thought she was a bit affected, or had a bit of a want. I could have told him she was just a bit airy as I found out when I took her to the Light Opera as a tiny child. The entire cast and chorus were hitting the high notes in the finale of HMS Pinafore when she leaned over to me with her jelly baby mouth and shouted "that's pure bedlam" and ran up the aisle.

In the interim the Fiancé had followed her home, although there was as little work in Ireland as when they left and realizing that they had better shit or get off the pot, they answered an ad in the Sunday Independent for a management couple to become licensees of English pubs. Now that she was armed with a piece of paper saying she could run a business and your man could cook, they were shoe- ins for the job with Grand Metropolitan Limited and were interviewed in a hotel in Dublin so the Aunts took the phone call to say they were hired before they got off the bus.

The Duke of Wellington was an old coaching Inn with a bar and lounge. The latter was filled with retired colonels in tweeds with double barreled surnames who lived in draughty mansions they had inherited which they could neither heat nor fix, and who spent the afternoons sooleying out gin and tonics and reading The Times. Evelyn Waugh couldn't have written this village. The public bar was filled with louts and boy racers with button down shirts, gelled hair and souped up cars. They tortured her on a daily basis.

Awwright dawlin they would shout banging the pool table, the fruit machine and the pound coins off the counter at the same time. Someone was always playing the Sex Pistols or the Clash on the jukebox. It was a trigger for mayhem.

She stood for hours behind the counter, listening to the problems of the world and learning to do a round of up to 20 drinks, how to pour champagne without having someones eye out or wasting a drop, how to dress Pimms with cucumber, knew the reds, whites and rosés, could whip an Irish Coffee onto a dressed saucer in 30 seconds flat, stud a clove for hot ports, fix cocktails and ploughmans lunches, decode the bags of cheese and onion crisps which were not green but blue, and regale people with stories of red lemonade, which they thought was fictional. In Ireland white was for vodka and red for whiskey and both were for shandies. In England the drinks round was a little different than at home where it was mostly a pint of plain, a Heineken or half ones. Now she had to get used to the average round sounding something like - Awwright dawlin', 4 pints of Strongbow, 3 pints of light and bitter, 2 pale ales, a St. Clements, 3 lager tops, a shandy and a flaming sambuca, ….. (*shouts back to the table *)You what, mate? Oh and a packet of pork scratchings and a saveloy. These were kept in a glass jar on the counter and smelt like 100 day old eggs floating in brine and she learned you can find out a lot by watching things eat.

One of the ringleaders of the worst of the bar crowd was a young blonde man who had modeled himself on a cross between Sid Vicious and Billy Idol. His name was Pippy and he had a shock of peroxide hair , ¾ length jeans with braces and 18 holer Doc Martens.He was the undisputed king of the back bar and like all bullies singled out the weakest chicken for the pecking order display that would end in a bloodbath of insults and piss takes.

Christ, she's fat that Oirish one, they must have built the facking bar around her.

His colleagues were aghast but lapping it up.

"Dyawanna hear an Irish Joke, Paddy?" He bawled in her ear when he had a skinfull.

The Guildford 4, she replied.

She remonstrated with him, gingerly, in case he took to smashing up the bar for diversion.Eyeball to eyeball she set out her stall and the feelings she had when he took pot shots at her of a most personal nature for the amusement of a crowd. At the end of her impassioned speech about giving a traumatised homesick girl a break she extended her hand to shake his. He laughed and walked away.

- You'll get facking used to it love, and all the crowd laughed together.

We were at home giving God thanks that she had a lovely job in the home counties with the

nicest class of people, and a good wage and a man who loved her, and I would lay down my **Dr Bruno Furst** *Memory Book and say a prayer for their safe keeping.*
She found out your man Pippy kept a bicycle in a hedge, a chopper, with red and white pennants flying from the seat and when he ordered a pint she slapped a lousy one up at him and when he remonstrated replied — You'll get facking used to it mate, while the bar roared and hollered.
Proper order.

April 2012 - Year 8

The dying woman with eyes like pale wrinkled raisins tell me she is afraid of the dark, and the unknown. I swallowed a lump in my throat and took a deep breath to say

- "You must never be afraid of the dark, it is in the silence and the warm darkness that you will be re-born into a life that far surpasses your present one, there is nothing for you to fear, you came here alone and screaming, and you will leave and go home, peaceful. There is much love for you there"

I closed my mouth in amazement as sometimes I appear to channel wisdom that is not my own.
She grabbed my hand in a firm grip, aware that she had to undertake this frightening thing *alone*.
And I told her about the twin babies talking in the womb.
One baby could not wait to be born, and begin a marvelous life, the other was terrified that leaving was dying, that their safe little world would be over once their cord was cut, and they would be lost and alone, in darkness, adrift.

- No, I think there is something beautiful at the end of this says the wise little twin sleepily.
- I can feel a benign presence looking after me all the time, and if you really listen you can hear it loving us.

His brother turned his head away and sucked his thumb
It troubles me that the very old have unresolved issues, and genuine fear about the act of death itself. They have been reared on the mushy pulp of the Gospels, named for Saints, schooled in the Bible, chanting Latin at mass, Good Friday a black fast, Lent a time to deny the self, the priests on high altars with their backs turned to ignore the parishioners who were throwing their money into the boxes, the children picking up pebbles as indulgences, to save the poor babies in Limbo, to take souls of sinners from Purgatory. I watched my Aunt take that journey last year, the Aunt who bought me the books, the Aunt who answered the phone, running across the road in her slippers to say they'll ring back at 6 on the dot, the Aunt who called me into the shop and bought me the red shoes I coveted, the Aunt who phoned me in London and told me to cop the hell on and come home. Her knees twisted together under the thin blanket, she raised herself again and again on her elbows exhorting all of us to "Pray, Pray, PRAY!".
Her heart may have been left behind in the stiffening remains but her spirit and soul had been released and was joyfully connecting with all there is, has ever been, or ever will be.

I placed a poem by John O Donohue under the pillow of my Aunt *Katie Daly* the woman
who named me Shellakeypookey.

On the day when
The weight deadens
On your shoulders
And you stumble.
May the clay dance
To balance you.
And when your eyes
Freeze behind
The grey window
And the ghost of loss
Gets in to you,
May a flock of colours,
Indigo, red, green,
And azure blue,
Come to awaken in you
A meadow of delight.

When the canvas frays
In the currach of thought
And a stain of ocean
Blackens beneath you
May there come across the waters
A path of yellow moonlight
To bring you safely home.
May the nourishment of the earth be yours
May the clarity of light be yours
May the fluency of the ocean be yours
May the protection of the ancestors be yours

And so may a slow
Wind work these words
Of love around you,
An invisible cloak
To mind your life."
Beannacht by John O Donohue

June 2014 - Year 9

There is a room where the carers and nurses go last at night and last in the morning. The lady there is a night owl and is put to bed and woken after everyone else. *Mary Glasses* was the nurse on nights and she was in overseeing the patient and chatting to a colleague. They were discussing whatever women discuss while they are working, weather, men, the state of the nation, particle physics. One of them is starting a shift, the other finishing.

- "God and I'll be glad to see my bed this night" says one to the other. The nurse is checking the **Bristol Stool** chart on the back of the bathroom door, a tiny series of boxes with checks or circles.
- "I hear you" says she making a note on her pad.

Another voice chimes in with a sentence.

A voice hoarse and husky from silence, a voice unused for an aeon, making perfect sense and in total context, Siobhán has spoken.

Mary Glasses goes white in the face.

"I was that shocked I had to sit down, it was so strange...... I have never heard her speak, never knew what she sounded like. We were both so completely thrown that if I was to be put on a rack I have no idea what she actually said. You have her voice!"

I didn't t know whether I needed a shit or a haircut when I heard this. I follow the nurse around the kitchen pumping her. "In the name of Goddle Mighty can you try to remember, what exactly were you doing or saying...... Put yourself back in the moment'1 beg.

Neither of us know, we were simply flabbergasted, I put it in the report and highlighted it' says she stirring a mug of hot milk.

I feel like weeping and gnashing my teeth and doing handstands all at one and the same time.

"*I just couldn't get over it and all night I told everyone about it and they were as shocked as I was - and in the morning I came in and said Siobhán, Siobhán, and pulled on her arm in the bed and she opened her eyes and looked at me and said "Not you, again" and smiled.*

Sweet Gentle Jesus.

On the night that the lady with the raisin eyes was slipping into the darkness, taking that solo journey, that despite the millions you may have you take alone, we were listening to MY voice, prating away on the radio interview about how I cannot remember what my Mothers voice is like.

"Look at you" I say -wiping juice off her chin and from the folds of her blouse - "as soon as I close the door behind me you are in here talking to the nation".

There is not a flicker. I squeeze her arm gently - "Siobhán, ... Siobhán".......... then "Ma am, Ma am".

Nada.

I never need to fear that I don't know what her voice is like as it is my own, and I am hers. Did the flickering light of the slowly fading christmas tree that is her brain boost and surge for a heartstopping moment, or did this woman try and get a message to the prodigal daughter she called a "divilskin" and a "scourge" by saying ...."Not *YOU* again" and smiling.

London 1989

Tom is the kind of man who will write down names and addresses and where you will be, and what time though, and who will be there all, and if you are not there where will you be, and whom you will be with, and underline, and draw rings around numbers as if this paper talisman could somehow keep his first and wildest child safe.

He may as well have been throwing darts at a map.

They sent them the length and breadth of the country on courses learning man management and manual handling which was how to carry a cardboard box around a room. Drug awareness courses that told them people high as kites would have the munchies and then they brought her to an industrial kitchen, all stainless steel and clogs and gave her a crash course in cooking, health & safety, food hygiene, HACCP, and a diploma from City & Guilds in catering.

And then they let her loose in an actual pub with the actual keys.

A relief couple is a pair who turn up to mind the gaff for you when you are on your jollies in Spain, or have to have a hernia operation from lifting kegs when the draymen come, or you are Scottish and have a heart attack drinking whiskey at a lock in. A holding relief was when your tenure was extended if the manager had run off with the potwash or left under a cloud having been caught rapid in a massive fiddle when the weights and measures men came and did random tests.

She came home on holidays in a blue Yugo Zastava (A605 GJT) they bought for a pittance and which had something wrong with the exhaust which meant they could be heard coming from 50 miles away, and a patient policeman finally caught them one morning in Bracknell and uttered "You're fucking nicked mate, I've been looking for you for weeks".

They would overnight on the Ferry, her getting a bacon sandwich, a brandy and a bunk in that order. She was as seasick now as carsick as a child, and would arrive in Rosslare, white in the face and weak as a kitten to drive home and surprise us, crossing by night, and arriving into town in the early morning. She threw the entire house into an uproar for the length of her stay, running in and out with friends and relations, telling off colour jokes in mixed company, ballsing up the running order of the round by buying out of turn and then getting drunker than the men. She won a years supply of Budweiser in a pub quiz and they carried the cases home and drank it out en masse. She taped the shenanigans when they were in their cups on a Dictaphone and played it back to them when they were as sick as a small hospital.

She brought Tom and I back with her for a week to a pub in West Wales, where I witnessed her performances first hand. Little Mrs Up and Down was still in situ, her playing to the gallery, carousing and late nights were obvious from the crawsick deflation of the morning after. I tried to have a quiet word with her about her drinking and her behavior but she always went up on a high note as a defense, and would never keep her voice down, the more I protested the louder she got, as she has never taken kindly to admonishments of either behave or perform, so if I gave her the nod and a warning glance to tone it down, she would up the ante and reach for the sky. Her default setting is outrageous.

She ended up carving a joint of beef on the Channel 4 News as they interviewed her about Screaming Lord Sutch who had taken up residence in the corner by the fruit machine Captain Beany was using the lid of the pool table as an office and was signing posters of himself sitting in a bath of beans in his knickers. They were contesting the Neath By-Election.

Due to the amount of takes necessary from her corpsing she ran out of meat and resorted to just *clashing the utensils together.*

Let's put the keckle on and have a cuppa lev says Joyce over her glasses every morning. She let herself in with her own key and cleaned up the worst of the excesses of the night before, and threw the roast in the oven. I watched in disbelief as a man got off the Valley Sprinter at the bus-stop outside the door every day and queued stoicly for his Honeyroast Ham in a shiny silver suit. He had an imitation hanky in the breast pocket, made out of cardboard, and carved with a pinking shears into pleated edges which fascinated me. As soon as he had wiped the last piece of sauce and cabbage from the plate with a soup roll, he stood up, straightened his cardboard hanky, fluffed the crumbs off himself and queued again for another dinner. Despite her protestations and remonstrating and pleas that she would fill the plate, or not charge, he would insist on queuing again and getting the exact same dinner replicated.

He ate 2 dinners every day.

She had a customer called Mikey Plump who was aptly named, who had a haircut like Oliver Hardy and a mustache like Hitler, who sang My Boy at the counter when he was locked, breaking down in sobs at the end and holding the last note impossibly while the men put their arms around him and called his ex a bleddy betch.

He wouldn't follow her if she sang.

She sang on counters and in corners and on table tops amid the pints of mild and peanuts. She sang old songs unaccompanied and songs from the homeland where Irish eyes were crying, and a woman was screaming out to sea from a cliff about a man who was lost trying to kill whales to make perfume for rich women.

She sang long after I had told her to call a halt to proceedings and get herself into the bed as the morning wouldn't be long coming around.

Oh, Peggy Gordon, you are my darling, come sit you down upon my knee,

Laughing turns to crying.

Hit her again, Brud, she's no relation.

Break yourselves, but don't break the furniture.

"She's one of our own Molly, don't be fussing with the tablecloth" said Toms Uncle Sean when she arrived out to see them in Uxbridge. She lay opposite him in the other recliner and watched as he showed her how to work the buttons. He took her to the Irish Club in Hillingdon and made her sing for the men.

Tablecloth me eye says he.

I will in me nickie nackie noo.

I will in me Na. - Raley and Truly hun.

September 2013 Year - 8

I decided to view a "*beautiful yorkshire terrier*" that needed re-homing on my way to Siobhán tonight, visualising scenarios where I would tote said dog around the gaff in a handbag.

All I know is that the number of the house is 6.

The first number 6 had a pensioner who looked askance at the sideways beret and the dress blowing up around my shoulders in a gale, and to her credit did not slam the door in my face.

The second number 6 was a man in the middle of eating steak & kidney pies judging by the smell and the flakes of pastry on his jumper.

The third number 6 is the right one.

2 fat fox terriers are looking at me in bewilderment.

I am looking back at them the same.

How did a yorkie morph into a fox AND a brace?

I am supposed to call them in the morning with my answer.

Then the broad who drives me drove off with the Baileys on the back seat so I gave Siobhán whiskey and lucozade till she had the hiccoughs.

I spent the rest of the time imitating the accents of the craythurs outside the door to make us both laugh.

I also played Fiachna O Braonain so loud that I may have kept Michael Winner awake Talking Heads, Bill Withers, Blur, Tracy Chapman, Dylan.

I'd say they were glad when I legged it.

A woman is standing in a hurricane looking wistfully up the road through a cloud of hair.

"Get in" says we, "I've a taxi" said she.

"Just as well" says the driver as I put on my belt, "last time I picked her up she opened the door in heavy traffic at speed and said "this'll do me" and tried to get out!"

We are lashing down the road when we see a gang on the path trying to lift a man.

And another man lying on the side of the street with a crowd around him.

"Lemme out" says I and run over to assist as if I was first response.

I am

The man is gee eyed.

As are the people helping him.

He has hit his head and cannot stand. I brace him on the path with my knees and try to put him in the recovery position. His mate is trying to drag him along the street by the leg saying *"He's grand"*

When the ambulance arrived and punches started to be thrown we retreated to the safety of the car. One young fella who came to assist us was holding a guy up against the wall with one hand and texting with the other and still didn't blink when I asked him to roll me a cigarette for my nerves.

I saw a rainbow over Mams room as I left and a shooting star when we parked and made a wish.

Summary 2012 - Year 7

When I was small there was no such thing as "babysitting".

That territory was reserved for summer holidays in caravan parks where you put an ad in the site shop and hoped not to get caught with a biker listening to Pink Floyd at 1am.

People *"minded"* children.

Neighbours, Aunts, random passing strangers, and everyone's house was full of their own and "*minded children*".

A woman I heard tell of used to call her son in for his tea with the remark -

"*Come in for your supper, Johnny hun, 2 boiled eggs - what no one else up here has!*"

Times were tough, and frivolities consisted of things like clothes and food - I grew up through petrol rationing, bin strikes- with the army clearing up the Dublin streets to remove the rats - apartheid, riots, The "*Troubles*" rolling blackouts and the RA. I lived in Guildford when the Guildford 4 were in prison down the road, and in London when Thatcher was enforcing poll taxes and they were overturning cars in Brixton, and in Germany when there was a wall. At times I felt like Forrest Gump.

A sitter was someone idle to the bone, who got "diamonds" on their legs from sitting too close to the fire, a Nanny was your Grandmother, and an Au-Pair was for that decadent shower beyond in France.

I digress.

I offer all this to explain why I was left in charge at home when I was about 10.

I was now the boss of the gaff but instead of relishing the role I fretted and sulked and worried the entire time they were out.

On a Wednesday night they would bank down the fire after the news at nine, put the guard over it, and leave the lights on. Siobhán would come tiptoeing up through the house to tell me and to advise me to stay in bed reading and be as good as gold and as quiet as mice, kissing me goodnight in a waft of perfume. "The barracks is right beside you, and sure aren't you as safe as a house on fire, we won't be long."

Almost before the door clicked behind them and they went tipping down the square to Travers for a pint and a glass, I was downstairs watching late films and eating biscuits. Of course then my brother would twig. He would come down and stand clicking his knuckles and curling his toes and announce that he, *for sure*, was staying up!

The noise of us shouting would wake the toddler.

"Ssssshhhhhh will you" I whispered and then gave him a curfew.

I was used to the scamper when I heard the footsteps across the silent Square at eleven and would horse up the stairs and leap across the room into bed where she would check in as soon as she took off her coat and scarf. A silk or chiffon square with polka dots or horse shoes would be worn over the hair, running downtown it covered a multitude, and post salon it kept the "*set*" in inclement weather.

My Aunts and Grandmothers wore Mantillas to Mass.

Usually Duckarse and Dickett brought home packets of steaming chips and battered fish wrapped in salty greasy newspaper and proffered it from a genuflecting position on clicking knees to a supine form under a pile of tangled blankets.

On rare nights they were late.

Caught up in a crowd, or a singing pub, getting stuck in a round that went on forever, and I would stand longingly behind the   letterbox listening for their footsteps and wishing them home. I would open my Mothers wardrobe and sniff armfuls of her clothing and imagine worst case scenarios where they had met with accidents and tragedy, fire and flood and I would have to take over the running of the house and my siblings.

I could easily make myself cry doing this.

It may have been the diva in me that hurled herself around the rooms and sat frozen on the stair steps waiting for the click of their heels. I should have been warm and asleep in bed. But I appear to have inherited my Fathers temperament, an emotional response to every situation and I have returned the favour to him many times over the years. He still has to be called when I am home if I am out late.

Siobhán had a lemon jersey. It must have been a gift from someone, maybe Easter one year. Every single time I have seen it on her, I have said I will take that thing off her and hurl it into a bin or bury it under landfill. It has that faux yellow consistency that makes the wearer look pale and wan and is the type of pastel that inmates of an institution might wear. *"Not a t'alla, not a t'alla"*

Last night it was on her again and I am reminded that I still have not made good on my threat.

"Thomasina, you may take that jumper out of the wardrobe and bring it home" say we.

Yis, says he. It never happened.

When the sister arrives to chauffeur me home I engage her assistance.

Between us we lift and hold and raise arms and support while the offending article is removed and Siobhán is left sitting in her vest with her hair frizzed out into a halo with static, looking surprised.

Nicola has it in her hand and I say "what will you do with that?"

"Light the fire" says she.

I would have brought it home and as I did a lifetime ago, inhaled the delicate smell of her, the perfume, and even the smell of the nursing home, wrapped it in tissue paper and kept it for evermore, inside the parcel that contains my baby matinee coat with her initials on it.

Tonight I am shaking cream in the carton to whip for an Irish Coffee and staring out at the sunset over the green hills.

 I am beginning to feel like **Randall P. McMurphy** after the big Nurse had her way and won the day.

I am immune to the calling from the hall.

Tonight I am not Bridie, or Pat, or the Nurse.

I am just a tired Michelle.

I have set a tiny tray with a schooner and spoon on a napkin, on a saucer, as if it was about to be proffered in The Horseshoe Bar, by a Dublin barman with a spotless linen towel and the gift of the gab for the Yanks.

"Did yee ever hear how they came to be made" he would ask as he polished the already sparkling *slim jims.*

"A buddy of mine ou at the airport was seeing all a dem gettin' off a da planes, FREEZIN' dey were ..." he would begin.

Someone has recently boiled the kettle and it is warm. I throw the water down the sink and fill it with fresh cold stuff from the crazy tap. It runs on air for 3 minutes and then a deluge. I have forgotten to take our own coffee from the room and sniff the communal jar in mild disgust. I realise that I am not breathing as I pour the thick cream over the back of the spoon, watching it settle and float with not a speck in the dark liquid, the beautiful white top settling into soft peaks. It just needs a coffee bean on top, the slightest dusting of chocolate, or cinnamon, to be perfect. I carry it back up the hall at speed.

I am a dab hand in a kitchen.Ditto a bar.

In previous incarnations I have shaved cheeses as a breakfast chef in Germany, poured gin & tonics in a west end pub in London for the luvvies and drag queens from the theatres next door, fried 150 eggs in one go on a rolling ship in a force 9 gale, served a rugby team drinks till 5am in Wales sans underwear, (it's a very long story) thrown men out of AND into pubs and off licences, run 200 seater carverys that turned over 5 times on Sundays, bars, managed cafes, bistros, hotels, hostels, and ships departments , read tarot cards online, and had my own cafe/wine bar at the height of my madness.

I know my way around a glass.

Siobhán is asleep when I come back.

Not just lying with eyes closed, but properly asleep, despite the trauma of the 3 person (plus hoist) lift she has just had to the commode. I thought it may possibly have woken her, but no.

"Oh, look what I have Mrs" says I.

There is no way I can get at her properly.

I am hemmed in and out by the gargantuan chair and I nearly break my back trying to lift her up a little. This is not good for me or her, as her osteoporosis will have made her bones sore and God alone knows the last thing I want to do is hurt her. I can't get the glass near her mouth without slopping it all over her neck and chest or dipping her nose in the cream.

In the end both things happened

I rummage in the drawer till I find a beautiful cerise chiffon scarf and knot it gently over her bare neck.

"Music, let's have music with the whiskey" I say and flick the remote.

There is a programme on TV that is so bad it is great. I know this because I watched it tonight. It is people singing on what looks like the pulpit of a church with a giant organ in the background.

And people dancing in front.

Country Irish.

Think Fester & Alien and imagine a woman in a **Heatons** blouse with a thick watch and a home perm singing in a wobbly falsetto some dirge about something or nothing.

By the time your one comes on to butcher The Voyage with an extraordinary arrangement that involves a 30 second musical interlude between each line, I am ready to hurl myself and the glass out the window.

The last time I saw people dance like this was in *Keegans of Broadway* when they had the big bands coming.

Twisting and jiving, and mugging into the cameras, the women with combs in their hair, A- line skirts with flesh tights and black court shoes and the oul' fellas with the shirts stuck to their backs, their combovers stuck to their heads and a large bottle of *Macardles* in each pocket.

It looks like I have opened the door to the 80's.

I expect there will be *Tayto Pub* Crisps on the table beside the untouched Irish Coffee when I look down.

A combination of exhaustion, sadness, nostalgia and temper hits me in a wave and my eyes grow hot and I can feel a sob about to burst from my throat.

Then it stops.

Dead.

Like someone stepped on a hose and turned off the flow.

"Well, this is new" I say aloud.

It is at this exact moment that the door is knocked, then opened.

Wexford 1992

*S*he ran away from from the London man in Wales to go to London with a Welsh man with a Swedish name. Then he ran away, and she came home, then he came here behind her and then I don't know what all but he left early one morning and I heard the roars and bawls of her in the shower and banged and banged on the door to get in at her and to say what's for you won't pass you when the worst of the sobbing had eased.

I told her she was a quarehawk to make her smile through eyes like a slot machine

There had only been one child in the house for years, what with the gap between them and the fact that the other pair had moved. The son was back from Germany too, and was now in college studying botany and landscaping, and I filled his rucksack with meat and vegetables every Sunday night, and emptied and washed and ironed the contents of it every Friday when he got off the bus. He was courting a nurse, and they were saving for their wedding.

Her Da was the very Garda who caught the Scourge courting in the county clinic long long ago.

The youngest and I became best friends, going shopping, or walking, or swimming at beaches, and driving off around the countryside in a re-conditioned Volkswagon camper van that Tom had turned his attention to. He had taken early retirement as his job was becoming onerous and he was under severe pressure to sell sell sell. Her ladyship went at her life like a bull in a gate and gave fodder to no-one and everyone. She lasted one day in a Chinese restaurant when they told her to spray the hot-cloths with 4-7-11 in a bath instead of washing them, and then went on to cook in The Bohemian Girl, Tim's Tavern and The Goal Bar, finally heading out to the country to cook in a pub while she was on crutches, sitting by the cooker drinking Finches Orange and issueing instructions to young ones, where she met and fell in love with the Doppelganger of Luke Kelly, moving into a flat over a pub with him, overlooking the oft remembered woodenworks and lulled to sleep by the tinkling bells on the mussl dredgers. She hid him in a wardrobe when we came to call as her Da would have lifted her out of it for living with a lad. (Messing one night, her sister opened the bedroom door and shouted in Goodnight Luke, and the looder forgot himself and answered her) Then she became a Tourist Information Officer, and was mistaken for a Ban Garda who had the same first name and the Detectives asked her to get ready to go to Wicklow to work on the Catherine Nevin case by accident. Then she ran off to the sticks to run a massive hostel, alone. An elective Mute Dutch man helped her cut down a Dub who hung himself with a belt from a chandelier and she waltzed in home at 7am having waited all night for a doctor to section him. We couldn't keep up with her, and neither could the men, Luke Kelly ran off with a young one he met when he was painting his Mothers fence and she cried for weeks and kept ringing him on Private Number, refusing to believe that the man who called her Babby and kept bacon and cabbage simmering on a steaming saucepan, had left her, in such a barbourous way.

He married the young one.

My son married his Nurse.

My youngest daughter met the Quiet Leitrim Man.

I became more and more concerned about my memory and found myself doing small ridiculous things that firstly amused, then concerned me. I told no-one. My Dad had gone a bit senile but not until he was in his 80's so I wasn't overly concerned.

Tom was in flitters that he had to speak at the wedding of his youngest daughter and was up to high doh for a week.

He took half a Xanax and made the after- dinner speeches before the dinner so as not to ruin his appetite, and we took to the floor for the dancing and waltzed and jived and tangoed all around the place while the crowd moved back to the carpet to let the dog see the rabbit and he spun me faster and faster and the Leitrim people rubbed their hands and said

"Jazus, sure they could give lessons"

"Go aisy on me now" I smiled at Ollie as I left to go home knowing I would hardly be in the car before he started fussing and complaining as I left by the back door in the Crescent.

The back walks, the back talks, the quarehawks.

"Dip it in the dip, Margie and lave the herrin' for Joe"

"Not a t'alla"

"Go aisy on me now".

January 2013 - Year 8

My sister was in a junk shop. The kind of place you might find a needle or an anchor, an upturned wheelbarrow without a wheel, a rusted bath with a hole in it, or a dusty bag of coloured wools.

She saw a bear that looked a little like a "*Steiff*" and nabbed it. He is heavy as there is machinery inside him that makes him do stuff. You press a button inside his fur to turn him on and then he basically does a heap of things.

Cries, yawns, cries again, puts up his arms to be lifted and then growls a bit and turns himself off by going asleep loudly.

He snores.

She thought it would be a great idea to bring it to Siobháns room and just leave it lying around the kip where it nearly put the heart crossways in me.

I have seen the women on my interminable treks up and down the halls for vases, spoons, glasses. I have seen them holding the soft toys and animals that grace the beds and window sills. I have seen one croon to a big eyed Disney Doll and hold its face close to hers in wonderment, mimicing the movements she made with her own baby a lifetime ago. The doors are always open to let the staff keep an eye on the residents during the long nights, as some are in bed and asleep by 7pm.

Some are not.

Some wander the halls with me - linking them or just walking slowly behind them - while I tell them to just sit down for a minute and I will get them a nice cup of tea. Tea is offered by everyone to everyone as a panacea.

"Come in and sit down and have a nice cup of tea" - they will say to the confused wanderers as they check their watches and look wistfully up the halls, waiting for a bus, a taxi, a reprieve.

"If I could just see one "D reg car out in that car park I would be away on a hack" says one peering through the fire exit doors. I wonder would they have room for me, I need to see my Mother - the woman in her 70's says with tears in her eyes. "She will be worried about me".

It finishes me.

Some nights I feel like I am a sponge that is saturated. There is no room for one more drop to go in, and what's in already is waiting to burst out in a deluge.

Siobhán herself stood at this very same door waiting for our car to come back and get her. Little Thomasina took the bear home to do stuff to him. Cleaned it up and brushed it, took apart its little fur limbs and found the opening to replace the batteries. And then informed me it was ready to take back out.

"Mam's bear is all fixed" he says on the phone as he drives to me with dinner AND it on the back seat.

I bring him inside and move him from chair to chair. *(The bear, not my Father)* I turn it on and listen to the sounds of him and the snores and then delightedly discover that he does a laughing thing when you press his paws.

Laughter is infectious even when inanimate.My driver recoils in horror when I march out the door carrying him last night.

"No, NOOO NOOOOOOO, not a dog" she wails.

"You're right there, missus" I retort as I strap myself in. "It's a bear"

Well, if he didn't growl and cry and laugh and snore the whole way out there so much as to cause her to shush him on a number of occasions - mostly at roundabouts - then call me a liar.

Siobhán has no idea that he has been on his holliers in town for 2 days. I smoothed her hair and fed her an ice-cream off a saucer and told her lots of outrageous things and then just sat holding her hand. We both listened to the sound of the little bear snoring on her pillow, maybe it is comforting, maybe if she could she would get up and hurl it out the window, and reach into her wardrobe for a coat and say –

"My name is Siobhán, I've been away for a *very long* time".

August 2013 - Year 8

I hear myself explaining stuff about Alzheimers to the driver on the way to Mam. I am boring my own tits off. He is interested and informed and we talk all the way from my door to hers. Siobhán is sitting in the dining room in her Stephen Hawking Chair.

I am beside myself with excitement to be taking her out and being in charge.

I wheel her out to the bus wrapped in blankets and scan the drivers face for a reaction, daring him to look shocked whereby I will be driven to give him a box in the face.

By the miracle of machinery she is hoisted aboard and belted in and we are off.

The sun is beautiful and warm and it's intermittent flickering -through the green canopy of overhanging trees on the mountain road, is dappling Siobháns face with sunlight and shade every fleeting second.

She knows she is out.

I hold her hand and narrate every single thing, each place we come to, the hills and dales, the highways and byways -

"There is the church in Barntown you got married in, there is Matts Lane and the Quarry, there is the house of the woman who makes scones for me on the Friary Gates, there is the house with the horses, and we are nearly there.................."

Her blue eyes are open and staring.

I text my sister who is flying home from Carlow with the baby of the Dooley house in the seat beside her that we are en route. God forbid I should end up at an empty house.

I angle Siobhán to be in sun and shade and plop the massive sun hat from the home on her. It looks like it may have been Wyatt Earps.

Little Thomasina and Keyhole Kate drive in......... their mouths a perfect "0" of surprise as they see us all at the table.

He leans into Siobhán and kisses her on the lips.

"Sure you know I love you, don't you hun" he says and kisses her again.

At the end of the day I had that lovely exhausted feeling where your bones are tired and lazy, and your face is a little burnt from sun and wind and you could curl up and sleep on the tiles.

I know Siobhán heard those Carlow voices and smiled.

Wexford 1999

There is another new baby in this house.

The son has 2 sons of his own now, and my baby daughter has also had a son of her own. The Quiet Leitrim man is as proud as punch, and was bunched the morning after wetting the babies head. The other scallywag is leasing a restaurant in an Arts Centre and is still up to her old tricks of being high as a kite one minute and at rock bottom the next. She is spending money like water, writing cheques by the newtime and everytime there is cash in the till she runs out the door to play. She seems to be going out with 2 men simultaneously and I am minding a starbaby who arrives every morning in a padded blue suit that matches his impossibly blue eyes. Her ladyship told her heavily pregnant sister to call her baby Keishy when she was prostrate across the table with the heat, the depression, the heartburn and the fear, her head matted with sweat and cobwebs having been mullocking around all afternoon preparing a nursery.

- Keishy? What does it mean?
- It's Indian, (pause) it means woman with beautiful hair.

Sometimes I see the youngest girl give me an odd look, setting the table for dinner I laid all the cutlery left handed. Tom too, has become increasingly frustrated with my repeated questions, most of which I am not aware I have even asked. He got himself into a knot trying to fold sheets with me and kept saying walk to me, walk to ME, no TO ME, for Chrissakes, and then I just smiled. Sometimes in the middle of doing something I will forget how, and then I forget that I have forgotten, and then it is ok. I read my book every night, and her ladyship goes through the phonetics of memory with me

Tea, Ray, Law, Jaw, Noah, Key, Tea, Ray, Law, Jaw, Noah, Key.
Tea, Ray, Law, Jaw, Noah, Key, Tea, Ray, Law, Jaw, Noah, Key.

I listen to music and do an easy crossword and watch the soaps and iron while Tom is up in the attic teaching himself to play the violin. He is 70 now. Who knows where the time goes?

Time, time, time, slime.

Parades and cloaks and Sheila of the O'Beirnes, put a napkin on that child, that coat will turn.

Do a few physical jerks.

Empty your can.

If I won the money I'd blacken me arse and go mad. .

On the millennium Christmas Eve the Scourge press ganged a number of men she found in a bar to drag a 15ft tree up 3 flights of stairs to her apartment and in the ensuing session blacked out the fact that she had invited us all down for the Dinner. She had spent the night carousing around the roads with a parade of hedonistic maniacs and so woke in a fog with the doorbell ringing on Christmas Day. First she booted a frozen turkey up the arse, which just happened to be lying around de-frosting in the hall, and then was confronted with a ring of us in the porch with babies in our arms. The apartment was like Beirut after the party and her brother looked at her in disgust and jealousy and said - she is still drunk. I'm grand says she and offered to change his clean baby and spirited the pair of them away down to the bedroom to lie down for "just one minute" She woke with him removing the child from her arms and telling her she had ruined Christmas for everyone and we trooped off home again to give her down the banks and cook a chicken to go with cold ham. I always loved the baking at Christmas, and would begin preparing in early November, stocking up on currants, raisins sultanas, mixed peel, glace cherries and marzipan. I always used to boil puddings and bake cakes for the brothers - pouring whiskey and brandy in with the soft fruits and brown sugar, letting them sit in layers of greaseproof rings in red biscuit tins, covering them with soft peaks of white icing and dressing them with silver balls and tiny reindeer. It didn't matter if they were only pulled out if a Nun called with a memory card, or if they were slathered with butter and washed down by mugs of tay. It's the thought that counts.

She woke twice of a Christmas day and sat contemplating the warchest of food and drink and boxes of crackers that she had bought in the cash and carry on a maxed out visa.

In the end she realised that she was throwing good money after bad and decided to take the advice of her Uncle Ollie, and "put the white on the window". She dragged a black bag of invoices to an accountants in Henrietta Street, and landed a biscuit tin filled with bills and receipts up on his desk and he took in the overflowing papers in the bins and tins and said –

"Do you realise I'm billing you by the hour?"

"Just organise that lot and try and pay yourself out of it" says she and he did.

She wrote "**No it's not**" under Today's Special on the blackboard.

And then closed the door behind her and ran away to Sea for 4 years.

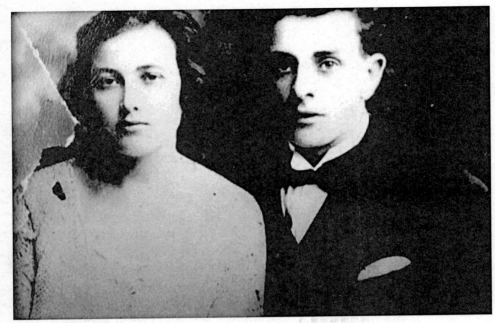

Maggie & Michael Mahon - Wedding Day

Tom & Margaret Dooley - Wedding Day

Tom Mahon of Wexford with Kitty 1941

Duckarse, Nana, Keyhole Kate, Tawnish,
The Baby, Handsome - Carlow 1954

The Scourge plots her escape 1965

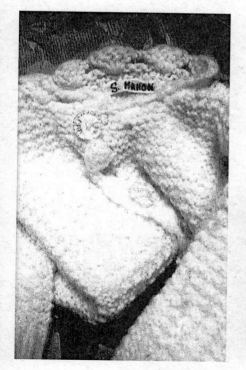

Strike a match - name of God tonight 1970

Tagged Cardigan 1964

*Your one has run out of leaves
again - Pantomime 1974*

Basking in Ballask - Carne 1979

*Meanwhile in Slade, the brother is
not demolishing walls*

*Little Thomasina plays with the Skin & Blister
- the **real** favourite 1973*

*Tom & Siobhán at the Church
they were married in 1993*

On this the day of my brothers wedding

Tom & Siobhán 40th Anniversary 2003

Tom's 84th Birthday Party

Tagged Cardigan - 50 years later

Siobhán at the field gate in late summer 2014

Spring 2012 - Year 7

I have exhausted myself from a surfeit of words, be they the ones tap dancing in my head or pouring forth incessantly from my lips.

A veritable fountain.

Today the witness in me watched the antics of the ego in me as I talked myself up and down and in and around the baking streets in the sun.

I live this life as if I was in a movie, and have my home dressed like a set, couches draped with soft throws, cushions,scented candles, nicky nacky noo things on every shelf and ledge that would be remarkable in and of themselves , the spines of a hundred books open and dangling off every surface - I have placed fresh-cut wild flowers in a white enamel basin circa 1940 in the living room, trying to harness a bit of rural atmosphere to a townhouse that thinks it's a cottage.

The director shouts "Lights, camera, action" and off I go, with an erstwhile commentator giving me feedback from the tiny inner monologue that is *not* the source within.

My first stop was my favourite book shop where I asked the assistant to go halvers with me on a magic spell.

"I need to be grounded and calmed. I need to be focused and I need you to march around here and find me something as big as a copy, but not a copy, and to hand it to me with joy and intent and tell me to write in it".

I would have brought chalk to draw a combining circle around us but I didn't want to frighten the horses *or* passing toddlers. I explain that I am a whirlwind of ideas and words and songs, that I am mopping my house at midnight with all the doors open, that I have painted over the 3 nudie women playing their instruments in a field and that when I woke, some had underwear on. And 2 had tattoos. My minute yard looks like Monty Don may be nixing behind the bushes or the strawberry plants - the 3 feet squared I have at my disposal I have managed to convert into a tiny meadow - one piece of this conversion involving taking a bus to Scalder Balls and hefting a spade in to the wet clay of a mans garden and bringing home dripping muck, weeds and daisies in a plastic bag on the bus.

Visited a homeopath up Wicklow way who held my hand for a brief moment and then flinched as if shocked or stung.

"Lord Lantern Tonight, it's like you were born without a top layer of skin".

I always watch, and listen, and dissect, I scan faces, I mirror body language, I watch tells and micro tells, I intuit, I empathise.

I can walk into a room and feel the energy, and it is precisely this that has formed a butterfly mind that will just fly away at the earliest convenience. Good night and good luck.

Despite trying to be present and aware, to focus, to be in my body, to channel my energies, my ego has run amok and I am speeding.

The sun has made me high.

The sun has also made me close the laptop and disappear out of the blue lit attic into the yellow streets, to be a part of the teeming life that goes on outside my door, to vacate the sentinel, the hermitage I reside in, and to engage.

It has taken a toll. The skin that is left is thin. It bruises easy.

All week I have been like a mule's tool - always out - and have been found on quaysides, on benches, in gardens, in houses, in cafes, on street corners, talking and talking and talking. My hysteria is the scream of a skier going over a cliff. I may as well be shouting at the algae covered crescent, or into the blueness of the *Kay* or out at the point of the raven where I could see the white sand and longed to be out there, out there where the clear air relays the conversations half a mile up the beach as plain as day, and walk straight into the blue, that despite being a scorcher of a day will still be ice cold.

This evening when I thought the top of my head might actually blow off and all the words and lyrics and snatches of melody and times tables might leak down the side of my face in a pale pink pulp and I longed for space and peace and white noise, I dragged my tri-colour body home and laid it down on a white quilt in a multi-coloured room to re-connect with my source and draw breath.

I forget that I need to do this, ironically.

Melvyn Bragg described in a beautiful line today that as his Mothers memories disappeared, his memories of her heightened.

Then I must be as full as a stuffed chicken as the memories of Siobhán are all over and all around me, and I sleep on them, and wake to them and other surprises. I may be sleepwalking but I painted a Universe on the attic roof, knit a hat for a nurse which I found finished, stitched and wrapped when I awoke, and have to trawl through my phones log to see who in the name of Christ and all his Saints I am talking to at 3am.

It was while I was looking for a box of letters tonight that I found the memory course box by **Dr Bruno Furst** that Siobhán was using, like the little dutch boy who put his finger in the dyke to stem the dam- to try to avoid - to re-jiggle the hardwiring of her brain by using formula, to retain, to salvage, to delay the loss of her memories.

She knew what was coming.

We did not.

The Tibetan Book of the Dead states that someone who has lost all of their earthly memories will be re-born without them.

Not on my watch.

August 2003 - 40ᵗʰ Wedding Anniversary

They told us they were taking us out for a meal and that they just had to call into the house to see how the children were getting on being babysat. They said just stick your head in for one minute and show your faces, and so I wrapped my cardigan around my shoulders as I couldn't find the sleeve with my arm, and then they opened the flap of a big white thing, rubber, you know the things, ah, they have them at a circus, you'd have one at a beach, we had one in Lahinch when the Down Syndrome child opened her top when we were camping, and the child had a boil on her back as big as a saucer, and then ....tents

It was a tent.

We had ho- ro and lánna bánnya in that thing, Tom was shocked but I was delighted to see everyone there and his band played and the drinks over- flowed on the bar table and it only dawned on me on the way home in the back of the taxi that the scourge had been on crutches. She has often been on crutches.

As a child she stepped wrong off a path and broke a bone in her ankle, then tore ligaments and muscles and had to be strapped and plastered and was on and off crutches for months. She was headbutted by a Travelling man when she tried to intervene in a row over a half dressed child, and the Gardaí brought her home with 2 black eyes, and said there is no point in the wide earthly world trying to arrest him as his wife will deny every screed of it. She was kicked in the back by a stranger walking past a fight outside a kebab house and the solicitor who helped her up wanted to press charges. She fell down a stairs at a party and woke up on a spinal board in A & E, discharging herself to go back and finish playing poker. She called me from a ward where she had been admitted after being nebulised for 5 days after taking an asthma attack at a session. She whispered into the phone on wheels to bring her nightclothes as she was disgraced in the blue ward filled with pensioners having enemas in her basque and stockings. She had a pain in a hip for a year and eventually the leg stopped working altogether and she took to dragging it behind her. Despite doctors, specialists and a bone scan, they could never find a thing wrong with it. In Wales she lost her voice for 6 months and had nodules removed from her vocal chords while the taxi driver eyed her in the rear view mirror as he drove her to Singleton hospital and laughed and said — "I bet yo arse is gowen li da" as he rubbed his fingers together.

On the night of our Anniversary she stood on the plug of a hair dryer conveniently left on the stairs for the next head in a house filled with secret visitors as she was running down in bare feet. I took a photo of her leaning over her fathers shoulder laughing with a bearded man.

April 2013 - Year 8

Day after day as I have been sitting typing, stopping to look out the skylight at the sunshine/ torrents speckling the glass, my view only of skyline and spires, I have been inhabiting a strange nether world that is neither fish nor fowl.

Memories are fleeting and intangible, and one can segue into another, and so while I am frantically trying to pin one to the page, another will pop up and like Alice through the looking glass, I am falling.

Today, Little Thomasina and I went for lunch. The place is heaving and I inform the waitress that he is in his 80's and not about to sit in the wind tunnel facing the door. She finds another space for us which is quieter (and marginally warmer) and so I take the opportunity to actually interview my own Father with a notebook and pen.

I know.

It has taken a long time to get to this stage, and a lot of Plamásing.

Now that complete strangers are shaking his hand and calling him *Little Thomasina* and making him feel like the Mayor, his tune has changed slightly. I suppose he feels that he may as well be in like Flynn, as he is *already* in, and so is prepared to answer my questions as opposed to waving them away.

Aside from an interval where I lifted my head to see the squalling rain lashing into the water under the bridge, I wrote while he ate, interrupting only to bark *"Spell"*.

He is the one wearing the 2 hearing aids but I am the one saying *"What?"*

I almost spat a sun dried tomato out on the table when he informs that his Aunt Katty died of putting on damp clothes.

The hotel around us is manic and we are an Island of 2, at a table for 6, and the language we are using is Wexfordian at its finest.

After listening to the memories and stories, evocative names and characters, like *Brass Lead, Ballsy, Baa Swift, Quaise and Sher, Filthy Paddy, The Bullet, The Yowk, The Drummer Boy, and The Big Fella,* I am amazed - when I lift my head to ask the waitress to ask the chef to introduce the chips to hot oil for a moment longer as they are as white as the driven snow - to realise I am not in the Wexford of long ago that we are talking about, but that is the year 2013, and that this little boy is in fact 83.

It is social archive, I tell him through hurried mouthfuls, as he has finished and is waiting for tea and a biscuit.

I know this, but the waitress does not.

I snort a noseful of coffee as he remembers that Baa, who lived in a one room house, had a huge painting of a grand staircase on the wall behind the front door.

There was always divilment happening in Carrigeen, says he in an exact replica of the line I used once. He tells a story of a man with a cork leg who they played an awful trick on with a corpse. He tells a story of dropping metal trays down a flight of stairs to disturb the card players in the parlour, and he tells a story of Baa on the stage in the Theatre Royal saying - "A horse, a horse .... my Kingdom for a horse!" and a wag from the Gods shouting down - "Will an Ass do?"

"Yeah, come down!"

We talked about nicknames and how every family in the country had them, some for reasons, some just because.

Siobhán was called Duckarse as a child because she walked with a waddle as a toddler. Little Thomasina has signed his cards to her all their lives as *Crinos*, and today I hear another one, the one he was called in Carrigeen all those years ago.

"Ah, here is little *Dickett* coming down from school".

He roots in his wallet and I say - "Now please, don't try to give me hundreds of euro, I will be mortified" -

But then he hands me a piece of paper, that has been folded and re-folded into creases many times.

I read it. It is the story of his life on half a page. I cannot stop the tears and am a mess over my coffee cup and need to blow my nose, but the napkin is gone.

He looks away while I compose myself and I place it in my purse. It is more precious than the winning lotto ticket.

The Scourge - August 2010

On the sunlit morning of my Fathers 80th birthday I watched my sisters tanned capable hands resting on the steering wheel of her BMW as she drove her fast car to an Asylum to have a battery of tests and psychological evaluations carried out on me.

An actual Asylum.

I had come crashing back to earth after a period of being so high a therapist who tried to heal me with Bio-Energy described me as not having my feet on the surface of the planet at all.

"*You are off playing with the angels and higher consciousness, and you must imagine your feet and legs grounded, like trees. You need to inhabit the earth.*"

I am lying on her treatment table and trying to breathe without gasping or sobbing. I am trying to still my egoic monkey mind and quiet my thoughts, which are racing. Nothing is quick enough, I can't type fast enough, high speed broadband seems slow. In the moment of doing one thing, I am planning 5 others.

I will write 4000 words, start knitting a hat, paint a wall, move the furniture, plant tulip pots, do a crossword, read 15 separate library books, cherry picking chapters, decide to go for a walk, surf the internet, cook, or set up an easel and paint chubby women.

I will talk and laugh and engage and fire one liners back and fore like rice at a wedding. And when all the painting and writing and watching and reading and singing and sewing ends...... well, it ends badly.

An empty sack won't stand.

After high comes low - as rain follows sun.

What goes up must come down and all that jazz.

Which explains why I am pacing like a caged animal in a medical clinic trying to get a GP to see me in a hurry and please diagnose, prescribe and assist me. I have not slept in weeks, and lie red eyed staring into a vortex of spinning black into which I could so easily topple. I feel there is a whirling energy in the room, and the bed resembles the scene of a battle royale every morning, my fingers tangled in the sheets.

There are scratches and unexplained bruises on my hands and legs.

My Mother was often quoted as saying "*That one's tearbag is too near her eye*". As I aged, the bouts of depression multiplied, and the fall out worsened. I became prolific as regards ideas and output but the fizzing thoughts were spiraling, feeding from the pain body, growing stronger and more debilitating every time.

By the time I had what could be considered a minor breakdown in the summer of 2003 -where I took to the bed, refusing to engage or do anything other than sleep, having my parents come to the door with hot meals as they had not got any phone response, shit got real.

I did not even class it as such, and would enquire wistfully of people what a breakdown actually *was*.

I quit my job, which had seen me work night shifts at sea in a small metal inboard cabin without a porthole for 4 years. I got on a plane to Spain and spent many weeks sitting alone outside pavement cafes watching the locals promenade with their perfect progeny in their little lace suits and dresses, and drinking too much.

Me - not them.

Many people will swap one addiction for another and most people with depression or mental health issues will try to drink the pain away, at least initially.

They do this so they can find that small clear space inside where just for a brief window, things are actually ok.

They do this so they can exhale in what Pink Floyd call a state that is "**Comfortably Numb**".

They do this until the alcohol becomes more of a problem, usually on a physical level, and so will often end up in The Rooms – sharing- and starting a 12 step programme.

I know.

I did.

I did sobriety for 18 months but the only upside was freedom from the bastards of hangovers that laid me low, and as the crash of the alcoholic waves of sickness and shaking turned back out on the evening tide - leaving a trail of flotsam and jetsam in their backwash - fear and loathing floated in on the foam.

I began to self sabotage, engaging in doomed smothering relationships with commitment-phobes, refusing to stay anywhere I was not comfortable, including and especially, employment. I would be off like a dirty shirt if the craic was not 90. I was the loudest, funniest, most outrageous girl, the one where the parties were at, the one who could manifest anything, the one whose ships cabin was nicknamed *Lillies Bordello* who could source cases of cold beer from closed off licences, drugs from passing strangers, favours, lifts and comedy situations you couldn't make up.

I think Ryan Adams may have met me before he wrote "*I wish I had a Sylvia Plath*"

I worked like this for 30 years.

It was exhausting.

When I stood behind the locum who was scanning my medical history onscreen that day in June, I was frantic and frazzled. My thought were spinning out of control, I was pacing and crying in the waiting room. I even lit a cigarette in the clinic and began to speed read the notices about counselors and Tai chi and support groups and wondered was he ringing an ambulance to have me sectioned.

Ladies and Gentlemen, Paranoia has entered the building.

A first.

He was only calling the Asylum to book me in. I almost fainted. I visualized myself in a padded cell restrained like Frances Farmer, I am nothing if not dramatic. He did not turn or face me once and typed my medical referral as I watched.

............................this 40 plus female presenting with significant depression on a regular basis, insomniac, please evaluate and get back soonest - query Bi-Polar /Manic/ ADHD?

He prescribed a mood elevator known as **Efexor** which morphed me into Randall P. McMurphy post lobotomy, pupils dilated, unsteady walking, drooling attractively, and a sleeping tablet that cut me off mid sentence dropping my head onto my chest, already snoring.

I threw the Anti-D's in the bin.

Stilnocht became my boyfriend.

Come on, it's not rocket science.

My appointment came a week later and we pulled into the car park of the hulking building with the turrets and the clock tower looming ominously against the skyline. She waits for me in the car, taking the piss and asking will she get me some sucky sweets for when I am on the ward. I huff and blow. I have dressed with extreme care and have been up for hours preparing myself, my clothing, my accessories, and my flawless make up. I am mistaken for a medical rep and sent into the wrong room.

A temporary hiatus, and then I am led through the locked wards where I stare from under my eyelashes at the groups of men and women in their fleece pyjamas and dressing gowns, some shaking, some morose, some catatonic, all chain smoking with their brown fingers curled under the white plastic mesh where they are huddled at the screen door. In the office I am left to sit while the shrink is sent for. An impossibly beautiful Indian girl about 16 comes in with a file under her arm.

In her soft dialect I find it difficult to understand the pronounciation, and guessed a number of answers, and told downright lies to more. She talks about CBT, Talk Therapy, Counselling Sessions, and advises she will send me an appointment for same. It is 5 years later and I have not heard a peep since. I could have gone over the Quay.

I fought back alone.

I fought back with words and alternative holistic spiritual ways.

St Therese is quoted as "If this be madness, bring it, Lord."

I read "Thresholds of the Mind" by Bill Harris and lent it to a Muslim Taxi Driver after a party. Someone had paid him with a bag of grass. He was distraught.

I read Oliver Sachs' book "The man who mistook his wife for a hat" about the human brain

I read "Women who love too much" and "50 Ways to let go and be happy".

I devoured philosophy, and re-incarnation and Karma.

I researched alternate religions and read avidly and voraciously anything that remotely resembled self help.

I read Paul Mckenna as he explained the persistant thoughts being like a virus in a harddrive but which can be released.

Remove and Replace.

Uninstall and reinstall.

Watch your thoughts. Watch the ones you are running sub consciously more as they are a deeper layer down.

I learned and read and learned and practiced. I signed up for courses about awareness and mindfulness and the power of now, the magnetic elements of thought, quantum physics, and about the beneficial aspects of meditation, something I had been claiming to do for years, but was in fact always in my head planning after minutes.

I flirted with Buddhism and became B.F.F. with Eckhart Tolle , John Moriarty and John O Donohue using his beautiful poem Beannacht as a mantra. I learned how to cast Runes and read Tarot Cards, read Anton Mesmer on Auto Suggestion, read people using auras and colour therapy, micro tells. I bought a course of Cd's from **Centerpoint** called Flotation, Immersion, and The Dive, that had a layer of embedded sounds under the white noise that tapped into the theta levels in the brain. You do each CD for 14 nights, and end with The Dive.

Christ, it was hard.

Everything in me reacted to the womp womp womp beat under the sound of lashing rain, and my eyes rolled back and I stripped my teeth from my gums, but I tangled my hands in the blanket above me and pulled myself back to my small centre and started again. I ended up kneeling with my head on the floor sobbing and saying - "I give up " – Ego hates to hear this, as it dies, and convinces you that you will do similar, which is complete tosh.

Surrender.

A homeopath up the country was brewing a remedy to treat like with like. She took my hand to do a pulse test and dropped it instantly like it was on fire.

"My God, you're a sensitive, it's like you were born without a top layer of skin" she cried.

The remedy gave me a violent migraine for a week but I kept drinking it from the metal jug with the metal spoon till it was gone, and so was the headache, and so was the stress.

Just FYI, I had a malignant melanoma removed from my arm by a healer called *The Deacon* in my 20s, after the application of mustard powder, roots and herbs and a bread poultice. Pleasant it was *not*, but it worked so I am on it like a bonnet. .

It was in this moment of surrender that a chink of peace came through, a spiders neck width, a shaft of clarity, a silence. Acceptance and Surrender are the two most functional qualities you can aspire to. What you will actually be is totally awake and aware in the present, in the Now.

NOW, I am so pleased with small things, the delight of meeting a human for coffee and having an actual real conversation, not small talk. I love the delight of seeing my Mother break through her late stage Alzheimers and open her eyes for moments, I love the bowls of fresh natural flowers on saucers in all the tiny poky rooms of this house, the smell of a giant stuffed chicken roasting that smells like home, warm scented laundry spinning in the tumbler, the hotch potch of projects started , the wordcount stacking and piling up on the blank screen, the gentle strains of Nick Drake singing *Northern Sky* grounding my feet in the sticky green shoots of fens and marshes so that I am wet up to my knees
Grounded at last.

When I don't create, something, anything, even if is only a flower arrangement, a cartoon, a story, then I am pent up and frustrated and impossible to be around. When I am producing reams and organizing multi media productions, and changing the bed obsessively, including its actual position in the room to face the moon, I am aware that I am high but I have learned to balance the comedown.

And I have learned the following – for what it's worth.

Every single thing you believe about anything is only a thought you had **once** that became installed.

You **can** change the thought. Be the rider, not the horse.

Most of the stuff you worry about will never happen.

"A coward dies a hundred times, a brave man only once

There is no angry vengeful God with a big white beard floating on a cloud judging you. We are the energy that the Universe and the stars are made of, and something with a consciousness that has the ability to create black holes is still connected to you on a daily basis.

When you are at the end of your tether and your head is demented, stop, take a deep breath and ask yourself – What is my next thought going to be? Wait. Watch. Notice what happens. Practice to extend the peace.

Everyone carries the black balloon of thought around with them and is so busy in their own heads they don't give a shiny shite what you are up to.

When Stephen Fry was asked would he swap his Bi-Polar to be "normal"he riposted –
Not for a New York minute
I concur.

I recognize the cyclical nature of the beast now, and detach and disengage when I am becoming ornery, maudlin, snappy, or running into exhaustion. Follow your bliss. Do what makes you happy. Lighten up on self criticism which is ego coming in the back door. If the self talk is all coming from the self, then who is listening? I am drug free and feeling my way day by day, allowing a higher power to create through me. It loves to play.

We are Eternal. You ARE what you are praying to. *Know thyself* says the Oracle at Delphi.

- Gnothi Seauton

My sister laughs in relief when she sees me coming out, tottering over the stony car park in my high boots. I flop into the car and light a Marlboro, hanging out the window to blow the smoke away up at the locked windows.

Well – she says, looking over at me with a bemused expression

- what have you got?

Bi Polar/ Schizophrena/Psychotic episodes/ or just delusions of grandeur? She smiles.

"Hysteria, (I cough) ....she says I am hysterical."

"Ah Michelle, I could have told you that myself" and she laughed and I joined her as we sped off in the hot sun to collect Little Thomasina for his surprise party, which he knew about.

Of course

March 2014 - Year 9

When I went out there first I was a veritable ray of sunshine.

I was all like ha ha and ho ho and all up in people's grills and all about their business.

I knew who was where and what was what.

I made tea and answered phones and held hands and pressed bells, as we were as familiar with the building as the employees. I even knew they kept the bottles of 7up in the locked shed outside and where the key was.

I sat in the staff smoking room and conversed with them about Christmas, or Easter, or the State of the Nation.

I entertained the night carers as I waited for a lift with ridiculous pronouncements and advised about classes, yoga, T'ai chi, accupuncture, homeopathy, NLP, Reiki, and the power of positive thought.

I was a one woman comedy review who would hold forth at length about acceptance, and awareness and meditation.

I was the all singing all dancing Michelle.

I knew the name and room number of everyone.

"She's hilarious" they would say.

"A tonic" they would say.

"A pure breath of fresh air" they would say.

Now, I walk in with my head down and try not to make eye contact.

I carry my small offering of a tiny trifle or mashed strawberries or a melting ice cream and close the door quietly behind me to shut out the clamour.

On October 2nd it will be 5 years.

I am a different woman now.

Then, I was blonde and slim having walked the pounds off on a trek to and from the hospital 4 times a day.

Now I am dark and massive.

My knees hurt from carrying the other Michelle around with me.

I sat tonight at the Courtyard listening to the water from the fountain while the business of hoisting and toileting was carried out behind the closed curtains.

And I thought how the opinions of these many others must have changed to reflect the change in the comedienne formerly known as the breath of fresh air.

I laughed and sang with men with guitars, harmonised with the Christmas Choirs, sat in the baking church for Mass.

Now I would rather gouge out my own eyes than engage, as the stories have filled me to saturation central.

Now I sit stroking my 3 chins and wondering how the hell my moustache grows back on a daily basis.

Could it be possible be that I am approaching middle age without even getting a handle on my teenage years? .

Stop the world, I wanna get off.

Please can we go around again, I was only messing.

I'll be good this time, no messin', scouts honour.

Now all the names and stories will have to go into some other girls head and she will have to carry them with her.

We ALL carry our stories, the ones that then we add to our basket of ourselves.

We put everything in the basket. Good and bad, and take it out to torment ourselves with it when we are feeling low.

There is no point in wishing for another better past, and as childhood is the only part of ones life that is not impacted on by one's childhood. I have to remind myself to let go, to let it wash over me, to live in the NOW.

I meet Little Thomasina for lunch and am amazed when he says he is getting a little puppy and has got a tiny coat for it. I stare at the white fluff on his 83 year old freckled head as he bends and opens the brown paper bag and my baby matinee coat comes tumbling out - hand knit and stitched, with the tag of my Mothers name sewn into the neck.

S.MAHON in indelible ink

He thought I might like to have it for the book, either as an aide-de-memoir or as a photograph.

Let her name be writ large.

It isn't hilarious any longer.

I spent a good hour handwashing it in the sink in cold water and then put it on a padded hanger and hung it in the sun.

Then I ran out to fetch it when I remembered reading -

dry flat

shape whilst damp -

and do not tumble -

on woolen care instructions.

I don't know whether those instructions should apply to the garment or me.

And I have no-one to ask.

The sponge is saturated and the eyes are filling up

I came home and listened to Mick Flannery singing "Boston" as loud as the speakers would go.

Hilarity - Moi?

I'd rather eat my own foot.

Breath of fresh air - if only ?

Tonic? Over ice and a slice with a slug of Bombay Sapphire

Flat & Dry   - Check.

Damp & Shapeless. - Check.

Do not tumble. Well, not in these heels.

 I came home and did a Paul Gascoigne behind the hall door

The sponge may have a crack in it.

"Please, no more therapy,

Mother, take care of me,

Piece me together with a needle and thread,

Wrap me in Eiderdown,

Lace from your wedding gown,

fold me and lay me down on your bed."

Shaun Colvin – "*Polaroids*"

Wexford October 2004

*H*er ladyship ran away to sea for 4 years and a clown bled to death in her arms on a cross channel ferry, and a young fella she drank with climbed the railings and jumped in the pitch black dark before the sodium lights lit up the harbor ahead. The ships engines idled and died as they threw flowers into the murky grey water and there was only the sound of the sucking sea and the sobbing of the crew. She moved into his cabin to remember him. My sister, the long one, Emeeeeeee Nash was found confused in her house, with a fridge full of rotting steaks and salmon, that she had been buying and not remembering to eat. Her ladyship moved in when she was taken into a nursing home to keep the house occupied and not long after took to the bed herself. She wouldn't answer the door or the phone, and when we called around would sometimes eventually grow tired of the knocking and calling through windows and let us in with a dinner on a tinfoil covered plate. She was pale and exhausted and appeared to be asleep all day and awake all night, as per. She refused to see a doctor and took herself to Spain instead, then quit her job and worked part-time in a bar, playing loud music and flirting with young fellas. Within a month she had moved in a lovely blonde lad she called Hewhomustnotbenamed and whom I called Owen. Which was not his name. She asked him to inflate the helium balloons at her 40th party and he moved in a week later.

He thought it was her 30th, which she didn't know whether to be pleased or offended by. She thought *all her birthdays had come together when she met him. She was wearing a black velvet dress again, this time a smaller size than she had ever worn in the last 20 years, and she ran from table to table like an excited child shouting what did you bring me? I tried to keep an eye on her from the booth the family had commandeered, and could see she was about to explode with excitement. It has always been my job to quietly remind her not to light cigarettes in the street, to mind her language, to behave like a lady, but she appears to have always confused behave with perform. She stood beside us at the end of the counter, passing the gift wrapped boxes and bulky envelopes over to me for safekeeping. A cousin of mine called Nan Dooley used to run a Huxters shop in Tullow, and would sit on a stool at the entrance, patting the customers down before they left in case they had robbed her blind.*

"C'mere to me, you're looking very bulky" she would say before she frisked them.

The bulky cards and presents had been relegated to a black bin liner and as I leaned over to deposit another one I saw her wave a roll of notes into the startled barmans face.

"I've a thirst you could photograph and the tide is out" said she with a grin and the red haired man eating chicken gougons beside her turned and laughed. He had been banging the counter to the drum beat in "Brewing up a storm" which she had a Waterford outfit playing on repeat like the Cantina Band.

"Jazus and it's a right night, and I don't even know whose party it is – I haven't had as much crack since the night we gatecrashed a 21st and stole the cake" says he.

*Her head spun so fast her beads flew around her neck and she informed him that it was hers, **and** her cake.*

- *Fuck says he. And I only came up here tonight because I heard **Brewing up a storm**. Another storm was brewing.*

A mild breeze had started to nip at my shoulders, and ripple through my hair. The winds of change were blowing around the house in the Square, and would turn into a hurricane that rattled windows that sad faces looked out of.

I lost my keys a lot, and I left my purse down town nearly every time. I got her ladyship to cut keys for me as there was no point in asking her for spare paper folding money as she never had any, don't tell Tom, I said. Don't tell Tom.

"Wipe the tears from your ears, baby dear"

"I'm a lonely little Petunia in an onion patch"

"Walk tall, walk straight and look the world right in the eye,
That's what my Mama told me when I was about knee high"

August 12th 2013 - Year 8

Siobhán and Little Thomasina have been married 50 years today.
I wheeled her from the room into the waiting bus with a ramp.
The nurses and carers have had notice of her departure and she has been lifted into a more manageable chair than the Stephen Hawking, and someone has kindly curled her hair.
I wrap the mint green throw around her legs as her curls dance in the breeze.

It must be such a pleasure to feel the air on her neck.

I am so excited to see her that I kiss the face off her and tell her all the secrets about who will be there – and who is coming from far away.

The mountain road is bumpy and we lurch against each other in the back, my arm around her shoulders, the radio blasting through the sunlit morning.

At the house, there is a small crowd of people standing waiting for the guest of honour, glasses of red wine to toast her arrival -

The dog disgraced himself actually by rolling in some horse shit, despite just having been washed so was literally in the doghouse all afternoon.

Cutlery and plates have even been borrowed from my madhouse, nothing matching, some cracked.

There are candles flickering on the table, and confetti hearts strewn about amongst the glasses.

Siobhán is fed a pureed meal and we wait for the Priest for dessert.

He wasn't for dessert but he should have been, after stopping Little Thomasina at Mass on Saturday to confirm the address.

It was supposed to be a surprise.

It was supposed to be a blessing for their anniversary.

It was not supposed to give Dad a chance to write a little speech of his own which he whipped out of his pocket before the Priest had put his back in.

I was perched on the side of the armchair, looking around the room, at the faces of the people who have been touched by my Mothers illness.

In some eyes I saw pain and confusion, in others stoic acceptance, and in at least 3, the tears that mirrored my own.

Little Thomasina stood with his head bowed as he listened to the words of the Priest, who is the same age as him.

We recited the Our Father, A Hail Mary and A Glory Be, as the old man called down blessings on this table, this family, the house and all who come into it, the voices soft and tentative in the quiet kitchen, me adding a whispered *Namaste* with my Amen.

Then my Father unfolded his piece of paper and read to us his thanks, and the blessings he has had with the love of his life, and reminded us that love, and family is *all* there ever is.

He ended with a quote from Mother Theresa about doing small things greatly.

I ended with taking my Mother back to the nursing home in the bus.

Tonight I have left a card addressed to them both on the locker in her room.

On the front are 2 champagne flutes and bubbles and horseshoes and golden number 50's.

It could not be more incongrous.

But the message inside is a blessing from another man in his 80's, which I wrote out for my Father to read tomorrow.

"The most precious gift we can offer anyone is our attention.

When mindfulness embraces those we love,

they will bloom like flowers"

Thich Nhat Hanh - Zen Master

Children are born "Cable ready" as they inherit the collective consciousness of all who have gone before.

I believe this.

Which is why my youngest Nephew is my tech support guy
and Little Thomasina's.

And why he was in the back of the car last night at the nursing home, en route to build a tree house.

I pulled him out by his runner.

"It's far more important that you come and play with Nana than tricking around in a tree" I huffed as I pulled his leg out the door.

He had been installing broadband and a high speed modem on Little Thomasina's new i-Pad.

"I'll get Pat Shortt to pull you out if you don't come aisy" says I, threatening him with the man wearing braces who is locking his car.

He tries to resist and stop laughing, but both are futile and I march him down the hall in a headlock, which is difficult for both of us, owing to the fact he is a foot taller than me, at least.

He lies on the bed laughing at the photos and videos on my phone while I attend to the face wiping and feet massaging of my Mother.

Siobhán has her eyes open.

The woman in the hall is crying for her own Mother to come and bring her home. I close the door gently as the Nurse lead her away.

Let's surround Nana with love and make a Trinity of hands - I say and he installs himself on the left of her, me on the right.

We unwrap her stiff hands and move her arms gently, and I put on the "Lovely Girls" for her to listen to the "Come-all-Ye's" and piano solos.

The Irish Jury has always been out on whether "The Rose of Tralee" is the naffest, cringiest, most toe curlingly embarassing programme ever made, or a slice of nostalgia.

It is our guilty pleasure, and even those of us who castigate it, deride it as a national disgrace, call it sexist, at best highly suspect, and at worst a pile of tosh, secretly watch at least 5 minutes of it.

We grew up with this.

Back in the day when the only thing in Ireland that was Gay was named Byrne, it was compulsive.

We bet each other off the couch to get a birds eye view.

There were wild swerves between respectful silence as the Roses were wheeled on to be grilled by Gaybo, or screeches of laughter when they stumbled over their words or their stilletos.

It has been our very own form of "The Gathering" for decades, bringing 3rd & 4th generation Yanks back to the old sod, to listen to their Harvard Graduate sing "The Mountains of Mourne" in a sash, wiping a tear from a tanned, white toothed face that never felt wet wind.

It has not changed one bit.

Siobhán held our hands as the quivering voice of the rose, the swell of the audience chorus and the Garda Band conjured up a slice of an Ireland long ago, and one, which if the tilt of her head was anything to judge by, she appreciated.

My Nephew, whose only frame of reference for the show is the lovely girls parody from Father Ted, is in the kinks with the stories I am telling him of long ago, and how as children we too watched this, his Mother and I, with our Mother.

"But, oh, t'was the light in her eyes softly shining....................

Siobhán's lap is covered in dog hairs/Lucozade and Hula Hoops.

YOU do the math.

That Walter, apart from being the tiniest dog I have ever seen, has a personality the size of Australia, and twice as sunny.

He has charmed every single person he has met and been in everyone's arms or laps tonight.

So many shaking liver, spotted hands reached out to him that I felt I should be wearing a Pet Therapy Hi-Viz.

The men in particular reached out to this tiny Chihuahua..

Normally, the men are the quietest.

Sitting idly, staring out the windows, parked in their wheelchairs, or lying on beds listening to matches on TG4.

Watching interminable episodes of soaps.

Tonight, men whose names I have never known called from rooms or the halls and reached out to this tiny animal.

- What's his name?
- How old is he?
- What kind is he?

A Carer places him on an old, old, mans lap and his face lights up.

As does hers.

"That's the first smile I have seen with him all week" says she delightedly.

I can hear them talk as I negotiate the Stephen Hawking chair, Siobhán, the Hula Hoops and the Chihuahua in a coat, out the living room door.

"She said he was fully grown" says one man to another.

"What?" says the other.

"The young one, she said that dog was fully grown, he's no bigger than a harvest mouse" he laughs and turns back to the TV.

I smile.

Another old man leans over and says - "he is a ringer for a day old pig"

I have the lead wrapped around Siobhán's hand for purchase, should he make a burst for the door.

Again.

I had already been like a woman at Crufts running her dog through the finals when he escaped on the way in. All I could think about was whether my bosom was bouncing the way theirs did.

Siobhán does not want to let the lead go and is being territorial about a dog she can feel, if not see.

I have to extricate him from her and brush her hair and tell her that I will leave her in peace, without the yapping.

His, and mine.

Archeologists and Anthropoligists research humanity years and years after the fact. They find a tiny shard of pottery and try to dissect an entire population, customs, practices and habits from it. Time Teams spend thousands on digs and research and conjecture. We put Preservation Orders on buildings to retain the history, and we are forbidden to alter a single feature.

And yet, all the history, the story of Us, the archive, the memories are sitting in chairs all around the country waiting to be asked.

Pepys, when he wrote his diary, wrote everything. How he felt, how things looked, or smelt. The minutae that make up an actual life, the memory that deserves to be preserved and recalled, as it tells us not only who we were, but who we ARE.

Their questions could have been asked of me about the old men -

Whats's his name? How old is he? What kind is he?

The death of an old man is like a library burning.

I received an email from a woman named Jessica.

She has a product that enables people who are ill or bedridden to wash without water.

Many people who have Alzheimers or Dementia or other illnesses can find it difficult to wash or be washed, and find the idea of water or showering traumatic, and it is as upsetting for the carer as the patient.

Many's the day I blessed Dry Shampoo.

The stuff is called Nilaqua. (Nil Aqua = no water, geddit?)

She says she is getting a huge response from people who have tried it and who have found it brilliant, and wonders if I might do the same.

"Send it to me" says I, who refuses nothing but blows to the head.

The postman couldn't stuff it through the letter box and I wouldn't get out of the pineapple chunk, as I looked like the wild woman from Borneo, wearing something highly unsuitable for greeting a male at nine am.

He throws a leaflet in the hall telling me to collect it myself in my own time.

I sent Little Thomasina up there this morning.

There is a distinct lack of a smell of bacon cooking when I walk in. He has decided against all that messing about and has dined in solitary splendour on a salad roll, which he insists on calling a *Spring Roll* despite my protestations, and my exhortations to him to put his seatbelt on *before* he drives away fall on deaf ears.

Literally.

"Where's the stuff" says I.

He indicates the parcel on the shelf. I am surprised he has not already torn it open. It contains the shampoo and shower gel, both of which work without water.

He reverts to watching youtube videos of accordian players and bemoaning the speed of his broadband.

The shampoo smells of apples and I pour the thin liquid into my palm.

"C'mere to me till I try it" I say and he ducks.

Regardless, I pour more onto his head and try to lather it.

He is bobbing around like a Jinnet.

"Christ Almighty, will you mind me hearing aids" says he as I nearly dislodge them from his ears in my vigorous attempts at scrubbing.

I lather up a storm while he complains and bobs about.

I have to see the funny side of this or lie down and cry beside the cooker.

I turn around to pull a clean towel from the pile and he makes a run for it.

"Where are you off to? " I enquire.

"To get this stuff off me and rinse me head" says he.

I explain again what it does.

And towel the head off him.

I cant find a hairbrush anywhere, and then I open the bathroom cabinet and see all of Siobháns brushes and combs, shampoos, and mousses, perfume and deodourants.

He removes a comb from his shirt pocket and settles his apple scented white fluff.

August 2012 - Year 7

The fat woman who says she is my daughter is back again. This time she is burning the pungent stuff that makes my eyes water. Peace, oh blessed peace where have you gone. My lovely dream of home gone and I wake again to this. I'm stiff from sitting. She is prating away while I watch bubbles of water running down the glass, catching fragments of words but the other voices are still there. Banging and clattering in the hall, sticks and wheels, an unholy procession of walking wounded. Sticks and stones will break my bones but words will always hurt me. The woman in white who shouts into my face with a breath that is pure minty tobacco is at the door. They talk about me as if I were not back from the dream, not here at all. Why won't someone feed that dog who whines at my feet Whose baby lies smirking on the bed? It has been grinning at me with its big teeth and black ears for hours now. When I try to talk the words won't come. They are pulling me now, pulling me up from the warm darkness and the memories.

Nancy D is below swinging on the gate. Oh, you'd a good innings alright. Break yourselves but don't break the furniture. Hit her again Brud, she's no relation. Black Mick from the Hill. A baby beyond in England , up in the sceachs with a savage scallywag, I'm going out to shed a tear for Parnell, light me Ollie, light me, don't tell TOM, don't tell Tom Thumb, she's very affected, he's rough out, Who burst your ball? I'd ate the balls off a low flying pigeon, your one is stone hatchet mad, and will you give me the woodworm as well, Mrs Dooley, this ship of a house, this godforsaken place, I'm sickened, in a heap, nauseous, naw shis naw shis NAW SHIS . Rise and Shine. Them are they. What else all. Je suis, tu est, I am being lifted into a chair. Bless me Father for I have sinned. Oh Angel of God my guardian dear. I promised not to tell. I'm like the wreck of the Hesperus without a screed of make up on. Bella won it and Bella'll keep it. Not a t'alla. Heck the beds. Getting in the window from the last dance in Tullow. Goodnight Dick. Whisht Nellie, excuse me May. Tom standing at the door in his pyjamas wagging his finger across the smoke filled room.

There are people sitting like crows on a washing line opposite me.

They laugh and talk and when I grow tired of watching the mouths move I shut them out to go back down. Daddy's pet, the white headed girl, apprenticed to the Miss Goffs, with a mouthful of pins and yards of poplin and silk and gingham. The make and model competition. Article 42. Fancy dress ball and a turkey at the pongo in the C.Y.M.S. That other heifir got into more scrapes than a barbers blade. Followed Key Hole Kate to town to get away. Table tennis and Bernie Bee with a smell of sweat that would knock you down. The Happy Ring House on the 8th of December with Tom sulking because I stole into the cinema to show my ring to the girls before his Mother saw it. "No Stir Yet" in the window of the small flat to placate the questioners. Dropping the big eyed baby slippy with suds on the bathroom floor. The midwife's admonishments during the screaming dry birth of a son. . . The old man in the bed rubbing his faeces in his hands banging on the pipe with the brass tip of his stick. His face advancing at me like a brass band under a wig. They have me on the toilet now. 3 of them in here. Even here a body gets no privacy. The fat one is wiping my face. If they don't stop I'll get the guards. Why are there so many people in this house this day. Cold meat and salad. A cigarette butt stubbed out beside the rind of a rasher on a willow pattern plate. China cups and strong tea. One for the pot. Jam and Cream sponge and Apple tart. Sitting on a cliff with the new baby while the other one dismantles the dry stone wall with boredom. Too small for her communion dress. En fumant pensez a moí, who burst your ball, who burst your ball, who burst your ball, There is a clip in my hair to keep it back and it itches my scalp. I can't tell them. The woman in white is poking at my mouth. How dare she? I keep my lips clamped tight. It's sore. She can feck off with herself. The woman opposite me moans and rocks and moans and rocks. I tell her to whisht. The fat one is singing now. She is pushing pieces of sweet brown stuff into my mouth. Tells me it will melt. It does. All over my chin. The big man in black whose face is familiar blesses me and places his huge warm hand on my scalp. He follows my eyes to the wall photo of the couple I can't place and says sure he had more taste than the taste in his mouth. At Mass the man beside me shouts that he has a sore arse. Sending the children to St. Anthony's and telling herself which crocheted loop to pull to open her bonnet because the big Nun gives out to her for being late lingering in the damp cloakroom, with the smell of sour milk and old coats frantically trying to open the black knot she has got herself into. Always highly strung that one. Hysterical for nothing. Thinks she has no friends and looks up at me with her tear soaked face. Am I ugly Mam? Laughing turns to crying. Mind the house. You're as safe as a house on fire. She'd rise a row in a barrack of soldiers. She was up smelling the clothes in the wardrobe as if we were gone forever. Over reacting to everything. Breda in the pantomime saying oh she's greased the boards before but she is pure ham. Playing to the gallery. At the strawberry fair a country man saying she's a fine lump of a child and her head against the window crying all the way home. The boy getting hay fever at the side of the lake with eyes swollen shut like a chinaman as we ate bowls of cold peas with brown sauce. Would you be interested in this? Have you seen my coat on your travels? Be honest in your dealings. Be active, be alive. Rise and shine. Rise and shine. Mince and onions with mashed potato. A small brown please and ten Gold Bond. A glass of lager and lemonade top. Tea and biscuits with the 9 O'Clock news. Eating chips rustling at the table while the lanky teen sprawls huffing and sighing that the end of the film is ruined. He'd give last to nobody. The fat one has me pulled and hauled. She drops me and I lie sideways in the hallway with my glasses hanging off while her face whitens. There is music on always playing, always playing. The voices rise and dip quavering in the sunroom for entertainment where the others squeeze my hands and sing and sing about the something sweet we get to eat.

Just a song at twilight, when the lights are low and the flickering shadows softly come and go........ though the heart be weary, sad the day and long, still to us at twilight comes loves sweet song, comes loves old sweet song............ That was Olivers favourite. Tawnish we called him because he couldn't say turnip. He put a black x on the bag of oranges the little girl brought him in hospital so he wouldn't eat them by mistake. Its time for her to go now and I see her at the door looking back in again. I pretend to be asleep. You give I the sick. Wouldn't that day just give you the pip. Rise and shine. Rise and shine, good night Dick, whist Nellie, excuse me, May.

October 2nd 2014 - Year 9

On this day 5 years ago, Siobhán was removed from the hospital ward she had spent 7 long months in
(- waiting for a bed in "Long Term Care" -)
buckled into the back of an ambulance and driven to her new home.
I was in the back of the ambulance riding shotgun with her and an elderly man heading to Waterford for an eye op. He had a big white plaster over his head and a carer travelling with him as he could not see, but there was nothing wrong with his ears, and he laughed a lot at the pronouncements and yarns I came up with during the drive.
We were cadging a lift as Siobhán had been sitting in a wheelchair in a reception area for hours on the one hundred and eighty first day of her stay. I spotted a man I knew walking down the corridor in an ambulance drivers green and white uniform.
There had been many pints consumed with him at a beach in another lifetime, and so I plamásed and cajoled and prevailed upon his good nature and he agreed to bring us.
By the time we got there I was strung out.
7 months in a hospital listening to the beep beeping of machines, phones, trolleys, visitors, travellers, elderly, youth, babies and the whole cacophony of humanity being human and vulnerable had taken its toll on all of us. The daily visits, the feeling of being neither fish nor fowl, subjected to HSE dictates about flowers on sills, visitors by bed, screens, rounds, meals, routines, the sights we saw, the sounds we heard, sobbing, screaming, a parade of broken bones and bodies at the A&E department, the boy who tried to hang himself and was cut down wandering the halls in a bare chest with a tracheotomy scar, the young woman who overdosed and turned herself back into a child, lying in a railed bed with a doll, the queues for x-rays and finally physio on an arm that was only found to be fractured when it was noticed to be swollen. I spent a lot of time in the hospital engaging with the other patients and their families when Siobhán who upon admitting CLOSED her eyes and didn't re-open them, despite the view of beautiful trees and the driveway of Emee Nash's house, who had died on an airbed after years with Dementia.
It is called **LTC** on a chart. Having worked with a Gynae, I knew a fair amount of medical jargon and also that **TCI** was - to come in.
Long term care. I noticed both first on the wall planner and breasted the nurse manager about what, when, where how ?
I can't see out of the back of the ambulance but I feel it turning right, and then right again, and know we are at the sliding doors of the Nursing Home.

There is nobody smoking in the porch or any of the window sills. There is no crush for parking or a fee, the glass doors open on arrival with sensors, and there is a tinkling glass windchime that blows when the door is open. There is a smell of dinner in the carpeted hall and a long line of window sills filled with red geraniums, a view to an enclosed courtyard with a fish pond.

I could have laid down and slept in the pond as I was emotionally wrung out. "I have seen things that nobody should see, or *everybody*".

The staff could have not been nicer and brought us to the newly vacated room of the woman that had become available only 24 hours before and I saw her name, and other relevant information on the back of the wardrobe door while we unpacked, and I closed the door quickly and exhaled.

We are squashed into the small room and I think I will implode with control freakery and send everybody else home.

Go, be gone, go, move, shift, sang Chrisy Moore and looking at my eyes they decided to take me at my word, and leave.

"Now, Siobhán says I, let's get you sorted for your new house".

I took her into the shower and sat her in the plastic chair while I soaped and shampooed and rinsed and then dressed her in her own clothes instead of nightwear and a dressing gown. I moistureised her face, put on her makeup and lipstick, blow dried her hair, and sprayed perfume on her wrists and neck.

You'll knock 'em dead, I told her.

It is shocking to me now to remember she was walking and talking and that evening I would have to see her face pressed against the glass door as we drove away.

That image never left me.

I carry it still.

I also carry with me all the images I took of her, that document the incremental decline from a woman who could eat, and talk and laugh and walk to what is now the closest thing to a cross between a baby or Locked in Syndrome. Siobhán is lying in her Stephen Hawking chair which can be tilted for feeding with the beaker and bib.

When it dawned on me the other day that the 2nd of October was a landmark day, I began to construct a piece of bedding that is as crazy as its creator, no pattern, a mish mash of colours, crochet pockets, buttons and bows, ALL from the premises she used to work in called Corrys, It is sewed up wrong and has seams facing in AND out and smells a little like a smoky room, a wet chihuahua and Febreze.

It is 9 years since diagnosis and a man remarked to me the other day that my life has been on hold since.

What do you do for a living? he asks.

Live, I respond.

After staying up all night finishing it all off and tying knots and stitching on the extras, I had it barely finished when the car beeped. On the off chance miracle that she may see it if she opens those baby blues from whatever altered consciousness she inhabits, then I would like to apologise that it took me so long to notice and make it.

In this instance what was in me is now *ON* Siobhán.

Sometimes I forget why I am in the room.

Something on the TV will have engaged me, and I will forget about the silent waiting presence in the chair.

I come to with a start, apologise and talk long- windedly about some palava, narrating what the actor is doing, or heckling the news.

Sometimes I am guilty of staring at the blue screen on my phone in the dusky room, scanning other peoples lives, photos of their dinners and babies, the wonderful times they are having all over the world, while I sit here in the darkness.

The neediness - the humanity.

It is better that I put on music.

When the music is on, I listen and sing along, filing away the back story of the singer or the year in case I am ever on **Who wants to be a Millionaire** and the million pound question is that very one.

I hold Siobháns cold hand, and move the chair with my knees so that she is dancing.

"Member the dancing, Siobhán" I will say uselessly to the woman who can remember nothing.

We like to sit in the dark, maybe with candles, or lit by the tiny pink solar lights that live on the remaining plant in the window sill.

Only the flickering strobes of the muted tv light up our faces as I sing, my voice cracking on the high notes, feeling a lump I can't swallow in my neck.

I used to be able to hit those notes.

In my youth I could stop a room when I sang, and Siobhán would lift her head sideways in pleasure and pride, my Father beaming when people said "She didn't lick it off a stone"

I sang all over town and in bars, at music festivals, at parties, in clubs, in packed West End pubs in London, in beach bars in Spain, Metal Clubs in Germany, accompanied by guitars, jazz bands, and alone lilting.

And then I just stopped.

I used to get so sick with nerves that I was beside myself before I opened my mouth, and during the applause would instantly think of a thousand ways I could have done it better.

The last time I sang in public was at a talent competition where a friend who is an amazing guitarist suggested we write a song. I wrote the lyrics in about ten minutes flat and he would drive down to the beach to rehearse with me, until we had a fairly passable little ballad down.

He harmonising with me on the chorus.

On the night of the competition I watched as more and more people turned up, every act bringing their own following.

In the jostle and crush as a hundred people asked me what I was singing, I beat my way to the ladies and stood swaying, white faced into the mirror till the publican herself turned up.

Bridget took one look at me and said -

- Put your head between your knees in the name of God

and came back with a Hennessy.

On the stage, as we are introduced to roaring, I think I will actually collapse, the blood rushing around me, the buzzing in my ears.

I am numb.

I realise that James has played the opening 8 bars twice and is nodding at me and whispering "*come on*" ....

I start - in the wrong key - and know I will never hit the notes in the mid section the way I want to. James smiles at me and whispers encouragingly, come on, you have this, ... and plays his beautiful guitar while I struggle on into the chorus and back, and then just as I am getting into it, and my knees are knocking, I scan the upturned faces for a heart stopping moment and then throw the microphone onto the floor in a screech of whistling feedback, and jump off the stage, and run out the back door.

There is a moment of shocked silence, and then applause, and poor Wee James has to extricate himself from the spotlight, alone.

"You see, the beauty of it is - he says in his soft Donegal lilt later - nobody knew what it was supposed to sound like and they thought that was the end"

We did NOT win.

This is not that kind of story.

This is the story of the girl who wishes she had recorded herself when she could, and who now only sings in attics, and at the bedside of her Mother, who also does not know what it is supposed to sound like.

Sometimes I imagine there is the tiniest lift to her head.

I spent my birthday alternately fuming and crying.

It started off grand but my mood plummeted by noon.

Nothing you could put an actual finger on, nothing to do with aging, just ornery and curmudgeonly and distraught.

I was beside myself with temper and contrariness at lunch and refused to engage, or banter, or even look at the menu.

And I refused dessert.

And coffee.

Alarm bells should have been ringing.

I put my head down and hopped off a meal I did not want because someone else was paying.

I escaped to the beer garden before I broke every plate in the hotel with the temper.

"That one could chop straws with her arse today" - was a line said about me more than once.

After a little cry over a full ashtray in the garden, I realised that I would have to get off the streets and into the house, fairly lively.

It may have been the millions of messages that combined to underpin the fact that this was not going to be an

"amazing beautiful wonderful" day - but would in fact - be like any other - with a side of underwhelming,a splash of anti-climax and a sprinkle of ennui.

When the letterbox flapped at 10am I ran to the door thinking "Hooray, cards".

It was my phone bill.

(Massive)

I walked into Siobháns' room that evening as usual, as it was "my" night, and I could think of nowhere else I would rather have been.

In her silent presence I could find the space to exhale, to stop grinning inanely, to cease forcing smiles and trying to remember things -
names, faces, pieces I have written.
No matter how much I love you, I have to run away sometimes and process the information - to pick over it with a fine tooth comb -
to tease it out like a tangled ball of wool.
And then to wonder why I didn't react better, bigger or properly
She has a catheter now with a bag taped to her leg. The morning carers, when they were lifting her up, noticed that her nappy was dry, and they are checking for a condition called Retention, where the message to the bladder from the brain stops getting through.
I place the tiny Chihuahua gently onto her lap.
I need a hug, so I bend over and hold her, and try to lean into her through the chair.
I try not to move or jar her.
Osteoporosis is a bitch.
I comb her hair and smooth her face and ask for ice for the Baileys. I do not drink any, birthday or not.
I line up the drink, and lemonade, and water on the arm of the chair to assist in the calibrated flow the nurses will monitor on the chart.
I can't sing or chat nineteen to the dozen tonight.
As I carefully place the rim of the glass against her mouth and fold the napkin under her chin, I watch the involuntary spasms which make her shake suddenly in the chair.
Parkinsons is a bastard.
2 hours have passed and we are an inch down the glass. The tiny Chihuahua cuddles into her, licking the curled closed hands, and rubbing his small head against her eye, the one that always has an itch she cannot scratch.
Alzheimers is a fucker.
I could not write this last week.
I could not write anything.
It has passed,
I have processed the information, teased it out, picked it over,
the tap is running again, and the words at least, are flowing.

Winter 2008 - Year 3

In the winter that the snows fell, Siobhán had been diagnosed for 3 years.
We coped.
I had given up work to be her carer, as things became harder and harder to deal with.
My Father was in denial for a long time.
He truly believed that if he could just keep doing regular things, and keep to a routine, then he could keep this monster at bay, and preserve some semblance of normality in their lives.
He believed if she was sitting in the passenger seat of the car with her hair done and her make up on, then it was ok

For a minute it could be ok.

He took over the housework long before I knew.

He washed and cooked and shopped, and filled in the gaps, and drew in the blanks.

He juggled while backpedalling and kept all the balls in the air.

The monster was lurking, rubbing its hands.

At the time, I was clueless, and would learn all the information that I pass on now through bitter trial and error.

And research.

Then, I was still a woman who worked, who went out, who had a social life, who woke from a lovers bed, and ran with tousled hair and bruised lips through the quiet morning streets with the hangover from hell.

I would let myself in and do my bit.

"She's waiting on you" he would intone on the ever ringing mobile. I was short with the pair of them at times.

And anxious to get back out and resume my so called life.

I would offer someone my kidney on a plate to go back now.

Recently, I saw the amazing Scottish actor Peter Mullen portray a man whose life is falling apart with Alzheimers.

The director had researched the science of the illness and gave a graphic representation of what happens in the brain as it is shutting
down -
the nightmarish quality of faces changing into other faces,

of being lost inside your own home,

of being confused and frightened and enraged by the moments of clarity when you realise that you ARE in fact, losing your mind.

It was at this juncture that Thomasina, after a medical consult, decided to build an en-suite wet room with grab rails and state of the art medical shower and seat.

He had been quoted a price and a finish date.

And so they vacated to the mountain where my sister lives.

And it was the worst thing ever at that time.

And then the snows came.

NOW I know that routine is the most important part of a patient's life, because what started off as a smallish plumbing job turned into grand designs, and I expected to see Kevin McCloud standing outside shaking his head about the weather.

The builders tore the house apart.

They took away my sisters bedroom.

Oh how Siobhán must have felt stepping around in the rubble, wrapped in layers and layers of clothing like a Russian Doll.

Her baby's bedroom was gone.

Because there was no kitchen we had to have soup daily. Despite my entreaties and pleas, he insisted on driving to town every morning on roads like sheets of glass.

He had to project manage the build.

But more importantly, he had to have his little 'oul bub' with him.

She has never used this room, as she would be hospitalised just after it was completed.

To anyone reading this who has a loved one with this illness then I beg of you to do the following -

Accept and deal with it sooner rather than later

Do not be complicit in denial

Do not try and help with answers, it is counter productive

Get and administer the meds, they help

Keep to a routine always

Label things and inform people

Get help

Love, reassure, and spend time with the person.

Be tactile, and hold them.

I can never see this soup or smell fresh crusty rolls without being back in that winter, in the shell of the house in the snow, with my childhood being demolished in front of my eyes.

"God does not play dice with the universe;

He plays an ineffable game of His own devising,

which might be compared,

from the perspective of any of the other players

[i.e. everybody],

to being involved in an obscure and complex variant of poker,

in a pitch-dark room,

with blank cards,

for infinite stakes,

with a Dealer who won't tell you the rules,

and who smiles ALL the time."

- Terry Pratchett - Good Omens:

The Nice and Accurate Prophecies of Agnes Nutter, Witch.

Sometimes, I think of those Gods from the movie who sat on clouds and amused themselves by throwing all sorts of curve balls at humanity.

Let's see how they deal with THIS?

Firstly, it must have been a bit of craic to make all the humans out of meat and bones, and then allow them to make machines.

"The meat made the machines?"

Oh, how they laughed.

"How did they come up with the idea of that?" they asked.

A small piece of pink matter, soft, fleshy, sitting inside the hard bone of their skulls controls everything -

their basic motor skills,

their functions,

their dreams,

AND the machines.

And if it is knocked, or injured, or a white protein creeps all over it like limescale on a kettle, then the whole process goes belly up.

It is 9 years since I shook my fist at the clouds and roared with temper.

I see myself as meat in clothes.

What's the point?

How does anyone have the Mirror of Mortality held up to them and not react in similar fashion?

My visits confirm this every time.

One of the known side effects for carers is that their own care falls away, the statistics are high for stress related illnesses and depression.

Losing a tooth has not stopped me eating sweets.

"Jesus, don't take my toffee chewing tooth" I exclaim to the dentist while he is briefing his assistant about how to hold my head as he goes in for the wisdom at the back.

And I find the gentle cupping of my head to be hypnotic and meditate by looking into the white light, and still I think – it's too long since I was held.

"I'll buy bigger clothes" I think, and also that it is well to be able to.

"Well to" I think a lot.

(Pronounced welta)

Welta be able to get up in the morning and go for a walk -

Welta be able to feed yourself -

Welta be able to open your own bowels.

The women I used to talk to about their lives, their children, their careers, are lying silently. One, who walked the halls nightly, wondering where all the fun stuff was happening, is sitting staring at the carpet now.

They quieten, and reverse inwardly, to the small still centre of themselves where they take stock.

She has made it as far as the porch but has stopped taking notes of the car registrations to give her a lift home.

I take her cold hand and call her by her name, this woman who knew me as a child, who taught me, and tried not to snort out loud at the wildness of my more outrageous ideas, this woman who rooted out the college forms for me when I sat in her office as a teenager talking about journalism.

And I WAS wild, the enfant terrible, a lost cause.

And now I am leading her back down the hall, reassuring, speaking in soft words and old familiar phrases, mentioning tea, guiding her into a soft seat with the rest of them, who do not even glance in our direction.

They have that frightened confused look in their eyes that reminds me so much of Siobhán. It is invisible.

The slowly creeping protein is invisible at first, but now I recognize it in the wide eyed stares, rabbits caught in headlights, so that when I chance across a photo online that someone has posted of their parent, my stomach lurches and I see IT looking back at me Since the beginning I have been photographing, filming and documenting the stages in writing.

Last night, while looking for something to read at an Alzheimers Coffee morning tomorrow, I found film footage of Siobhán walking.

I sat snuffling over the keyboard and thanked those very Gods that I have railed against - that in my orneryness and stubborn wildness - and contrary to my sisters demands that I put down the camera and give her a hand, that I carried on telling the story.

It is gold dust, and we are stardust, and eternal.

I need to remember this most of all.

"The Gods may throw a dice,

their minds as cold as ice,

and someone way down here,

loses someone dear"

- Abba - "Winner takes it All"

They've asked me to be the voice of carers in a new Advocacy Programme being launched by the Alzheimer Society in December at the Aisling Hotel on Park Gate Street in Dublin.

If I start, I may not stop.

In the fabric shop where I am trying to get plaid and fur to have a coat made for a tiny dog, I am interrupted mid-rant by a woman looking for buttons.

She is standing holding the old fashioned tubes of buttons and scanning the wall for the elusive big grey one she needs for her cardigan.

I always stand back in the various shops and let actual customers get their 5 minutes, and in at the counter, letting the dog see the rabbit, if you will.

If not I could be monopolising the counter staff and the conversation for the best part of an hour.

I was told to remove myself from the window display in the book shop the other day as I told the harried manager a thousand times that he was doing it wrong. He was painting a sad snowman who looked like a refugee from a Patricks Day parade onto the glass.

The woman is well dressed and her hair is perfect, the coat and scarf matching, and I scan her from head to foot.

This is what Siobhán would look like if she was well, I think.

Something about the style of her, the go of her, reminds me of the silent bent presence in the chair.

I often find myself doing this, noticing women of a certain age, who could possibly be peers of my Mother, or who could BE my Mother.

Her name is Alice.

I stop rooting in the basket of cut price wool and prick up my ears, and then she says two words that confirm it.

Table Tennis.

It is how my parents met.

- Tell me this, says I, did you ever in your travels come across a woman called Siobhán Dooley?
- Oh, Lord............says Alice and I know it is her.

All through my childhood and later, Siobhán had a bunch of friends with impossible sounding names who became the stuff of legend.

Zilfa, Alice, Madeleine Le Strange,..

Alice looks at me in amazement.

- I'm her daughter, I say.
- Oh, Jesus, I saw her in the hospital and I knew, she said.
- I just knew, she was lost. I was visiting someone and I saw her and it broke my heart and I didn't go over.

Christ, I think.

- You should have - I say.

Alice tells me things about Siobhán and how close they were, and how she loved calling for her and all the good times and laughs they had. She knows Little Thomasina and all about the fact that they met playing table tennis.

- He taught her, I say. He said - wait till I show you again hun and held her hand to show her to follow through on the serve, and he told me he didn't want to let it go. He is holding her hand still.

I tell her I am so glad I met her, standing surrounded by the old fashioned buttons and fabric, and at the very counter that Siobhán would have stood at, peppering to get out to the table tennis match, to meet the man with the smiling eyes.

I tell her that I am writing a Memoir, and that it is so lovely to have someone to be ABLE to ask, as she gives me her number.

I showed her the photo of Siobhán on my phone and watched her react.

"How's such a one?" says Alice.

Dead says I.

How's so and so?" says Alice.

Dead says I.

Life is short says I and try to swallow.

A falling leaf is a whisper to the living.

Siobhán has been on the Dopamine patch for the Parkinsons for a week now, and I like to think it is helping. It may be giving some form of muscle pain relief and appears to have ceased the darting shocks that rippled through her suddenly, first stiffening and then shaking her down to the tips of the tiny fingers resting in the hand that has held hers since they met.

I never had time to call Alice.

Christmas 2007

I can't remember what to do at the table.

I am confused and frightened. So many in the house, I hold the small child on my lap and let the other women do the work. There are ladybirds crawling all over my arms and sometimes I see her face, then HER face, and sometimes the face is the giant teddy she came off the ship with.

It's lonely in here.

I said it's lonely and if I don't want it, I don't want it, simple as that. Oh, if you wouldn't be better off in a cows stomach, this ship of a house,

Tea, May, Jaw, Law, Tea for two and 2 for tea,

You for you and you for me

Me me me me fa so la ti dooooooooo

I'm a lonely little petunia in an onion patch.

93, ...86...................em 79 72

Key fee pea key fee key feeeee K
Keishy — the woman with beautiful hair
087 98 26 472
I burnt the arse out of a pot of carrots as there was no water in them and I told Tom to feck off when he said sit down and have a nice cup of tea. Lying to me he was, trying to tell me the shops were shut, and that it was eleven o clock at night. Does he think I am mad, does he think I am stark staring mad, stone hatchet mad, like a burst yolk, brutal, savage, dead to the world, or gone around the effing twist, and the cheek of him locking the door, by Jesus, Lord Divine Jazus, I know where the key is anyway, well fuck it and bucket, I don't .
Sundowning my arse.
That other one is running a hotel now out at the beach. We go down there to pick her up, your man and I and they get me a half dinner and they cut it up so I only have to use a fork. She brings me to the toilet and waits outside as if I was a child. In the hotel I forgot to lift the seat and drenched meself. I met meself in a mirror and I met other people in the mirror too, my Mam was there and plants and animals and the clouds on the bathroom paper that looked like dogs and heffalumps and the wan, the WAN wouldn't let me out of the shop though I pushed on the 2 way glass for ages, and she whispered and whispered and the woman with the badge came over and asked me to sit down to get me breath. She wools the head off me when she washes my hair and takes lumps out of my soft head with the brush, I'll tan the hide off her if I get hold of her. I had to dress her stinking hand as the cauliflower grew out of her wrist, and the hole grew wider and I could see white bone when I wrapped the boiling poultice in a gauze bandage around it, and she screamed when I said as hot as you can bear it, offer it up, offer it up, offer it up. The Doctor wouldn't look at it. It's out of my hands now says he, and eventually it was out of hers, not before she broke a window in temper and agony. That scourge.
....................93..86
Apple, car, tomato, green,
Apple car, tomato, green,
Fried green tomatos at the whistle stop café
The Taoiseach is ....em .... em............... your man, no, what's this his name is, em ....eh,.................ah, you know with the ....
em
1934, no, oh, THIS year? ....em..........................
Apple
With a score of 7 out of 20, I can confirm my diagnosis of Alzheimer's Disease and suggest the appropriate medication for that and underlying Parkinsons Disease, and Osteoporosis says your man to my man.

February 2012 - Year 7

Siobbhan watched me all weekend.
I couldn't get up to her room but she watched me in mine.
There was a litany of reasons -

inclement weather, no lift, a sibling away, deadlines.

Blah.

The real reason was the shock and impotence I felt at my last visit. I needed a little time out to detach and process.

Despite having deadlines up the Wazoo and 2 imminent speaking engagements, where there was nothing written to speak of, I quieted my monkey mind with house husbandry.

At midnight I looked around the kitchen in frustration, trailing plugs and extension leads hanging from every wall, surfaces packed and overflowing, towers of paper and lists, phone numbers, things to do urgently, if not sooner.

There was also a considerable pile of tiny dog clothing and bedding to launder forthwith.

I got stuck in.

When Siobhán had been in hospital about 5 months, a woman was wheeled in who resembled "*The Scream*" by Edvard Munch.

As someone who will follow you down the wrong street to see where you are going, or hear the last lines of your phone conversation, then seeing a parade of humanity pass by on a daily basis was just Manna from Nirvana.

This woman frightened the bejesus out of me.

She was so old and thin she resembled a figure carved of knotted wood, her knees raised and twisted like twigs, her mouth stretched wide into a permanent O.

O

OOOOOOOOOOOOOO.

Oh.

Don't make me look.

Please don't make me look!

I looked.

"Ah Jesus, it's just not *fair*" I railed in my own head.

It's not fair to get so far, and so old, against so many odds and ultimately lie twisted and corded with your mouth stuck open in a permanent scream.

I edged nearer and nearer the bed, my innate curiosity winning out, and watched as the implacable Nurse cleaned her mouth with a soft pink foam stick, moisturising and wiping and smiling into the gums as she talked nonsense about the weather

I have edged so close that I can almost feel -

the soft mist from where she is going, the otherness, the quiet beating of gossamer wings, and the bed resembles an Island,

with just me and she and she and me,

and all hell gathered all behind us.

I have edged nearer and incrementally nearer like a feral kitten being offered chicken

As I am taking it in, all of it, the nurse, the stick, the mouth, the twigs, a hand grabs mine and won't let go.

Her grip is amazing.

The nurse laughs -" Oh, Molly likes YOU" she shouts in that overly pleasant loud voice that medics use when they are being jolly and think that everyone is Mutt and Jeff, when they don't want to hear the quietness and the stillness of the other place, winding it's way round the room like a ribbon.

It was this, more than the dry twig grip that I found nauseating.

At 4am I was balancing a full fridge on my chest as I tried to take the strain and IT down. It was my own fault for balancing it on top of a tumble drier, and then using the top as a shelf. My motto appears to be *"Do it first, then work out how"* which explains how only a number of hours after the initial thought, the entire kitchen is transformed, a wall painted, pink muslin curtains hung, prints mounted and framed, keepsakes and memento mori dusted off and ready.

Before I started painting however I hung a photo of Siobhán, sitting on a Castle Keep, her blonde hair blowing in the breeze, bang in the centre of the wall, and so she became my Mona Lisa, her eyes moving from one side to the other as she saw her daughter manhandle furniture, a chihuahua, paint trays, newspaper, and a tiny brush.

"I'd rather be looking at it than looking for it eh, Siobhán" says I.

She laughed.

She is used to my spontaneous decorating and would often remark that there was masking tape and white spirits in the press as I painted over cobwebs and picture hooks. I laughed in her press.

"You've a few pound on you in that photo Mam" - I thought.

I finished at 5 am and with paint in my hair, and fluff and damp plaster and spiders eggs all over the floor, dragged the mop bucket down the hall.

Siobhán had been my witness and companion, although I had not returned the physical favour.

A man stopped me the other day and asked -

how do you know how to do all this stuff?

"I'm expanding with the Universe" I replied and ran off laughing.

The irony is that although I was playing and creating, the tools of my trade, the words would not come, well, not in the way I wanted.

Then something about the Universe reminded me of words, and that my grip is strong too, maybe enough for both of us.

I stood back to take a photo and as I lined up the camera a perfect circle floats by slowly, like a child has been blowing soap bubbles from a tube, playing, and I whisper "Jesus Christ, did you *SEE* it?" to nobody.

I hope I caught it on camera.

In the morning I am taking myself to Dublin to talk to people in a hotel about this bastard of a disease. Because I spent so long mooching and painting, I may have to write the piece on the train.

"Words are flowing out like endless rain into a paper cup,

they slither while they pass, they slip away across the Universe,

Pools of sorrow, waves of Joy, are drifting through my open mind,

possessing and caressing me" –

Jai Guru Deva

Om.

John Lennon

Christmas Day 2013 - Year 8

The bus met us out there.

I am travelling by car with *Hewhomustnotbenamed*, Little Thomasina and Walter.

Despite protesting that he is a gay dog and that he will be disgraced - *Hewhomustnotbenamed* has the lead wrapped around his knuckles and the dog wrapped around his little finger.

It is a bright beautiful morning and the men are making an effort to converse for the day that's in it.

"I got Mass twice" says Little Thomasina, who although has already attended on Saturday afternoon, has still watched 2 more on the television, answering the prayers in his head, respectfully waiting to boil the kettle till Communion is over.

Siobhán is sitting ready - still and silent in the Stephen Hawking Chair, and I know we will be lifting.

I send the Father off with the dog, hoping that he will not use his miniscule head to change gears, again.

Leave us, I say, we've got this.

The Carers and the two of us do the transfer from the big chair to the wheelchair, raising, moving, bracing, and flinging the rubber cushion from one to the other before she is replaced.

I wrap her in throws so as not to have to deal with the intricacies of sleeves, and after a short pause in the porch, we are winched aboard and trundle off through the green lanes.

The bus bumps and sways around the tiny bendy corners, climbing higher and higher till the checkered fields and the blue sky converge, and in the distance the sun sparkles off the shining sea.

I watch my Mother rocking.

Maybe she loves it I think, imagining the feeling of movement and speed even though the body is at rest.

At the Mountain house, instead of drama - reversing and beeping, winching and a crowd around the door, we drop the ramp and I wheel her down the drive.

I do it backwards in high heels.

A point that was brought to my attention when it was remarked that I should maybe keep an eye out for parked cars and plant pots.

I've come a long way.

The house smells of cooking, and fabric softener, and the fresh snapping wooden logs on the stove, lined up in waiting rows under the paintings of James Joyce and a disappointed horse.

We rearrange the seating so Siobhán is warm and included in her family, but not close enough to the fire to swelter in her blankets.

I take over and start bossing about in the kitchen.

"Rest that Turkey - have you stock? where is the masher? what do you want done with these? get out of me way"

I want to cook today as I don't think I am able to feed.

I tried.

I couldn't get in properly, I couldn't do it from the wrong side, I was too hot, my back was broken, I had to stop.

I folded the napkins and boiled the kettle about a gazillion times for tea, roast potato, gravy, washing up.

The Sister did the necessary.

God be good to her and all belong to her.

In the afternoon I heard the plaintive sounds of a piano as Little Thomasina played his one handed repertoire in the child's bedroom.

He begins with "Hey Jude"then segues into "Mise Eire" followed closely by Jigs and Reels he normally plays on his violin. He finishes with a version of Molly Malone that ends up as "My Grandfather's Clock was too tall for the stairs"

I have been recording him for 12 and a half minutes but am already bored and gatching on the bed with the nephew.

Sometimes I think I may be an idiot savant as the smallest of social mores and normality alternately escape or bore me.

I call my nephew *"Spoiler"* because he is, and he calls me *"Rager"* because I am.

I am just settling into the normality, the loveliness of heated rooms, the plates of meat and cakes, the men playing chess at the candle-lit kitchen table as the sky darkened.

Then I remember we have to leave.

"It's a Wonderful Life" is on the TV on mute and we have music on for our Mother, so that she can hear the children's voices carolling, the strains of the strings from the orchestra playing the old refrains and know that it is Christmas, and she is *home.*

The frosty starlit sky had deposited an inch of ice on the windscreen which my Father cleaned with a small blade and then the 2 men and the small dog drove away.

I travelled alone with Siobhán in the big bus. She is wearing a Santa hat with a fur trim to keep her head warm, but the bus is heated and we rattle and roll back down the black mountain to the flat lilac lands, to her other home, and I wheel her down the hall and kiss her goodnight.

Little Christmas January 6th 2014 - Year 9

Little Thomasina drove slowly away with the tiny Walter staring crestfallen out the window in his fur trimmed hood.

He wants to come in but he doesn't think he can handle it.

My Dad feels similar.

Her room is empty when I look in, and seems oddly sparse, the Stephen Hawking chair that takes up more room than a sofa gone, the presence, the colour of the patchwork blanket around her legs missing.

The light and contrast have been erased.

Siobhán is parked in the corner of the packed Oratory where Mass will be celebrated for Little Christmas, and the Annual Party.

I release the brake and manoeuvure the giant chair through the slippers and wheels and handbags, back out the door and up the hall in one fluid movement and the nick of time.

I tell a Nurse on the way that we will celebrate ourselves.

And at the top corner outside her room I run smack into the priest in his vestments carrying the silver bowl with the sacrament in it, trailed by nurses.

"Hello, Noel" says I. "Could you leave a bit of Jesus under Mam's pillow for me and I will give it to her when we get back from gatching?"

The Nurse who hates me gives me a scandalised look as if to say you are outrageous.

He smiles and nods and we turn into her room.

Her hands are cold and she opens her eyes for one second to look at me, and I smile into her blue eyes.

"Wait till I take off the hat, Siobhán, then you'll know me" -

There is a smile on her own face and I almost faint.

I skip over to the wardrobe to hang my coat thinking today will be an excellent day, and I will work hard at trying to remember, and be present, and listen and record salient points and facts.

I will be the Witness.

Then the door opens and Siobhán's Little sister Keyhole Kate comes in.

She has been redirected from the Mass to find us hiding out in plain sight.

We talk and laugh and goster between us while all the sacred holy stuff is happening a hundred yards away.

The door opens and a Carer pops her head in.

"Would Siobhán like a blessing?" says she.

"Begob and she would" says I.

"God love her anyway" says the Priest with the white shawl as he leaves.

Soon, we see the hordes descending on the room where the food is at and I brave the throng to get my Godmother a glass of wine.

Little Christmas was known as the Women's Christmas, as it was felt that they could have a rest from boiling hams and stuffing bread up turkeys arses, icing cakes for biscuit tins, and flaming brandy for puddings and could sit down in peace by the fire, on their own arses, eating all the above leftovers, until as full as their own puddings, they could relax and have a jar.

Madge watches me feed Siobhán and is inflicted with random bursts of me reading stuff off my phone, showing her photos, and ranting about the minutae of my life,

".........And the Dog is found, thank Christ" .... says I drawing a breath.

I have a spoonful of bashed up trifle on its way to her mouth when Siobhán opens her eyes wide, smiles broadly, and slowly raises her small arm, uncurls her hand and points.

I am speechless.

There is a light around her.

"Madge, Madge, Madge"............ I say and reach for the camera.

Madge is staring.

Siobhán continues to stare and smile, her finger points into the very corner of the room and She seems transfixed.

I am snapping and snapping, the dark, the flash, the shutter speed, I can't get it, I can't get it, ...I'm getting it

"Who are you seeing, Siobhán......... What are you seeing Siobhán?" I ask as the spoon falls to the carpet.

Her finger moves, barely, imperceptibly, and then shakily around and around .... until it is pointing at *me*.

I snap and snap.

And then, like a clockwork doll winding down, the lights go out, the hand slowly drops down and the blue eyes close.

I am delightedly shocked.

I am shockingly delighted.

Michelle Shocked.

When I bring the bowls back to the kitchen I lean in over the giant chair and say - "Tell your sister the 3rd Secret of Fatima for the Little Womens Christmas" and my own walks down the hall to bring me home.

2 pairs of Sisters,

Mother and Daughters,

Aunt and Nieces,

Godmother and Godchild.

Godchild.

October 2009

N ights drifting
Days shifting,
In a blue and white ward.
Beeping and creeping and everybody sleeping,
Trollies and feeding and everybody needing,
Bowels and tumours and young women bleeding,
And old men in wheelchairs,
And all my thoughts speeding,
Porridge and shite, in black and white,
Porridge and shite in black and white
I close my eyes, I close my eyes.
Apple.
93.....................................
087 ....
Eeeny meeeny miney mo...........................
That lad has a head like a wingnut,
It's done and dusted and it will stay done till the trumpet blows.
Bugsy Malones and Too Good to be Threw , the pinstriped suits for Hudson and Joe Scaff and the black and white minstrels in the tea caddy in elastics and Mr Pink Whistle, and Sambo the Pig with the broken tail, and the Golliwog and Mister Mitchum, and Roberta -
Snowy, Basil, Herbie, Midge, Chloe ....and Sid.

August 2013 - Year 8

A woman I have been running away from for months, never having the time to engage, or ever actually MEET for the coffee I have sworn and promised faithfully every single time, finally caught up with me the other day.

I was ready to trot out an excuse about having to leg it when she unzipped her bag hastily and handed me a piece of paper with this on it -

"People who have Alzheimers are living breathing examples of Mindfulness, of Presence, and of simply BEING - as they have no past, they have no future, they have only the NOW that they inhabit."

These are my words as she took the piece of paper back to keep. You get my drift though.

For 3 nights I have had nightmares and woken up crying, the tail end of one this morning was of Siobhán sitting pretty on the end of her bed, dealing a hand of cards, wearing her glasses, and with her own teeth - (not rotted away from medical and dental personnel being unable to brush) a full smiling mouth of delph)

She spoke to me and asked me how I was and then smiled and it was not the talking, or the glasses that threw me, but the familiar shape of her mouth with teeth still embedded in the gum, and altering utterly the shape of her face.

A terrible beauty is born.

And then I woke.

The nightmares take until at least noon to shake off, and at least 2 pots of strong coffee.

Last night I alternately laid steaming or freezing cloths on her face, rubbed her nose and left eye (always the itchiest) and applied a liberal dose of the creams and unguents she received at Christmas, while she had a baby Gordons and tonic.

The room smells like a candle-lit spa and makes the woman who doesn't know about ice stop and ask what it is.

Not the ice, the smell. .

There would be more chance of finding an oil well under the land than ice cubes in the freezer.

Did the woman who knew the recipe die? I ask in jest.

No, we have to tell the girls in the kitchen.

Siobhán was intent on seeing whatever she was seeing in the far corner and sat like this for a number of minutes.

One of these days I am waiting for her to say something, anything, and pray to Christ, I will be sitting by the bed.

She got the hiccoughs after the few sips of Baileys.

I pelted the length of the hall in my inside out jumper, to get a cold drink, from the woman with the trolley.

"You should do the lotto tonight" says the girl in the Supermarket this morning, eyeballing the label scratching my throat.

It is Sparrowfart O Clock and in a rare flurry of largesse, I am getting fuel delivered.

My Skin and Blister had been fascinated, hawing in the kitchen.

"I can see my own breath in here, Jesus" says she before cleaning and lighting my fire and driving away.

I stare back at the shop assistant.

I appear to be like the *Two Ronnies* - always answering the question from the question before -

"Oh, you mean my jumper" I offer and she laughs

I will idly think - I must wash all those things over there, and then find myself drying the last spoon.

I will wildly think - I must have a shower in a minute, and then, quicker than an Ethiopian at a buffet find myself stepping out of it, done.

Or not.

Did I wash my hair, I think, put my hand to it and feel that it is wet, and presume yes, I must have.

And then find out it is only conditioner, when it is still not dry 4 hours later.

This is a first even for me.

Where am I?I am obviously not present as I am operating on auto and only watching it unveil before me, and after the fact.

They buried a man this week who was in a coma for 8 years.

Years ago, in another lifetime, I sat on a moonlit grey stone bridge in Wales with a man I loved very much, as we rawmaished about life, and death, watching the icy black water racing far beneath us.

In our defence we were very drunk at the time, having just come back from watching The Scarlets in Stradey Park, drinking Felinfoel Ale, or as we blithely referred to it - "*Feeling Fowl*".

He had opened his thumb like a banana, putting his hand out to stop me falling over a tailbar between 2 parked cars, and fallen himself instead. We ended up heading to Chepstow Hospital in an ambulance on the motorway, as they thought it might need stitching at the special grafts department there.

They put a big Edward Scissors Hands Dressing on it."*Shell, I gotta tell oo, you gotta unplug me if that ever happens me*"

The talk has led to people who are in a suspended state, and are lying in comas, being kept alive on machines and respirators.

"*If I'm not in yere*" says he tapping the side of his head with what appears to be a white boxing glove,

"*And I'm naw out there*" says he throwing his bandaged arm wide to include the starlit sky and almost toppling backwards off the bridge,

- "*then, where*" he leans down closer and whispers ....

- "*where am I?*"...........

He smiles and I nod.

"*Don't leave me there*"

I never forgot it.

He left me one morning while Siobhán stood in the kitchen of the square, in her blue cotton dressing gown, making tea and toast for the giant handsome visitor, who was catching the early ferry home.

I had thought that showing him Ireland, and me in it, would have had him overcome with love and joy, amazed by leprechauns and shillelaghs and comely maidens dancing at the crossroads, and *Ryans Daughter* being re-made in every village every weekend, and it would make him stay, and we would be happy ever after in the land of Saints and Scholars, and the 40 shades of Green.

I keened like a Banshee when he walked away down the hill.

I turned the water pressure up on the shower and slumped under it as the water ran over my face and into my open mouth.

"Jesus, Shell, SHELL" says Siobhán as she bangs on the door.

I can picture her face still, as I opened it and came out, bereft.

I cannot recall what she said.

Siobhán has always been the polar opposite of her hysterical needy first born - and a lady, and believed you did your crying at home, behind closed doors.

I didn't so much close doors as slam them, and then SLAM then again, louder.

The guy in the market shop asks me can he have a rub of me as I'm so lucky.

The label is obvious to him too.

The Nurse advises me to buy a scratch card as I will surely win,

"when" she laughs "your jumper is on inside out and back to front"

I know - I tell them wearily, as I have not had a minute idle in 18 hours to change it.

Where am I?

Where have I been?

Then, as I tell Siobhán the news that I created an event where I will hold the floor, and have had a phenomenal response, I know she is listening and processing as I whisper, into the pale pink rims of her seashell ears, and laugh at the line -

"We're gonna need a bigger boat"

and I hear **John Grant** on the Creedon Show on the blessed radio singing" Glacier"

"This pain,

it is a Glacier,

moving through you,

Carving out deep valleys,

creating spectacular landscapes,

and other stuff."

Your Jumper is inside out they said,

they should see the inside of my head,

Now, THAT is upside down.

Siobhán ate well and I left her wrapped in her patchwork throw, listening to Bob Dylan and Johnny Cash.

Dont leave me there said Richard, but nightly I leave Siobhán, and know that she is serene in the essence of herself, and that even if there were the memory of tears, they would not be shed with an audience.

April 2014 - Year 9

The Dog had my Aunt for 13 years.

He was a tiny black Pom with a tail like a Peacocks fan, and he strutted around the place like a Lord of the Manor, surveying his tenants.

He had chocolate brown eyes and a set of paws no bigger than knitting needles and she loved him unconditionally and totally from the first moment she met him.

The first time she used a piece of tissue on his tiny shirt button arse was because he had a bit of poo stuck to him, and all the millions of times since was because she had set a precedent with the first time.

Oh Mrs Brennan, what is your dog doing? said the visitor in the kitchen one night as my Aunt pressed the tea and she watched him reverse repeatedly into her leg.

- I have no idea says she mortified. ("God, and I would have been disgraced if she knew I was wiping him like a baby")

In "*Good Behaviour*" by Molly Keane, there is a line about a character saying to her little dog -

"*Oh, Chang, why do your tiny paws smell of mice*" which resonates with me daily

They do.

My Aunt called her little baby Moby, either after the whale or a Dj.

The jury is out.

He was a clever little dog, with a ferocious tenacity in warning and protecting his Mistress, and a creature of habit who was a homebird with tendancies to lie down and sulk on various mats in various halls when he was forced to abandon his patch.

As he aged, he developed arthritis and "a bit of a chest" which meant he was on heart tablets and she had to help him jump up the 2 steps into the living room.

I remember sitting sideways on those steps as a child, leaning to the door and swinging out of the way to let the mens pinstriped legs pass up and down.

My Aunts husband went out the door for the last time one day to coach a match that his identical twin sons were playing in, and remarked idly to a friend on the bench - that he had" a whore of a headache" -

"Play on, play on for Christs sake"........shouts the referee as the young boys stood around the field, glad of a reprieve from the baking sun that August day to catch their breath, watching the speeding ambulance bumping across the grass.

As a little girl I used be given a pound to sing the twins to sleep.

They wore identity bracelets because the wrong twin would get fed twice, or be given double homework, and various other shenanigans you can hazard a guess at.

The dog continued to bark and whirl around the floor in a fever, and scratch to be let out at the exact time to void his bowel, regardless of whether the binman or the Bishop was in situ-

taking off at a sedate trot like a Borrowers horse, his basil brush tail erect, to cock his chicken wing leg on a rose bush.

On Thursday, she thought he had the vomiting bug.

He settled in the early afternoon and was in good form and was cosy in his basket and she thought I'll feed him tomorrow. She put the basket beside her bed, piled high with his fleece blankets and cushions, balls and toys, and was awoken from a cat nap at 4 am where he was "Agitated, his paws going ninety, and he flopped out of my arms like a 2lb bag of sugar, gave two big gasps and was gone."

Gone.

I imagine she cradled him for ages while she cried. She says she thought she was having a heart attack herself with the shock.

She mentioned his forehead getting stiff.

She arose and went and wrapped him in a brand new yellow blanket and wondered who could she ring.

Even though, she was distraught and kept peeping in at the tiny black stiff body wrapped in the little yellow fleece on the end of her bed, she observed the social mores and didn't ring until the streets were aired.

Her nephew arrived at 12, which meant she spent 8 hours with the lifeless body of her beloved pet, and was in tatters.

They buried him under my Uncle Ollies Tree near the back door with the latch that people came in and out of all day and night.

"I'll miss him forever, he was my best friend for many years" says my Aunt today as we leave to make a different visit.

The Cemetery in Carlow at dusk, in Mid-Winter is bleak and stark, the crunchy ground crisp under the alloys, the green edges weighed down with growth and heavy rain.

Here and there are isolated spectators with their heads bent reading ivy covered stones, some kneeling tending, some visiting here for the first time, others for the last.

I stood at the Dooley Plot, shaded by a Yew tree that has grown 20 feet since I was a child. My Uncle Ollie kept the water bottles in its cool green centre, and we would pluck them out and re-fill them from the tap on the wall, while he raked the white stones, in his shirtsleeves and braces, clipping the saxifraga back from the cornerstone edging, clipping the grave back to gravel in jig time.

I pulled the tree apart today and found not one, but about 14 water bottles nestled within, and so took the green one, reeking of stagnant water, home with me.

He always had a green one.

I felt that all 8 of the occupants of the graves we saw today, came back to their home with us, that they filled the car, and filled the kitchen, balancing their cups and bottles on window sills, filling up all the rooms, filling up the house, filling up the entire Crescent, drinking porter, calling for songs, and opening the warchest of memories and archive we share with them still, letting us know that although they are not here, they *are* here.

And that we are eternally connected, and they are broadcasting loud and clear if only we would tune in.

And that they are only one more notch up on the buttery dial that connects us with *Hilversum, Prague* and *Budapest*, and like the 3 degrees that never cooled, are present, singing still in the white noise.

After tea, I carried the emergency chair back up to my Grandmothers bedroom, the one she was carried from 30 years ago, and I swear I could smell her perfume, and in the darkness of the drapes could almost see her lying under the eiderdown, waiting to ask *"would they give last to nobody"* and laugh her sideways laugh, the beautiful Kennedy woman from

Gowran who married an Asylum Keeper, her shoulders shaking against the feather pillows.
I told Siobhán all this tonight as I bit the chocolate sweets into quarters, and she smiled.

Christmas 2010

087

"I'm still inside"

I leaped from the car in fine fettle and up to high doh.

I had a pretty productive day and had managed to accomplish a fair few of the tasks on my to-do list.

So, I swung through the glass doors with a bag of yoghurts, filled with a sense of my own amazingness and ready to impart all sorts of palava to Siobhán.

The Matron is sitting inside the door and she calls me.

Siobhán has slipped.

I watch her mouth moving as the blood roars in my ears, and my stomach heaves,

I refrain from bending over as the piss and vinegar rushes out of me, leaving me spent like a burst balloon.

I walk to her room with my heart in my mouth.

She is tilted in the Stephen Hawking chair, and all I can see is white -

her hair, her blouse, her face.

Her hands are icy and flop back down onto the blanket.

"Let's get the hot cloth" I say and run into the toilet to cry while the water runs.

Jesus, Jesus, Jesus, no, no, no, I can't, I'm not able, no, no, no, I think as I try to get a grip.

Her mouth is hanging sideways.

No, no, no. Please in the name of all that is good and holy, I'm not able, I think.

The water falls back out.

I ring my sister.

She is bright and breezy on handsfree as she is driving over anyway. She calls me out to talk in the hall.

Through sobs and ragged breaths I try to fill her in. The crying keeps stopping and starting as if a bit of me wants me to cop the hell on.

A larger part wants to lie down and screech on the carpet.

The roles have reversed.

I preach acceptance, and awareness, and detachment but am shaken to the core. "It is what it is" says my sister.

The nurses tap her chest with their cold hands to provoke a response, and use a syringe to administer fluids.

Normally, I have only the candles lit, and the music on.

Now, in the bright light of the overhead, and in silence, with the medicine trolley parked at the door, the whole dynamic of the room has altered as much as the roles. I leave anxiously.

I call later that night.

I call at sparrow fart in the morning.

I hear the 2 words "*brighter today*" and only realise I have been holding my breath when it bursts out in a long sigh.

I have been back again and again since, the work I so desperately thought I needed to do falling by the wayside.

"One-woman show my arse" I thought when it looked like the bottom was falling out of my world.

The next night Siobhán was showered, and responding, sitting with her hair blow dried in her beautiful blue blouse.

She swallowed some 7 up for me, and held my hand, hard.

Oh, to have her strength. *She* is a One Woman Show and so mine will forge ahead regardless.

There may be tears.

February 2014

The wind is howling.

I rang the Mayor for sandbags earlier.

He arrived 37 seconds later wearing his Marine Watch jacket.

I wonder should I cancel my lift to Siobhán as the bins blow around the street and limbs of trees dot the road.

I mention it to Little Thomasina and I can hear the pause as he says - "Sure, whatever you think yourself".........

"Wouldn't it make more sense that you could relax knowing your children are in off the roads beside the fire?" I ask.

Clair has been a friend of mine since I was knee high to a grasshopper, she responded to my plea for a new driver when my old one relocated to the City in a futile attempt to get away from me.

She has never come in.

Most people don't come in.

"I'll come in someday" they say.

"Not tonight" they say.

"Tell Siobhán I said hello" they say.

Some just say they are not able. Mostly my brother says that.

I look at my phone and know it is too late to make the call as she will have left her home and be navigating through rain and floods and storms to come get me. Instead of texting or beeping she gets out and runs to my door.

"Get in the CAR!" I shout.

She can't hear me with the wind as I try to lock the door and my hat blows backwards off my head and down the street.

"GET IN THE CAR!" I roar.

We set off while I tell her that I won't stay long, just ten minutes even, and ask her will she not wait instead of driving in and out, and out and in, and out again.

"I'll wait" says she - "I can catch up on my calls and texts".

She tells me how amazing the show was on Sunday night, even though I had to edit one piece as I performed it, knowing that I would dissolve into floods as my chin was wobbling and my voice faltering and I knew I had to sing a song called "Aeroplane".

"Aeroplane" is a song about Siobhán - inspired by the piece I wrote likening Alzheimers to being strapped into an aeroplane seat and never landing, never going home.

It is hugely emotive and very personal and Little Thomasina, the Sister, my Aunt and the lesser spotted Brother were in the audience.

So, no pressure then.

They all cried.

I performed it with the man who wrote it, and you could have heard a pin drop as the last notes faded away.

I played it from my phone to Siobhán as the Sister needled me on Saturday night.

A nurse opened the door and found me stripped on Siobhán's airbed, the dog playing with my abandoned tights on the floor, the song playing and with the needles of my Accupuncturist Skin & Blister sticking out of my legs, stomach, and hands.

They are used to me so she didn't blink.

I cried a lot as the energy moved.

Tonight, Clair came in to say hello.

She has tears in her own eyes.

"Ah, Jesus, Siobhán hello, it's me, Clair, I used to be knitting on your roof".

She leans down and kisses her.

All of the things I have written about are here, the scented candles, the photos on the wall, the woolen blanket, the music on the radio, the plants on the sill.

And Siobhán.

She looks beautiful tonight, her hair freshly washed and blowdried, her skin clear and unlined, her hands folded under the patchwork blanket.

"How old is your Mam now" says Clair as she watches me hold the glass to her lips and wipe her chin.

She will be 80 in 2 weeks.

I can't even process that myself as she began this illness in her late 60's, and so in my mind she is framed forever at that age.

We stayed for 2 hours.

As I put the key in the door tonight, I hear Joni Mitchell singing -

"Come in from the cold"

and I realise that it is an ill wind….

I don't even know what country I was in when I sent my Mother home a little card, that I thought she may find pleasing.

It was not my usual style so I must have been in a tearing hurry to catch the mail collection.

My normal style was saucy beach scenes, busty blonde barmaids in striped dresses, small men with big overcoats and shiny red hooters ,cards that were "suggestive", and had every likelihood of stuff falling out of, or popping up in,the middle, to disgrace both recipient AND donor.

On a visit home I spotted the card I had bought in Oxford Street in London, mounted in a small black frame, hanging in the hallway.

"Whaddy ya want to keep that old tat for" says I.

"I'll get you the actual picture."

Siobhán didn't do cats or kittens as she was a dog lover then AND still. Her first born daughter was allergic to cat hair, pollen dust and cleaning and would need to be nebulised if her chin got itchy.

Something about the little girl moved her enough to mount and keep it.

Fast forward 2 decades later.

When I met *Hermione* in the home where Siobhán has lived for years, I thought she was staff. Her companion was a large green watering can that lived in an outside shed, and so we walked the halls together, She and I, as she showed me which ones to leave by pressing her thumb into the clay, which ones needed light and shade, which thrived in the dark, how to spray and mist the succulents, the cacti, the orchids, explaining that the dead flowers would rot down into the compost and enrich it. We commented on the perfume of the old roses, their pale velvety petals hung with the scent of yesteryear.

She wore a twin set and pearls and I schlepped alongside in a smock splashing the water over my bare feet, as we did the passageways and windowsills, porches and mortuary, running back to the room with the big sink to fit the can under the tap.

On my way last night to get a glass and a spoon - through an open door, I spotted what I thought was *Hermione* slumped in a chair -

I asked the tealady and then went in.

I bent down and said "hello Hermione, how are you" as I reached for her hand. She is wearing a pale green cardigan and her once bright blue eyes are milky and opaque from cataracts.

She grabs my hands and won't let go.

"I'm nearly dead here" she says and the enormity of this statement shocks me into laughing to try and chivy her along, and bolster her mood.

The lady is not for turning, and so I mention that the plants are looking great and being well minded.

She pulls me down to her face and I stare into the milky orbs that can see nothing now, and she says in a furious whisper - "YOU have the power"

Eckhart Tolle in conference in silent auditoriums likens the flower to the human, albeit with a difference. Flowers need light and food and water to grow, but that is all they need.

They have their own sense of presence, of awareness and have no need to be anywhere else, doing anything else, with anyone else, other than simply being.

"When you can truly be with a flower, can feel its essence, its serenity, then you can feel that state of consciousness arise in you, and you can never go back to mindlessness" says Eckhart.

Hermione cannot truly be with a flower as she has no sight left to witness their presence, only the memory of their colours, their styles ,their positions.

Back in Siobháns room I scan the window sill filled with Polyanthus, Saxifraga, Tete a Tete Daffodils, Ferns, and the tree of yellow roses and realise that here is a woman who could see them - if her eyes were open - but can't remember what they even are.

The portrait of the blonde child with kittens bears more than a passing resemblance to my Mother as a young child, the white blonde hair, the pale skin, the skyblue eyes, and I wonder if it was this that drew her to the schmaltzy card at the outset.

I have the actual portrait in a beautiful mounted frame with artists twine ready to hang and I shall be sticking it on the back seat of a car tomorrow to take out there.

It was handed to me by Keyhole Kate, as it was gifted to her by her own daughter, in a bizarre co-incidence.

Siobhán is very much a human being while we run around like humans "doing"

"Remember, man, you are but dust, and into dust, you shall return"

Maybe Siobháns eyes will open long enough to see the little blonde girl on her wall, and remember she has no need to be any other place, and that she is home, and very very loved.

A picture speaks a thousand words.

Siobháns cheeks are flushed so I wrestle the giant Stephen Hawking Chair out of her room to give her a breath of air.

I wheel her to the front door and stand on the pads that make the glass doors slide open, so that she can feel the wind on her face.

The Nurse comes out of the office and spots us.

"I'm making a break for it" I say while she laughs.

Sometimes I'm not even joking.

We do a circuit of the building, the internal corridors, the doors open to the familiar rooms, knowing each occupant by the covers, the quilts, the cushions, the fluffy dogs, the porcelain dolls.

We head to the church.

I usually behave a little like John Denver in here, talking to George Burns in the movie "**Oh God**"

I walk right up to the altar and staring at the small locked Tabernacle usually begin by saying in a loud voice -

- "Hello God, it's Siobhán and Michelle"

and then I ask him to mind us and bless us and all belong to us. It is my prayer for her, and the one she cannot say.

I know God isn't an old man with a beard on a cloud watching us, but I do know that there is something out there, a benign presence, a loving energy, a consciousness that is aware of us all.

I just call it God so that Siobhán knows who I am talking to.

There IS an old man watching us though.

In the silent space, with the evening light filtered softly through the stained glass, an old man is sitting quietly at the back fingering his tiny Mother of Pearl Rosary beads.

So quietly that I am launching into my Hello God speech before he coughs.

His coughing is prolonged and outrageous and it leaves him spent and gasping.

"I started smoking as a child" he told me, and his addiction would continue for 3 score and ten, and then some.

When he was admitted here he was still smoking and I often palmed him a lighter knowing that it might be more of a shock to his system to stop than to continue.

Those days are gone.

He can barely breathe.

His shoulders rise with every intake and his laboured breathing and wheezing are painful to watch and it strikes me that it must be simply awful to fight for every breath.

I am a smoker with asthma and had to be nebulised before Christmas as I had a chest infection, so I have a small inkling of the frustration and stress that it causes.

I turn over the shocking tumours and horrific photos on the boxes and live in a fantasy land where I will stop tomorrow.

Always tomorrow.

Breathe they will say when women are birthing babies.

Breathe they will say in meditation and yoga classes.

Breathe and count to 10 they will say when stress threatens to overwhelm. In through the nose - out through the mouth.

He is on an oxygen tank that falls off his face when he sleeps and he wakes gasping for air. The Breath of Life.

In deep meditation one is advised to focus on the breathing, the gentle rise and fall of the chest that goes on all day and night all by itself.

We don't wake up at night to breathe, something is breathing for us

"The lungs are the soul of the body" he says sadly, staring at his shiny shoe tapping the carpet.

"I have destroyed mine".

He is furious with western medicine and the way it treats the elderly. "2 good women are worth more than any doctor." He describes his life now as being on a see-saw where he is balanced on the top, knowing he will slide down at any given moment.

Siobhán is curled sideways in the chair, and although to a passer by she appears deeply asleep, I know she is listening.

A confused man passing us earlier had pointed at her and said to his daughter - "He is dying".

We are all dying, a little every day.

It is in the breathing that we connect with the divinity within us and realise that we are one with what we pray to.

"Be still and know that I am God".

Little Thomasina took his old pal out for an errand and he wheezed and coughed the whole way into town, the 2 deaf men in their 80's shouting at each other in the small car.

Dad brings him to a music shop and waits outside, the engine idling, 2 wheels on the path. He comes back out slowly and lowers himself gently back into the car angling his stick over the back seat and begins to put his belt on.

"Did you get sorted J" says Dad as he checks the mirror to pull out into the street, and looks across at him, he has opened his hand to display the reason for their mission.

Lying across his palm is a harmonica.

Christmas 2011

I'm still inside

June 2013 - Year 8

The phone didn't answer.

For a heartbeat of a second I allowed myself to think outrageously and then realised he probably just didn't hear it.

Then he rings back, and I exhale seeing the familiar reassuring name flashing on the screen.

"Dad" it says.

The Blind Man from Howth knows that I call him Little Thomasina.

He is in the Care Doc's Clinic with chest pain, and so begins my day.

Through the lashing rain we drove speedily, the tyres shushing the tarmac, our breath fogging the windscreen, and waited with all the other humans in the rows of fixed plastic seating,

the Polish baby called Marta,

the old man on the walker,

the footballer with the busted eyebrow,

the girl on crutches.

The radiators are hopping.

Little Thomasina comes walking out and I smile, and notice he is blushing, probably about all the fuss, and I think this day is fine, we will have dinner, and this day is fine.

This day is fine.

He has a prescription in his hand and I am in a hurry to chivy him through the thunderous shower to the safety of the warm car.

It is his admission slip for A&E and my heart sinks.

Oh, God in heaven can we not go home?

Can we not just put him in the bed,

and bring him up a dinner with gravy

and a bit of trifle

and let him sleep.

Give us a tablet there and tell us to go home, I think as we drive to the hospital.

The jury is out on how I feel up here.

It has so many memories for me after spending every single day here for months.

I got to know everyone, their families, all their visitors, and every name of the staff and who was on where, when and nights.

That's just how I roll.

But now we are coming back with the Father, and I want him to behave more like me.

If my leg was attached to my torso by a single filament of skin and tissue, I would insist they bandage, release and medicate.

I'd be off like a dirty shirt.

Preferably with a bag of drugs for pain, I'm not an idiot.

He is wheeled into A&E and then seen, and then parked in a corridor, and then seen again, then bloods are done, and we are back on the corridor, we are told it takes 2 hours for the results, like a washing machine on spin.

You can't stop it to get a single hanky out.

So we are back in the corridor much to the annoyance of the porters but we had nowhere left to go.

He is uncomfortable and flushed on the trolley but when I show him that it can be raised at the back or lowered he tells me to leave it.

"*LEAVE* it"

He won't eat anything despite me marching to the garage in the rain for sandwiches, water, his Sunday Independent, and so I am taken home to pack a bag for him and spend 45 mins walking up and down the stairs getting things, pyjamas, razors, foam, his dressing gown (*hanging on the side of the wardrobe tell her*) as he relays information, and I find all I need and then some. The packet of rennies he had on the mantelpiece, the small dog with the wet coat he had on a sleepover that smells of his aftershave.

the Buy & Sell Magazine he likes to read in bed at night in the vain hope of finding a beautiful german fiddle for half nothing, or an old VW Van lying in a field of daisies, with its split screen and its roof height bed, his earphones, phone charger, and prayerbook.

My own heart was aching on the way back up.

He throws his head back as the nurse searches for a vein and I call him a wuss.

We take turns sitting at the curtains while the mayhem plays out a foot from us, all we know is the feet of the players, the women and men in pale blue scrubs and Crocs, the Consultants in brogues, the Doctors in normal shoes and so we watch them approach, open the curtain and then I hazard a guess as to what is happening looking at the positioning of the feet.

I take a break to run for the hills and visit Siobhán as his broken heart will break again if no-one is with his little bub.

Siobhán has been propped up on pillows and is still sitting in the dining room in her blue bib when I arrive.

The Nurse says she was left facing the windows out to the car park after tea.

Did she know?

Has she missed him?

She appears oddly alert, stroking her own lip, as if lost deep in thought, her hand never gets that far to her face without assistance or coaxing,

It is a gesture that unsettles me.

I wash her face and brush her hair.

Siobhán drinks an inch of fluid for me, as I wipe her neck with a chiffon scarf, and the bit of a throw that covers her stockinged feet, rubbing them, pressing on acupressure points that may relieve blocked channels of energy and spray my own wrists with her perfume and dab it on her earlobes and under her nose, that she may smell it over the other smells in the room.

I dial Little Thomasina's phone and he answers it.

"Say hello to your favourite girl" I tell him, and his voice lifts, and through the tightness in his chest and shoulders he says "Hello Siobhán" while the lines from Stewart O'Nan in "*Songs for the missing*" go through my mind -

..... **"the two of them separated by fate,**

Surrounded by night,

A pair of voices and ears ...... connected by invisible waves,

Travelling the cold air between remote towers"..............

I leave him curled up in the Cornonary Care Unit, a department store bag by his bed, his shoes and coat peeping out over the top, and in the tiny locker drawer, his new phone in its case (turned off because of all the machines) the pair of tiny hearing aids, the pack of rennie, and a prayer book. His hair is white and fluffy on the pillows and his face is still pink. I walked all the way home in the mist carrying a ham sandwich in tinfoil and cried every step of the way.

We will all know more tomorrow.

I send him so much love and peace and apologies, as I am as outrageous and unforgiving of him as all the other humans around me, and instead of letting go, get stuck in, encouraging him on by going toe to toe with him, challenging, informing, refusing to allow him to go down the dark roads he worries about.

I am positive he can return the favour.

As I walk in home, the tiniest male in my life, a miniature pup whose fraying bandana smells of his Grand-fathers aftershave, runs up the hall.

I bawled when I picked him up.

Next Day

Little Thomasina is holding court in C.C.U. and has the Nurses wrapped around his little finger. Following the hellish day in the halls he is hooked up to the machines that beep when he even moves his head - which has led to some bizarre yet hilarious moments.

"Fiachra, you're flatlining" I say to the man reading the jockeys autobiography, while he scans the machine above his head in consternation.

The fault is in the machine, not his heart.

Once I stopped sniffing in the hall, I reverted to my default setting of nuts and rule breaking and so tried to present a man with a heart condition and awaiting an Angiogram-

his phone and charger,

and then his iPad and charger,

(despite the notices all over the gaff saying NO ANYTHING IN HERE!)

and then as a Coup de Grace, his radio and earphones.

All of these were handed back, as was the battery operated toothbrush.

It was me who searched out his nightwear, underwear, socks and toiletries while the clicking engine of the Jag idled in the rain.

I tore the house apart for slippers.

In the Coronary Care Unit, there are only 4 beds and the Nurses look after the people who present as if they were fragile cracked glass vases that need gluing back together.

Their hearts are being minded and they are being taught to listen to the body, and to hear its tiny call of enough already.

They are in silence, and have a Siesta - the lights turned off and the curtains drawn in the middle of the day so as they can shut down and sleep, and heal.

There is nothing from the outside world to stimulate the senses, to startle their already vulnerable hearts, to frighten the horses.

He is lying in a white sheeted limbo, with every move (including bowel) being documented, and so can feel the peace of a safe space where instead of lying alone at home, enduring the long dark night-time of the soul, is being cared for and monitored so he can exhale in relief, knowing that he is already IN the place he needs to be.

I sat in the chair in the hall awaiting my entrance and watched the play of the humans walking and talking, limping and wheeling along.

A male nurse comes breezing through the swing doors with his bag on his back and is confronted with Michelle, in an impossible dress, and a hat tilted rakishly over one black lined eye, and breaks off in the middle of the song he was singing loudly.

"How lovely that you come to work singing" I remark without so much as a how do you do.

He is Little Thomasina's new B.F.F.

I watched my Dad in the wheelchair waiting in the Echo room for a porter to take him back to the ward as he scooched his shoes up and down the floor in boredom, and pondered the amount of time we spend together, caring for Mam, breathing in and out, and the calls - the early morning calls to ask him how he is,

the late night calls to bid him goodnight

and all the calls in between to ask him has he eaten?

Will we eat? *WHERE* will we eat?

How is Mam? What are you watching? Did you go to music?

Will you bring me coal?

Can Walter go to your house for a sleepover?

Apparently, my Father is my B.F.F.

He is missing Siobhán like a limb, and I reassure him that I am on it like a bonnet, running down the hospital hill in my platform boots to catch the car that will take me to her bedside, and document *her every* move, for him.

March 2012 - Year 7

I love uncurling a new baby's hand inserting my thumb and feeling them grab it, and latch on.

Some of them just clench, some try to suck it through their own hand and some just wave it about from side to side.

Tonight, I played that game with Siobhán as I uncurled her small pale cold hands and pressed my own hands under and over, instilling the warmth and presence from my own into hers.

I willed it into her.

I lifted her small light arm and gently bent it at the crook of the elbow to re-arrange the pattern she sits in, like a crinoline doll, with its hands joined.

I peppered my fingerprints up and down the pressure points on the curve of neck and shoulders and watched from the slow blink of the good eye, that this was pleasing and comforting

I knelt on the ground to make eye contact, looking up through the flop of white fringe and trying to tilt a spoon covered in chocolate mousse into the mouth of my baby.

I find myself saying "that's the girl" as if I was the Mother, not the child. While my small

Mother Siobhán has been sitting sideways in her Stephen Hawking chair, listening to the comings and goings in the hall, my small Father Little Thomasina has been lying in various wards in Wexford and Waterford Hospitals doing the same. Despite his worst fears, they have told him he needs no procedure, no interventions, no surgery.

Go home they said and we will review your meds.

He was discharged this evening and gone to the sisters house where he is basking by the fire watching *Primetime* and hugging his Grandson, as God forbid he would be sent to the hippy with the madhouse covered in words and sketches with only a blanket over his knees for a bit of hate.

I think he feels it is an anti climax.

We, on the other hand are delighted.

Siobhán was delighted when I called him tonight on speaker phone and he told her how much he loves and misses her, and that he will be back soon to kiss and hug her.

She knows, Goddammit, she knows.

A carer at the end of her shift in the hospital last night washed a bed from mattress to castors in 5 minutes flat, including the rims of the wheels and every screw and lever in between.

"Jesus, I'm that tired I don't know whether to have chips or brandy when I get in" she sighed.

"Have both" says I, reminding her that life is short

It's been a long week.

August 2014 - Year 9

I went swinging through the glass doors on a high.

One of those exhausted highs where there are never enough hours in a day, to talk, to answer the phone with the full mail box, to scan the messages, the emails that I keep deferring.

Later.

I will do it later.

So crazy from laughing, and talking, and wheedling things out of surprised shop assistants, trying to organise a one woman show when I am only one woman,

ranting and tilting at windmills and begging people to give me lifts to collect things so that I am hoarse and red in the face.

In fact my face is the same colour as the dress in the bag with the duo of chocolate mousse pots.

Siobhán loves them and it is my concession to a combination of chocolate and ice cream and she eats both as they are deceptively small.

The Matron is the first person I see and she wants a word.

I follow her upstairs to the office with my heart beating loud in the quiet space and she ushers me to a swivel chair at the desk.

Apparently, because of Little Thomasina's recent hospital stay it had become apparent that there was no "End of Life" plan in place for my Mother.

"Laughing turns to crying" - Siobhán would say to me as a hysterical child and her words were echoing in the room as I read the plan that has been drawn up with my Father, holding a torn tissue to his eyes.

It is about what will happen when the time comes.

She is only reading the second line aloud when the tears start to spill from my own eyes and down my face.

The Matron is not hysterical though, nor does she react to me.

Her calm unwavering tone continues as she says the monstrous words I never want to hear, about swallowing, and feeding and J pegs, and funeral arrangements.

Sweet Jesus, the bag with the scarlet dress and the twin chocolate pots is gaping open on the desk, beside the forms, and the writer in me wants to photograph the scene, as if by documenting it, I will make it real. As if by staring at the photo of the pots and the scarlet dress I will process the enormity of this, and come to terms with the reality.

Scarlet ribbons for her hair

I seem to be processing everything in this way and appear to be living so completely in the moment that I can only actually deal with the reality of each moment.

I cried signing it.

In her room I kissed Siobháns head and hands and cried there too, turning my head away, stifling the sob in my chest.

I cried in the carpark and on the way home.

And then put my head in my hands as I remembered that I was supposed to be writing a piece about art for an exhibition opening the following night.

I think people think I am joking when I say I never have the pieces written until the night before, but the laugh was wiped off my face as I booted up the computer and prayed there was enough ink to print it.

NOW

You don't take a photograph - you make it says Ansel Adams.

The most brilliant photography lens in the world is the human eye, and it's ability to imagine, dream, visualize, place, envision and capture moments to challenge our perception, to show us a sliver of humanity, to reflect ourselves back to us.

You don't paint a painting - you allow it to be created through you.

You step out of your own way.

The Universe uses you to channel its magnificent energy into one single focused point,
- drawing the inspiration into and through you,
- to the fibre of your being, and nailing it to the page, the canvas, the film.
- It becomes you.

You become It.

We have a responsibility - those of us who create - to the ones we display ourselves to, and to the ones who come after us, to document, to remember, to illustrate, to capture - the moment.

To allow the thing that breathes through us to make its presence felt here, in the Now.

There is only ever Now.

And it is only in the Now that we exist, or remember all the other Now's.

The Now that existed before you walked in the door this evening has left for ever. The

Now that will exist after I stop talking hasn't happened yet, and may be altered in some minuscule way by our collecting, by our combined presence.

Anybody can look at something beautiful and see beauty.

It takes a gift to look at a pretty child and visualize the old woman she will become. It takes a capable Artist to do this.

But a great artist-a master- can look at an old woman, photograph her exactly as she is, lines and wrinkles, and allow us, the viewer, the voyeur, see the child she used to be –

An artist can afford even those amongst us with the intelligence of a turnip and the sensitivity of a Geordie bouncer, the ability to notice that this lovely young child is still alive, not older and ravaged, but simply imprisoned inside a battered body. They can make you feel the hushed, endless tragedy that there was never a girl born who ever grew older than 16.

Any fool can be happy. It takes an artist with a heart to make beauty out of the stuff that makes us weep.

"Do you not see how necessary a world of pains and troubles is to school an intelligence and make it a soul" **John Keats**

Creators must never be afraid of the white space.

Stain it, mark it, claim it.

It takes the chaos within one to create Art without.

For one beautiful moment, while you are harnessed to the work,

bent across the table,

reaching to the corners,

kneeling on the cold tiles,

you are in tandem and in step,

hand in glove,

with the Creator itself,

and it is holding its breath,

looking over your shoulder, and sometimes

.............sometimes,

when you least expect it,

you can feel it's warm breath in the tingling at the nape of the neck,

in the silence,

in the nameless peace,

in the formless becoming formed,

in the abstract becoming physical,

Creator and Created,

Creating,

Together.

NOW

January 2010 Year 5

"Paddy Fortune, Paddy Fortune, ...
where you gone with the water,
where you gone with the water,
you've been so long,
soooooooooooooo long,
so so long" -
This is not the verse of a song.
This is the voice of the woman in the hall I can hear,
while I am holding the glass to my Mothers mouth.
I have to investigate.
As much as I have tried to become immune,
to the voices calling from the halls,
on some days,
such as these,
I am drawn out the door by a hollow note,
a tone, an answering bell.
The humanity within me responding to the call.
Maybe it is the voice of the woman,
rising to a note of panic,
frustration, impatience and holding the note,
holding the soooooooooooooo.........
so long that it feels like a stage production,
a director in the dark wings encouraging the performance.
The woman doesn't see me when I hold her outstretched hands.
She sees through me and the fine mists of time to the day she waited for Paddy Fortune
and the Water.
"Try the one with the red on it,
the one with the red on it,
the one with the ...."
She stares at me.
The man checking the radiators and running his hands along the walls ignores us as if to
say -
Nothing to see here.
"Don't mind me, I'm just checking everything is shipshape and coolaboola here" -
imagining himself back in his home,
his space,
King of the Castle.
In the candle-lit room I have been explaining to Siobhán what I am up to,
this impossible child of hers,
this case of arrested development in her upturned hat,
this girl in the spinsters body.
"So I rang the hotel and booked the biggest room they had and I am going to put on a

show there" I continue breathlessly.

I have been speeding for a week on the steroids and a high that makes me feel I may just blow off the side of the planet like a dandelion clock.

I am hysterical, and hilarious by turns,

trying to harness the thoughts, the pieces, working out stuff in my head,

trying to stage the show I would like to attend.

Despotic Diva, Demented.

Siobhán listens, as it is all she can do.

The last thing left, the hearing.

"Do you hear that woman?" I say and scan the face that I know better than my own,

seeing her fingernails on my own hand,

the criss cross of pale blue veins on her ankle that mirror my own,

recognising the tiny sounds as I dry my own face from the shower,

the similarities in Mother and Child.

Trot Mare, trot Foal.

There's no one to bury me, I think.

There is neither chick nor child,

no-one to remove the beard in my coffin,

no one to lead the singing,

or milk the reading,

stage manage the choir,

to muster and corral, to brow beat and press gang,

to hector and bully, send me off with a bang.

"Wrap me in black plastic and fire me over the quay"

I have said more than once to those who would need -

to know.

Michelle ends when she ends.

No lineage, no heiress, nothing to pass on.

Nothing to see here, move along.

Paddy Fortune is still missing with the water,

and the woman still walks the halls,

wringing her hands, the man still checks the radiators, and I check that I am breathing,

and try to be still,

to come back from out where I have gone,

out on the edge,

Alone.

"We all know that our time in this world is limited, and that eventually all of us will end up underneath some sheet, never to wake up. And yet it is always a surprise when it happens to someone we know. It is like walking up the stairs to your bedroom in the dark, and thinking there is one more stair than there is. Your foot falls down, through the air, and there is a sickly moment of dark surprise as you try and readjust the way you thought of things."

- Lemony Snicket - " Horseradish".

"This is happening, come to Peace with it" -
Cleveland Brown - Family Guy.
Siobhán surprised me AGAIN tonight.
In her awareness, and her ability to communicate with her oldest child, from her Stephen Hawking state.
She is a powerhouse of a woman,
bloodied but unbowed,
railing against the odds,
rolling with the punches,
reeling from the blows like a boxer that won't hit the canvas,
she is still swinging back.
In the 10 years that this bastard of a disease has been de-constructing my Mother, making her forget, even the smallest of abilities, and making me forget who she was, who she IS, I have watched and noted and written as like a rug being rolled up while you are standing on it, the memories went sliding away.
Tonight I arrived in up to high doh.
Hoarse again and spent from mucking about, behaving like a minor deity, wearing a hundred year old hat I found in a vintage shop and telling the broad I would break her leg rather than leave the shop without it.
"Never mind the paper folding money" says I.
I whisper to Siobhán what I am up to, and with a fine sheen of perspiration on my head from the steroids AND the hat, while feeding her strawberries and cream, narrate the tamer exploits of my day.
I need no filter here
This woman knows me inside out.
She has been dealing with the enormity of Michelle and her hysteria since the day she birthed me.
When I realise she is looking at me, I take out the camera and put the hat on her head.
She is really looking at me.
We both have the Dooley eye.
I had noticed it as a child in my Uncles, her brothers.
A tendancy to wander off on its own, or roll indiscriminately of its neighbour, as if it were trying to see something somewhere else.
"I know you are drunk" - says Hewhomustnotbenamed one night.
" - You are only blinking one eye".
My eye wanders off to the left when I am wrecked so I must be positively wall eyed tonight.
I could read a book and watch a film simultaneously, if I had the time.
Tonight, Siobhán turned both of her Dooley eyes on me and I snapped and snapped.
I put lipgloss on her and sprayed her wrists and neck, brushed her beautiful hair, and said "Come on, hun, let's do this, let's get a photo of you for posterity, not sympathy".
She helped me.
I swear to Christ, she helped me.
Although curled sideways like the legendary Mr Hawking, and bearing more and more of a resemblance to him on any given Sunday, she stopped the Ref mid count and came back

swaying to be present.

My God, it was beautiful.

The Nurse comes into the candle-lit room with her trolley of meds when it is all over and Siobhán has retreated back out to the foggy edges where she lives and says it smells gorgeous in here.

I tell her about Siobhán, almost as much to hear myself say it as to inform.

A friend asked to see a photo of Siobhán the other day and as I passed her my phone there was a heart stopping moment of silence as she took in the image and involuntarily started to cry.

"Where is She, Michelle?" she asked.

"She's IN there" I responded.

Tonight, the Nurse wiped her own eyes genuinely moved and amazed.

It is nothing to how I feel.

I was meant to have that hat for this occasion.

I have my foot on the rug, and can only aspire to have her strength, her fortitude, her presence.

I hope that she is out at the edges of a stunning sunset and she can hear the sound of the sea, rushing to the shore.

She humbles me.

Down, but not out.

April 2014

I'm still inside.

April 20th 2014

I wanted to film
To narrate, to document, to sing the Song of Siobhán.
I did NOT want to take footage or images that would sadden or shock, bog standard file footage of a Nursing Home,
feet in tartan slippers, wheelchairs, walking aids,
people slumped sideways.
I wanted something beautiful, and profound, and momentous.
To that end, I climbed hills and hung out of cars with no seatbelt on -
the window wide in the rain and howling wind,
or chasing sunsets,
bossing the driver around with a rotation of my finger,
knowing I would have to edit and add sound,
running like a headless chicken to get the footage that would be projected at the *"Shellshock"* Show.
My entire family would be present looking at their Mother, or Wife.
It was a big ask.
The jury is out on whether they would jump up and down.
Or an involuntary tear would form,
or they would be annoyed and pissed off about the violation of privacy, and wondering where will she stop?
Between all the palaver I had to sort - the venue, the press, drawing the poster, micro managing every detail, rehearsing, learning, not to mention actually *writing* the show, I was worn out.
Between the shouting, singing, and hoarse practicing in Siobhán's room, telling her every detail,
and who said what to whom and when,
AND the implosion again of every electronic device I laid a hand on, there were more cuts than Copolla,
and more versions than Toy Story.
Will I use the one with the stars,
the one with the church they were married in - it's red door gleaming against the grey stone, the mist on the headstones,
the countless minutes of what I wanted to call *"The Journey"* showing the view from my door to hers, the one Little Thomasina makes every single day, in all weathers.
Between showers, on a day when my driver had borne the wind in her ears and a spray of fine rain on the left hand side of her face for miles, I dropped the yoghurt I was spooning into Siobhán and ran for the doors, to capture a few minutes of evening light that I thought might be nice.
The film is jerky and awkward.
It is filmed on a broken phone with a smashed screen.
There are no attempts to be Art Malik.
The sound is unedited, the film untouched.

It represents a small tired woman walking around the car park of a nursing home, capturing light.

When I watched it I was mesmerised

It is enough.

Light came to play with the birdsong, and the massive clouds in the Montana Sky, the sound of passing cars sounding like the shoooosh of the sea as they drove by.

It was projected on a big screen while I read the piece called "Shape Shifter, Dreamer of Nightmares" that I had written for it.

And it closed with the image of Siobhán that she helped me capture, in her 100 year old hat, with her Dooley eye open and listening.

She has *always* been listening.

I dedicated the show to her - saying it was not a One -Woman show, but a 3 woman show, the child in me who runs the whole thing -(*showing off*) -

the middle-aged me who has to pull it together,

and my Mother, who inspires it, as She has done all her life.

The audience raised a toast to her and said her name.

To Siobhán they cried as they lifted their glasses,

and the lights on their glasses reflected back to me alone on the stage,

in the spotlight.

August 2013 - Year 8

There is a crack where the light gets in.

And so I chase it,

the tiny dog resembling a Gremlin astride the headrest,

his red lead trailing, his blue superman t-shirt pasted to his body, (bought at a Ploughing Match for a teacup chihuahua)

his flying ears pointed in the wind.

I heard Siobhán cough last week.

Any noise from her silence is remarkable, and so it is with delight that I bless her when she sneezes,

or when the involuntary sigh I remember from my childhood, escapes her lips when I rub the hot cloth across her face to itch her eyes.

We are late chasing the sunset as the aforementioned tiny dog has caused pandemonium in the sunroom.

As per.

Anyone that could stand up, did, and the rest held their arms out beseechingly.

I walk from wheelchair to chair, handing him down to the laps,

the tweed skirts, the suit pants, the soft fleece blankets,

to legs that are swollen, or twisted and bent,

to the man with the huge hands that are all knuckles,

to the woman with the elongated pianists fingers, to the man whose nose is wider than his mouth,

and watch as like a placid baby he curls into them

and licks their ears and cheeks,

and they inhale him, and feel the tiny beating of his tiny heart.

To the woman he may have been the baby she once or never had.

To the man he may as well have been a newborn spring lamb

To them all he was a tiny breath of normality, a bundle of warmth.

In Siobháns room, he licks her ears and mouth too, as he climbs all over her to say hello,
and stands on the top of her head to look out the window.

"That's a tiny dog on your head, Siobhán, and I am your first born and favourite child,
Michelle. You may know me better as the scourge, that little rip, or the changeling baby who
was swapped by travellers. "

I remove his pencil legs from her head and place him on the bed to entrance the nurses,
and then wrap Siobhán for the off.

We are going out.

It took a fair bit of negotiation to install us in the very far corner of the courtyard with the
sliver of sunlight stealing over the slates, notwithstanding the size of the Stephen Hawking
chair,

the dog hysterical with excitement as I remove his lead for the very first time

and he can smell grass and air and hear the tricking of the rushing fountain,

the foaming water cascading over the mossy green stones,

the sudden flash of vivid orange in the dark gloaming of the deep as a golden fish the size
of a salmon weaves through the water lilies.

Siobhán can feel it too, the sun on her head, the sound of the spray.

I ring Little Thomasina on speaker so she can hear his voice and he can hear mine, and
know I am there.

"We're in the sun" I say holding her hand and watching that the dog doesn't take a flying
leap in after the fish.

"Jesus, I hope you have a blanket on her, Mam has a cough, you know" he says getting
fussed up.

Getting fussed up is my Fathers second favourite thing to do,

after "Waiting for the Man" - who is always some random guy that he has asked to do
something for him that involves staring at a clock, a phone and out the door as he waits for
a price, an estimate, or a truck.

Sighing............. "Yes, I'm on it like a bonnet" I inform him

and turn to see where the dog has run off to, now that he CAN run, and he is leaping
through the grass over imaginary jumps like a prize stallion at the horse show in the RDS.

And then I see the faces at the sunroom window,

the small hands waving,

the pointing nurses turning the chairs towards the outside,

and the smiles.

June 2014 - Year 9

This family seems to be moving after a state of stasis.

I appear to have consented to fly to Stockholm and take a hilarious number of trains to lie around by a Swedish lake and think.

My skin and blister has just returned from a whirlwind tour of China, where after a number of hours spent cursing in the wrong airport in the wrong country, was left reeling from the public conveniences and the sheer scale of the gaff. I told everyone she had gone for a takeaway.

She has gone to Shanghai for a chicken ball and curry sauce.

The Quiet Leitrim man had to prevail upon her to unpack the various and motley items she had purchased for all and sundry the very night she returned, as he was leaving for Budapest in the morning and needed the case.

En Famille they are vacationing En France, and the only reason Little Thomasina does not know this is because his Hidden Hearing Aids were playing up that day, and they told him *very very* softly in case he had to clutch his chest.

The Nephew is off to Lourdes to push people around the churches and lift them in and out of water in the hope of a cure.

A Pilgrimage if you will.

Siobhán continues to sit by the window in the Stephen Hawking chair.

Some days she is too deeply asleep to swallow the melting ice-cream her husband has brought her, and it lies uselessly draining onto a saucer, while he watches the snooker with the volume turned up to the loudest, or walks the halls for a bit of a chat.

Some nights I kneel and massage her small feet through the padded socks, clasping her ankles, willing the centre of me, into the centre of her.

Her legs jump like she is electrocuted.

I rub the ponds cream into her face and brush her hair and call people on speaker phone so she can hear the voices, and their stories.

A Pilgrimage is a journey, sometimes of a personal nature,

to a place of being, of birth, and re-birth,

other times it is a connection to a deeper spiritual realm,

to reconnect with the essence of oneself.

I notice that her wrists are thinner.

Siobhán always wanted to travel - advising her offspring to do similar, and so saved pin money to see the world, lodging her few pounds into the Credit Union every week.

It is for her that my Sister jets off hither and thither, flying to Cuba to cycle hundreds of miles for the Alzheimers Charity, wandering alone with maps in taxi's through the teeming streets of Shanghai, or on holiday lying bronzing by a tourquoise sea while the warm evening air fills with the smell of Marlboro, garlic and steaks.

It is for her that my Nephew will be assigned to care for someone on their *own* pilgrimage to Lourdes, assisting, carrying, dipping and drying.

It is for her that I will attempt to remove myself from this cluttered sentinel and take planes, trains and automobiles to a different space, a different view, clear air and wild flowers, sunlight on water, dappled pools, and blonde strangers, to exhale and work on the writing

that Siobhán was the first to notice, and encourage.
I am a Pilgrim too.

Golden Stockings

**Golden stockings you had on
In the meadow where you ran;
And your little knees together
Bobbed like pippins in the weather,
When the breezes rush and fight
For those dimples of delight,
And they dance from the pursuit,
And the leaf looks like the fruit.
I have a many sight in mind
That would last if I were blind;
Many verses I could write
That would bring me many a sight.
Now I only see but one,
See you running in the sun,
And the gold-dust coming up
From the trampled buttercup.**

Oliver St. John Gogarty

When Siobhán moved to the home she lives in now, there was another woman remarkably similar to her moving into the room one door down.
The same size and height, style of clothing, the same short ash blonde hair, the same way of holding their heads at an angle as if they were hearing music in the distance. They were so alike that in the beginning some of the carers mixed up their names and would say" Goodnight Lilly" to Siobhán and vice versa.
Except for the fact that Lilly sang.
Lilly sang in her armchair, and in the halls, and at the dining table and as her illness progressed and sporadic outbursts of confusion and agitation became more constant, she still sang.
A high soprano voice singing along with the pile of Cd's stacked by the little grey stereo with the tinny sound,
operas and crooners, tenors like Caruso, Carreras, Pavarotti and Domingo.
"Wait till you hear Lilly sing" says the lady who is drawing room numbers and surnames on my Mothers clothes with an indelible black marker to ensure they are re-hung in the proper room post laundering.
In the intervening 6 years I heard Lilly sing a lot, and sat in her room listening in awe as the small body and tilted head retained the memory of the lyrics while the memory of spoken words was unraveling, the brown plastic innards of a cassette tape unspooling itself.
Once, long after there were words from Siobhán, I almost dropped the phone one night as

I called out my phone number to a person and began ......"087"............

"9826472" said Siobhán and smiled.

The body retains the memory of all the events that have preceeded and they become installed as the hardwiring of ourselves.

They make us who we are, and who we think we are.

I'm pink therefore I'm spam.

As Christmases turned into Easters, and Summers, then Autumns I watched the seasons turn and the decline of these 2 small women, one whom I document here faithfully and one who only gets documented on the last night of her life.

In this lifetime.

Over the last year I have kept an eye on the soft singer in the room down the hall, as if using her as a yardstick for my own Mother, her neighbour.

Some nights I stole in quietly on tiptoes, through the open door, and pressed play on the small stereo, filling the room with the music she loved and informed the small shape in the white bed with the patchwork throw, that it was me, Siobhán's daughter.

There was never a response, just a sideways glance from the face turned to the wall, the pillow bolstering her body, in the small of her back.

A nurse informs me that when a person is crossing they move the bed away from the wall and into the middle of the room so the family can gather, to witness and be close, to say goodbye, to pray, to hold, to retain a memory, to assist in the passing.

I am smoking in the drive waiting for the jeep that will take me home, staring at the impossible sky, the moon, a space station, the heavy charcoal clouds flitting overhead, when I meet a woman from the night crew turning in to work.

I vent about death for about 16 minutes without drawing a breath while she tries to look at her watch discreetly a number of times.

"How do you deal with it, how do you cope, has it changed your perception of your own mortality, what and where and when and how" - I tail off running out of air.

"Acceptance, they all get it, all of them. Acceptance, it has changed my thoughts about it, and has negated the fear of death I had" she says calmly while looking me up and down, this ragged woman in mismatched clothes and wild curls, smoke streaming down her nostrils.

I knocked the closed door and was about to launch into a stream of introductions about stuff when I realise the room is empty and Lilly is lying alone, her eyes sliding sideways to give me the glance.

"I want to say hello, ... and goodbye" says I to the staff when I asked permission earlier.

Her eyes are cloudy and unfocused as if she is already looking into somewhere other, and the room is silent.

There is no music here tonight.

All of the pronouncements and thoughts and prayers I had thought to offer or say disappear out the window like a puff of smoke, and I place my hand on her small shoulder and feel the heaving in my chest and swallow the burning tears and the brick in my throat and say "God Bless, Lilly" and close the door behind me.

Tonight, I walked past her room to get a spoon to feed Siobhán a choc-ice and saw the "Do

Not Disturb" sign hanging on the door.

On the way back the door opened momentarily and a nurse came out.

The bed was in the middle of the room.

Tonight, I offer a prayer of safe passage and delight and joy to Lilly as she makes her solitary journey , and hope that a choir is leading her across a bridge of sighs, home

"Just do the dance that you've been shown,
by everyone you've ever known,
no matter how close to anothers,
your steps have grown,
there is one dance you'll dance alone"

Jackson Browne.

Little Thomasina arrives every day at the same time with the small paper bag. Lately it has been the giant blue cornetto with the whipped cone top, sprinkled with flakes of dark chocolate - a nod to "summer" - sometimes it is a trio of tiny trifles, albeit sans or with the minimum of actual fruit, which has to be plucked out with the back of a spoon and left to harden on a saucer, minute cubes of pineapple, little chunks of pear, a trail of crimson slime from a single strawberry, decorating the plain white plate.

Knowing he had already brought the Cornetto (wrapped in plastic to keep it from melting all over the car seat) I arrived with a fancy trifle last night and on greeting her, placed the vases of scented stock - smelling like clove rock sweets - on the hospital table, the top of the press and on the green shaded window sill in the late evening sun. I kiss her and tell her I am going to get a spoon to give her something delicious.

In the visitors tea room I burst in on a pair of women drinking tea with a giant tray of fresh hot baked scones cooling on the table.

Somebody is dead.

They must be, as the hospitality room is set for the mourners, the crockery, the biscuits, the fine china jugs of cold milk, sliced cheese and homemade brown bread, the kettle boiling.

Back in her room I feed Siobhán the trifle, alternating with sips of ice cold lemonade, both to open and refresh her mouth.

"Imagine if there was fruit in this and they caught me and the nurse had to come and root around in your mouth and take it out" I tell Siobhán as I wipe the trail of custard from her chin.

The carer after remarking on the smell of clove rocks refuses the profiteroles despite my pleas that they are fresh cream and that I live alone, and they won't last pissing time. She runs down the hall laughing while I follow her waving the plastic triangle, begging to no avail.

My shopping is all over the bed, the meatballs smelling of garlic and tomato, the strawberries warming under their sellophane wrapper, the bottle of lucozade losing its fizz from being all shook up all over the gaff.

My sister arrives with her accupuncture needles and some pungent sticks that she lights when cupping.

"Mam is chewing something" she says and when I stop eyerolling and sighing and saying there was no fruit in that trifle, I place my little finger into her mouth, and feel the warm cheeks, the nubby gums, and the look of surprise on both of our faces.

There is nothing here that I can feel.

I take advantage of her presence to walk down the hall to the church and now that the mourners have driven away, I open the door to the silent space.

For years now I have been tiptoeing across this carpet alone, drawn and repelled like a magnet, to whoever is lying in the box.

Twice I have stopped in my tracks, and refused to go further, blessing myself and reversing back out the door at speed.

Usually, I am drawn as if on a pulley to the side of the coffin, where I look on the faces of the men and women I knew - from the chair they sat in, the room they occupied, the glasses they wore.

I am the child they taught.

I am the neighbours daughter.

I am the witness.

Last night, I looked down at the face of the man of the cloth, lying pale and silent under the flickering sconce of the tabernacle, the last light filtering softly through the stained glass windows, the smell of the bouquets of white lillies around his head, the masscards at his feet, the plain wooden crucifix on his chest.

I place my small warm hand on his icy alabaster ones and ask -

"Are you there yet?

"Is it what you thought?"

I think I can see the smallest smile at the corner of his thin lips.

Back in the room with its smells of home, and sweets, and pungent sticks, with the music on, and my Mother sitting with her trousers rolled up to her pale white dumpling knees as if she is about to go paddling in a warm sea, I notice the sister has been busy and there are needles everywhere.

I am lying on my back on the airbed as quick as Johnny wrote the note with needles in my head, neck, hands and legs, to combat stress, to aid with sleep, to revitalise and re-energise. The nurse comes in and takes in the sight and laughs and then asks who has the clove rocks.

Whether it was the needling or the releasing of the dam I keep blocked with my little finger, to enable me to narrate and document, to witness and relate, or whether it was just the enormity of life and death, and the memory of my little finger but I cried in the car all the way home.

There is nothing here that I CAN'T feel.

June 2014 Fathers Day - Year 9

I had spotted the beautiful bath in a momentary superficial glance through an open door one day and as all the rooms are en suite, I pondered its function.

At that time Siobhán was walking by my side, then linked, later it was on a walking aid, and then later still, a wheelchair.

We would yet have to graduate to the Stephen Hawking recliner she lies sideways in now
The bath reminded me of its presence even when the door was closed.

It called me from behind the wooden portal, promising benefits, and healing and therapy.
I never forgot that it was there.

Last week I passed it again and sought out a Nurse.

"Whose leg do you have to hump to get a go in that bath?"

She agreed to put my request in the report that the Matron oversees each morning.

I was sitting with Little Thomasina when I got the call, and was both pleased and shocked, pleased at her speed in getting back to me, and shocked that I had to take the call with my Father sitting opposite.

The Matron is direct and straight. She is not overly familiar, she is not a larger than life character that gushes and exclaims and calls people love, or darling, describing everything including humans as delicious, in short she is not Me.

"Well, the only misgivings" she begins.........

"Let me stop you there, there are no misgivings to have, it's hydrotherapy and it will be amazing and she will love it"

My father is watching me. I mouth the name of the Nursing home and watch his face change, the sudden pallor under the beginnings of the tan he has attained by sitting with her in the baking afternoon sun, both of them wearing the sunhats that have graced a hundred other nameless bent white heads.

I motion with my hand that everything is ok and this is just a routine call.

I walk outside and listen as the Matron talks about spatial awareness being absent and reassure her that this will be beneficial, and much appreciated and that I will help.

She cannot know what I know –

That Siobhán has always loved water, mucking about on the River Barrow as a child, and when she moved to a coastal town, the endless beaches, the indigo seas that crashed to shore.

That my sister and I removed her from a sweltering hospital ward, wearing an ankle tag and a nappy, and supported her to the edge of the ocean, dragging her up the slippery dunes with an audience staring at the woman in the blue dressing gown, the trinity of us reflected in the late evening sun, the white foam drenching her slippers.

That only last week I had placed a basin on her lap filled with warm soapy water and entwined her twisted hands into the soft flannel and watched for the tiniest movement of her fingers, possing.

That I had watched Stephen Hawking in an anti gravity chamber smile a smile of unutterable joy as he floated freely, unencumbered by the chair, and his broken body, and bobbed and weaved in freedom, at liberty, unrestrained.

It would bring tears to a glass eye and so I was lost.

How wonderful is the anticipation of a bath filled with warm water, standing into it - feeling the temperature on the shins - lowering oneself down into the foamy suds, sitting first, clasping ones legs and then easing back, little by little, splashing the water over the body, reminding the self that we are water and that we come from it, the soft feeling of it lapping, the release of tension in muscles and joints, the slackening of taut tendons, the involuntary sigh when the back of one's head finally touches the ceramic and the neck relaxes.

This womb of water.

This womb that birthed me.

My Father has to drive me out and so I bring the world's tiniest dog to engage him.

The curtains in the room are closed despite the noon day sun, and I imagine them undressing her and open the door.

Her chair is empty.

It takes me a moment to locate her in the shaded room.

She is in the bed facing the wall.

I touch her gently on the shoulder and smooth her hair back from her face and tell her that I am her firstborn and favourite child, and that she is having a bath.

It reminds me of nothing so much as waking a baby, and I lift the patchwork quilt I knit for her and look at the bent white legs.

Suddenly, we are 4 in the room and the harness I have christened the parachute is placed under and around her with much gentle rolling and placing of limbs and straps and buckles, tightening and adjusting.

And then she is hoisted into the air and the tears start as my heart breaks.

Although we see her on a daily basis, it hits me like a frying pan in the face, that there is not an ounce of mobility of any description left, and that a team of carers carry out the most basic of human functions for her, as Siobhán is always in the chair when we arrive.

The enormity of the scene shocks me and I wonder how I will cope as I am already in flitters.

"*That one's tearbag is too near her eyeball*" she would have said.

If she could say ....

Positioned in her chair, her blue dressing gown on, she is wheeled away from her sentinel, past the banging and clattering of pots in the kitchen, the smells of lunch cooking, the glasses of milk poured, the comings and goings in the halls, and into the quiet room where I forgot to bring the scented candles.

I pour the vanilla bath foam into the gushing water while my Mother is undressed by 2 women, leaning her forward, balancing and supporting, bracing a limp shoulder against a firm stomach, and I want to avert my eyes, to afford some privacy to this most private of women, this woman I write about on a public forum, and reveal her most intimate moments to an audience, because I am her witness.

The landscape and geography of a lovers body become as familiar to us as our own, but it is my Mother's body that I am now more acquainted with, it's dips and folds, it's creases, it's secret spaces, the little toes that resemble my own, the fingernails, the set of it, the familiarity.

The Surita hoist is an indispensable tool for lifting but at moments it resembles a crucifixion. Siobhán is winched across to the bath and gently, gently swung over the water I have poured, the bright yellow rubber duck the only colour in the clinical room, not a nod to nostalgia but a temperature gauge, and she is inched down, lower and lower, until I can reach her legs, and guide her swinging form down, and then I see an arm moving, waving, and I don't know if it is agitation, trepidation, or tremors from the Parkinsons, or an awareness of what is happening as her eyes are open.

Not waving but drowning.

With infinite care we sink my Mother into the welcoming water which suckles and pops around her still form, and then there are 8 hands in the liquid, 6 busy ones moving and tenderly washing, rubbing cloths and flannels over the quiet limbs, 2 idle hands floating on the foam. Her head is cradled like an infant in a sink basin and our three points of focus and combined energy are directed totally to the helpless body of my Mother in the bath. I wash her hair.

For many years as a child, I had my own hair washed at the kitchen sink, the old stainless steel measuring jug that was used to heat the baby bottles, poured over my bent head to rinse, while I clamped a soaking towel to my face, inhaling the laundered smell and feeling the rough nap of it while exclaiming, - *my eyes, mind my eyes*. In a mirroring image, a towel is bunched and held to her eyes as the cascade of water streams through her hair, flattening it to her head so that she resembles a sleek otter, a water baby, and the child I once was, ... that she has now become.

The matron hands me the small curved scissors with the very sharp blades and indicates that I should cut her fingernails, as she has already pushed the cuticles back with the sides. I demur. My sister and I are the Mary & Martha of sisters, she does the essential maintenance and I do the flitting around with the lemongrass burner. She does the removal of foreign bodies from orifices, I do the lighting of candles and the singing. She however, is in the south of France and I am here in the room.

The Matron is pleased how well the event is progressing and is imagining possible future scenarios where the hoist has some minor arrangements made to wheels and mechanisms to facilitate easier transfers for late stage patients who are normally not bathed.

- Did you ever use the foot spa on your Mam? she enquires.

All too soon, the parachute is making a second appearance and I realise with a start that our time is ending. In my mind, it would have been only she and I, in a hushed candle-lit room, maybe a little incidental music on, my arm around her as the water reached her shoulders, gently lapping at her knees, running more hot water and relaxing while I spoke of old times and they had come whispering in and ranged themselves like pictures around the tiles, a communion of Mother and Daughter in a room filled with memories.

This is a busy space though, and these women have other patients to attend to.

Siobhán is wheeled back down the corridor to her room wrapped in towels, and again we reverse the practice of the winching, swinging her through the air to lay her back down on her unmade bed, to pat every inch of her dry, to rub the lovely scented cream into her skin, and then she is winched up again and swung across to her place of residence, her chair.

Thank you so much says I, touching each of the women on the arm, trying to impress on them the importance of the time we had shared, the honour of the allowing, and how that honour had my own restored.

It was a pure pleasure, says the Matron.

I took advantage of being in this space, at this time, and removed the hairdryer from its perch in the locker to blowdry her hair. I moisturised her skin, and put dabs of eyeshadow and lipstick on, draped a silk scarf and perfume around her neck, and wheeled her out into the sun of the courtyard by the fountain where a small white headed man sat patiently waiting, and presented my Father with his wife. It was the best possible gift I could have given this man that I love as much, on Father's Day.

July 3rd 2014 - Year 9

A veritable plethora of people take me to my Mother.
Some have been doing it for years, some not.
They have picked me up in rain or shine, sleet or snow,
high as a kite, or downright low,
never flatlining or medium, or straight,
never on time, always late.
Last week the woman looks at me askew,
as I am wearing a nightdress and shoes.
A wardrobe malfunction I say as I strap the belt on, looking at her looking back at me.
In Siobháns room, the sight of me slumped in the chair in the reflection of the tv screen
decides me to go the whole hog and roll some pink velcro curlers into my hair, for a laugh.
"*Laughing turns to crying*" Siobhán would say when I was small.
I kick my shoes under the airbed and put on her slippers.
For the laugh.
Walk a mile in my shoes............
Despite feeling fragmented and brittle and pulled in every which way, writing, performing,
playing to the gallery, drinking at my one woman show, and dealing with a parade of men
and their needs and an all pervading exhaustion that manifests as a bone aching physical
pain, I am laid low.
It is 11 years since I was on a plane.
My ten year passport was unused and out of date.
Despite my best attempts at self sabotage, this is happening.
Nothing could ground me but the wearing of my Mothers shoes.
In the warm fur, I felt comforted.
"*Head and feet keep warm, the rest will take no harm*"
In the ankle support, I felt braced and grounded.
A treatment of bio-energy healing includes the gentle support of ones ankles by a therapist.
Ditto the gentle holding of the head between cupped palms.
It is comforting beyond belief.
As humans we need the reassuring touch of another.
I am tactile and touch people a lot, feeling and squeezing your hand to see if it is
cold, touching you on the arm to make a point, hugging humans and holding them.
Being held.
The little fur slipper boots held me and rooted me.
I must write this, I think and then instantly forget.
I am supposed to be packing to get on that plane tomorrow - to fly to Sweden and take
buses and trains up the country to an idyllic spot on a lake, to behave like a responsible
adult human female.

To write.

Instead, in the mayhem of the tiny bricks that surround me, and in a flurry of lace underwear, sundresses, hats and boots with a list that grows longer by the minute, I visit Siobhán tonight.

To tell her what I am doing now, and to kiss her goodbye for the longest time in the last eleven years.

She does not wake for ice-cream or a drink, and I spend the visit staring out the window at the scudding grey clouds that I will fly through tomorrow night, wiping the tears off my cheeks

I forgot the slipper boots, again.

"Mind her for me" I tell the carers as I leave through the glass doors, a tin of dogfood and a bar of chocolate in my bag.

Tonight I deliberated about stuffing the boots into the case and bringing them, and thus her, with me.

"*Walk a mile in my shoes*" ....

On the back in stitching is a word that I only read tonight -

it says **Moon.**

Despite the ego trying to cancel the whole shebang, and due to an enevelope from my Father containing paper folding money despite his worries that his child, another woman from his family is leaving him, my id has stepped up to the plate, to reach for the moon, to do it for herself, *AND* her Mother.

Maybe, this once, crying can turn to laughter.

Sweden Summer 2014

Although I am a thousand Swedish miles away,
Siobhán never leaves me.
These last few days I have wanted to call her,
to hear her voice,
her quiet reassurance.
Even though I know I cannot.
She has not spoken for years
and I have not stopped.
"I'll ring her in the morning" I think, and realise.
"I'll ring her when I get to the restaurant" I think and realise.
"I'll ring her when the interval is on............................
I can't explain other than that I want to share my experiences of the residency and the new country, and all the crazy shenanigans I have been up to.
And that the last time I was away anywhere she was living at home answering the phone.
I asked Little Thomasina to put the phone to her ear,
and spoke into the silent feedback,
the tall towers between countries,

the satellites carrying my voice
down fibre optic cables
into the small ear in the big chair.
At a poetry slam on a beautiful sunlit evening on a tree lined street I had to perform a piece
of my own poetry which I composed that afternoon watching a woman walk by.

Marknad

Sashaying in summer sunlight
in stillettos smoking
the woman with the heavy
coil of hair
stoops to kiss
the childs face
angling the cigarette
away
twin plumes of scented smoke
dispersing slowly in the Swedish noon
hips straining through sheer skirt
calves stretching
white ringleted children
in pink shorts shriek
as a golden cadillac splutters
on the crosswalk
seagulls screaming for strawberries
as they wheel and bank
across a marshmallow sky
and then the child
begins to cry.

MDM July 2014

- If the past is a story we tell ourselves,
then are we still
forever
caught in that moment,
condemned eternally like a fly on sticky paper.
Hot from the car and wielding the crutches I have ended up on again,
I arrive at the glass doors of the nursing home after 17 days trouncing around in Sweden,
behaving outrageously with P.R. people, punk bands, poets, and persons unknown.

My luggage and Ikea bags are strewn around like confetti on the back seat.

Little Thomasina is sitting in the armchair in the hallway so I know Siobhán is being swung to the commode in the Surita hoist.

He stands to embrace me,

this limping child,

this enfant terrible,

this prodigal daughter who has returned to the fold.

"I missed you" he says as he kisses me.

He looks pale.

In her room Siobhán is lying sideways in the Stephen Hawking chair, a ring of dried chocolate around her mouth from the melted ice- cream.

I am moved and reassured simultaneously.

Although I have been behaving like a responsible female adult in the snowy country that has been sunsplit for my stay,

temperatures reaching 32 degrees,

and an impossibly blue sky at midnight,

the child in me has been amazed and overwhelmed.

In the depths of winter and depression and suffering from SAD with a capital S, I could never have imagined that I would travel so far.

In my mind I've gone to Carolina.

The visions of me in the knobbly green cardigan hunched over a single firelog and sleeping with the frost creeping up the windows have been miraculously replaced -

with a tanned woman cycling into town to post cards and drink espresso, people watching, photographing strangers and the crows who ate a Panini from the restaurant table -

with a woman producing and presenting her own radio show, recording in a studio with an engineer,

writing the intro and links on the wall on the way in,

deciding the music and the questions as I went along -

with a woman who performed pieces of her own work and held workshops in creative writing and performance -

with a woman who made it to the last round in a poetry slam despite repeating that she is NOT a poet to anyone who cared to listen

singing a ballad when she ran out of poems,

with a woman who finally cycled to that Swedish lake in Sommen and heard the voice in her ear that said Trust the Universe you believe supports you, and laid back her head and surrendered and finally, finally, floated on her back in the greeny brown water, allowing hot tears to flow from her greeny brown eyes,

as she spread her arms wide,

in surrender,

to the Universe.

No matter that I sat on decking drinking till dawn,

that I laughed and cried,

that I sang and partied,

that I blagged a heap of us free into a closed nightclub with the aid of a big camera and a bigger mouth,

that I looked on paper as if I was "on it like a bonnet" -

a part of me was always present in this room,

hearing the quiet hissing of the airbed at a waterfall,

hearing the soft rustlings and creakings of the machinery over the noise of the punk bands rehearsing,

hearing the quiet whispers of love and tenderness that my Father repeats to his soul mate daily over the shrieking of the endless trains that screamed by to Stockholm,

smelling her scent in the spray of the tiny perfume I brought with me,

in her scarf that I wore around my head,

I am the fly that has come unstuck,

and is learning how to fly.

Again.

"Blackbird singing in the dead of night,
take these broken wings
and learn to fly,
all your life,
you were only waiting for this moment to arise,
you were only waiting for this moment to arise,
you were only waiting for THIS moment to arise"

Lennon/McCartney

September 2014 - Year 9

The room is newly painted.

A shade none of us can agree on what to name ....

Depending on the light it looks light grey, pale green, mint, or charcoal.

During the week, I was so exhausted and ornery and wrung out that it escaped me what colour it was.

Or where I was.

Huge swathes of time would tick by while I listened to the sound of my own breathing, the voices in the halls, and the small ragged coughs from the giant chair.

On a number of occasions, I snapped back into the room from wherever my head had wandered, and sitting up in surprise would apologise to my Mother in the silence.

"It is Michelle, your firstborn and favourite child, I'm still here" I would announce softly and grip her hand.

Leaving after these visits always makes me sad, and mad.

"Jesus Christ, can you not be present?" I will berate myself in someones car on the way home.

"Can you not watch with Me one hour?" said Christ once to a companion who was also not fully present.

When I have behaved like this I am rueful about going back,

making up reasons about having to write,

or no lift,

or a parade of half arsed excuses that I can trot out as quick as a blink.

It does not assuage my guilty conscience though.

Last night, despite the fact that my presence was required in about 17 premises and events, I spent the Bank Holiday Saturday night at her bedside, in the chair still warm from my Father.

I have brought a "champagne" magnum ice-cream and am initially repulsed by the chocolate, the colour of it, the grey bloom on the icy coating making it look like something that should be in a bargain bin alongside broken biscuits.

It was delicious though.

Siobhán ate all of it from a paper cup with a little spoon and the use of about 837 tissues.

My Sister takes over on the juice.

"Move then" says she, watching Walter dismember the wooden icepop stick on the carpet.

And so I lie on the bed.

It's an air bed and many's the night I have laid on it to ease my aching joints, feeling the pressure of the electric motorised air pushing against the small of my back, under my legs, hearing the small wheeshing and shuushing noises it makes.

But I feel bold and giddy and my head races for mischief, so I find the controls hanging over the side of the railings and elevate the bed into every position it was ever manufactured for and a few it was not.

The machinery protests in a series of cranks and creaks,

whistles and sighs.

"Begob and it's been a long time since it did this eh" says I to the bent back of the Sister who is leaning over the giant chair with the glass of orange liquid, and another roll of tissue.

She turns around to survey me with a raised eyebrow.

I am lying off like a Lords Bastard propped up on memory foam pillows about 8 feet in the air, with my knees raised, my calves elevated and my feet dangling.

"You'll break that bed yet" she says holding the glass to my Mothers mouth and tickling her lip to get her to open up.

This is what passes for love and affection between sisters as if to ever start talking would instigate a flood of sorrow and burst the banks of the Dam we try so hard to keep from flooding.

I lower the bed slowly, despite the din, and then wonder for a split second what the view is like for this woman on a nightly basis.

Siobhán sleeps curled to the wall on her airbed, with the railings up, and a pillow in her back to bolster her.

In winter she is snug in a fleece pyjamas, a woolen patchwork quilt tucked in around her shoulders.

In summer, she is cool in a cotton top, a sheet pulled halfway up to cover her modesty.

And the nappy.

On the wall, the brush has immortalised a tiny blob of hard paint into a tinier mountain, and a number of inches away, its twin.

I stretch out my index finger to touch these.

And in that split second realise that this is something Siobhán will never do. If her eyes are open,

whether it is on a long sleepless night,

or in the morning waiting to be winched from the bed to her chair,

this will be her view.

These 2 tiny paint mountains.

This woman who painted - who drew clouds and skies on the bathroom wall at home when the wallpaper was stripped for painting

"What's up with you now eh?" says the sister when she sees my face.

I tell her.

"It's 2 totally different scenarios.

Siobhán is probably seeing colours, or dreams, or children.

She is not seeing what you see"

Nobody sees what I see.

No two people watch the same football match.

"To hear never-heard sounds,
To see never-seen colors and shapes,
To try to understand the imperceptible
Power pervading the world;
To fly and find pure ethereal substances
That are not of matter
But of that invisible soul pervading reality.
To hear another soul and to whisper to another soul;
To be a lantern in the darkness
Or an umbrella in a stormy day;
To feel much more than know.
To be the eyes of an eagle, slope of a mountain;
To be a wave understanding the influence of the moon;
To be a tree and read the memory of the leaves;
To be an insignificant pedestrian on the streets
Of crazy cities watching, watching, and watching.
To be a smile on the face of a woman
And shine in her memory
As a moment saved without planning."

Dejan Stojanovic

August 2014 - Year 9

He doesn't like to talk about it.
It seemed that the point was moot about taking my Mother out for the afternoon,
on the day of her Wedding Anniversary.
Her 51st.
I had mentioned it over lunch in the tiny red cafe with my sister in attendance,
and watched as his face changed, like a hurrying charcoal cloud flitting across a golden beach.
He puts down his cutlery and before he can draw breath I seamlessly change the subject and move away, move away from the glaringly obvious and onto the subject of dessert,
Ice-cream or shortbread?
And tea.
A great man for the cup of tea.
The last anniversary I remember celebrating with my parents properly was their 40th.
We hired a Marquee, we children,
And installed it in the garden, between the bouncy castle and the trampoline
With a floor, after much debate and ominous forecasts of twisted ankles,
amidst much muffled cursing and sibling tantrums on a roasting August afternoon.
A number of hours later, after standing on the plug of a hairdryer left on the stairs of a manic house filled with secret visitors, while running from a shower wrapped in a towel, I was removed by taxi to A&E to be strapped, medicated, and crutched.
Twisted ankle.
A number of hours after that, the image captured for posterity is of me in my default setting, where out of my mind, on Ponstan and wine, I flirt with a beardy musician.
And my Father tries to pretend he is not delighted that not only have I brought the entire Wexford Folk Orchestra, but also his beloved violin.
He always pretends not to smile, often turning his head away to laugh, and I feel it is a legacy of a childhood where beatings and punishments in school and chapel, were considered not only normal but in fact, de rigeur.
"Spare the rod and spoil the child"
"Children should be seen and not heard"
"Don't speak until you're spoken to"
"Sit down and whisht, and mind your manners. "
"Get down on your knees and pray for redemption and salvation from the fiery furnaces of hell and its flames for all eternity"
He remembers getting a box in the side of the head from a "Christian" Brother for writing with the butt of a pencil, all he had.
There was a war on.
I am asking the Musician to play a certain song, one that I know he knows, one that my parents will love.
We told them we were taking them out to dinner, and then for a few jars in their local.
"I don't want any fuss, mind" He remonstrates giving me the eye, which I blithely ignore and rustle up a whole world of fuss, and food, and drinks, and people.

The sister pretended she had to call to the brothers after the meal, on a pretext of checking on her 4 year old son.

In the warm summer darkness, they walked around the side of the house on the hill and straight into their own Céilí -which was in full swing and at full throat - my Father pulled back the flaps and saw all of us there, cheering, and shouting, our hair plastered to our heads with the heat, and the drink, and the water running down the marquee walls with the sweat flying off the band, giving it socks.

In the photo I managed to take in the split second that he does this, I captured their frozen images forever, my Fathers face a mass of conflicting emotions, shock , surprise, mortification and pleasure, my Mother - smiling and pointing in delight.

Pointing.

It's been a while since we saw movement and the wide open spaces of our hearts stretch and contract when we notice the smallest of twitches, a finger moving on a soft fleece blanket, the tiniest nod of a bent white head, a muscle flickering beside a closed eye.

Bring her *OUT*?

The jury itself appears to be out on whether it would be traumatic to hoist her broken buddha body, with its fizzing synapses *not* travelling down the endless miles of muscle and memory, into her chair, and try to wrap her in blankets and throws, a pashmina fashioned into a makeshift scarf to keep the breeze from her hair, and whether it would be invasive and pointless and just heartbreaking.

Or whether She would love it.

It could not be much more heartbreaking than their 50th last year, when I prevailed upon the head honcho of the Franciscan Friary across the road to come out and bless her.

And collect me and an ornery needy Chihuahua who thinks he is people.

And have the tea with us.

To his credit, he played a blinder and shared stories of his youth and vocation while we waited for the Nurses to wheel in the cake, the table of ham salad sandwiches and cream sponges laid waste by the hulking teenagers high as kites on fizzy drinks, Pavarotti blasting *Nessun Dorma* on the Nursing home tape deck in the window, Siobhán being spoon fed a lukewarm bowl of mush.

He even re-blessed her bowed head, curled sideways into the giant chair, when I told him he was like Speedy Gonzales with the hands and I hadn't even got the camera open on my phone.

Oh, the humanity.

Oh, the documenting.

We took him out for lunch on the day of the 51st to a building like a barn, with screeching infants, piped Muzak, chrome counters and the deafening din of chairs being dragged around, trays banging off tables. I thought longingly of a small warm café and sighed. There was a lot of us though, all the children and grandchildren present and correct.

I use the term loosely.

The missing space at the table was occupied by a soft cardigan.

I left it behind in her room one day. It was laundered and labelled by the time I remembered.

I saw her in it on a visit and thought how lovely she looked, the pale pink contrasting with her hair, the ruffle at the neck and cuffs making her look like she was heading out somewhere.

Anywhere.
I left it there for a year.
One night, cold in a sleeveless dress, I extricated it from the wardrobe and wore it home.
"That's Mam's cardigan" says he when I get out of the car, and I show him the small button pressed into the label, that the girls in housekeeping have attached.
It says *"Siobhán Mahon"* on it.
He reaches out his index finger and rubs it, squinting over his glasses, while the jugs of iced water rattle on the trolley beside us.
"Leave it on it" says he.
Sometimes I wonder does he know me at all.
Late that night on the phone I try to pump him about the actual day in 1963, and where they went, and what it was like. It's like pulling teeth.
Oh, it was all so long ago he sighs when I persist and I tell him goodnight, and to pour himself a half one, and that it is a milestone day, and he should be happy.
The wide open spaces of his heart have a lonely wind rustling through them, and the plaintive sound of a curlew, calling.
He doesn't like to talk about it.

Pale Pink Purse

As life grows longer - awful feels softer,
but some nights
some nights
the mountain in me
feels magnificently monstrous.
"your tearbag is too near your eye"
Sighs the Angel of Collections
on a night
when the Sky
was a fat blue mushroom,
splitting asunder
with slanted rain,
and purple thunder,
the wide open spaces of our hearts.
Slowly teasing gossamer wings,
memories flying like butterflies
and flutterbyes
who sing
into his outstretched mesh
the formless and the stillness,
in the maelstrom of dancing illuminations
that surround my Mothers bowed head.
Sparkling iridiscent pinks, lilacs, greens and golds,
a myriad of coloured vibrations

that as they leave her fizzing synapses
and the night gets cold,
he captures for all eternity,
never to grow old.
As I tenderly wipe
the steaming cloth
over her itching face
she releases the sound of my childhood,
a protracted sigh.
It is my final gift to her,
No time to reason why.
And down through the years
the childrens voices echo and cry
"Ever this night be at my side,
to light, to guard,
to rule and guide,
Amen".
As the Angel does not have a mouth
he speaks his mind
and tells of the forgotten things,
and I watch them appear,
in sprinkled shafts of sunlight,
creamy rays of moonlight
and in the flecks of sudden rain
that speckle the glass like plump tears.
He prompts me to chase
and catch all the tiny things,
to access the vast recall
that entwines us.
Wiping the food from my Mothers mouth
They come to mind, these
images and moments
plucked from a pale pink purse,
with a red satin lining,
that smells of medals and coins,
released on tippytoes into the room,
and I watch them stretch and mingle
with hers,
in a pirouette of an imagined ballet,
swooping and whirling
in a dance of remembrance.
Some nights there are so many spinning lights
in the room
that my Mother smiles.

October 2013 - Year 8

I had been typing in the silent kitchen for hours.
When the sun goes down,
even though there is light in the sky,
a small breeze creeps in the open back door
on little fog feet
and wraps itself around you.
The kind of sneaky cold that makes one rub ones bare arms and look for a cardigan -
or sleeves.
So I closed the laptop and wandered inside.
It is 8 minutes to midnight.
I flick on the TV in the hope that something interesting,
informative, or amusing will while away an hour of unwinding.
I have 8 minutes to kill before the onscreen menu changes.
And so I watch the images unfolding-
in a blur
not really thinking,
still in my head
in the memories of long ago that I am dredging up,
and I am bathed in a soft silt of them,
so it takes me a moment to realise I am watching real life unfold.
I don't do soaps.
Or chick flicks.
I do documentaries, and real life.
My guilty pleasure is people watching,
real people being real.
NOT Jeremy Kyle who should be shot with a ball of his own shite for crimes against
humanity.
So I watch people .....
watching us watching them watching us,
cooking for each other, painting each others houses, staying in each others B&B's, and
pushing infants into the world.
The messy business of living -
breathing in and out,
as humans on a whirling dot in space so vast we can't comprehend it.
Tonight I am watching an end of life piece.
The cop is speaking into a walkie- talkie while looking up at a window.
The 999 call explained there was the body of a woman on the path outside a block of flats.
We are in her space.
The camera crew and the police are marching around looking at the flat.
It is spotless.
There is a chair under the open window
and the policeman notes this and leans out to look at the drop.

She cleaned up before she jumped.

She washed and cleaned and tidied.

She ironed a pile of towels and sheets and left them folded neatly on the back of the couch.

And then stuck a post- it note to the window sill, informing them to look at the TV screen.

Her daughters number and the letters were stuck there.

The cop takes the lift downstairs and lifts the rubber sheet to ascertain that there were no ligature marks on her.

His face contorts for a millisecond.

"Catastrophic Injuries" he pronounces and the firemen turn on their hoses, and the camera pans to the foaming water bubbling around their rubber boots.

And I am undone.

I saw her home, her life, and her final view before she jumped.

The high rise blocks of flats, the orange lights, the motorways, the night sky of Manchester, a planes tail light winking in the distance.

A small Jack Russel Terrier on a blue lead is lifted into the cab of the fire engine, and his tail wags uncertainly and his ears prick as the lighting rig of the film crew blinds him.

Last night I sat rubbing my Mothers head and talking softly.

Despite everything, and all that has happened she is now 80 years old, although for me she is framed forever as a young woman.

I trace my fingers down the curve of her face..

I am so blessed to still have her.

Could the woman who cleaned, and wrote letters, and kissed her dog goodbye, have found comfort and release in staying,

not leaving?

- if she could have known that although you might never be rid of the blackness, you can be friends with it, - make peace with it - would she have put the chair back in under the table and turned out the light and gone to bed?

One can come to peace with awareness and acceptance.

In a Zeitgeist where anyone on the planet with a phone can watch footage of humans beheading each other and being unspeakably cruel, often in the name of religion,

would it not behove us to mind each other a little bit more,

to love each other a little bit more?

- knowing that we are all only specks of light and shade,

Chiaroscuro on a canvas of space,

and that although we are minute, we are infinite and everlasting energy.

January 2015 - Year 10

Now is the time
when Siobhán resembles every image of any old person ever slumped sideways in a big chair.
She used to heave her own Mother up,
and brace her and put a pillow behind her back.
Sometimes I helped her,
marvelling at her self control and stoic acceptance,
and the easy way the sisters had of helping,
and sometimes laughing through the lifting.
Her Mother had a stroke,
and although was physically incapable
was still as sharp as a tack.
She would laugh along herself at times,
times when the trio of women would be in the higs,
giggling in the face of adversity.
Now, it is my turn,
and I have no big- eyed, soft faced child to witness,
or help,
or hold the pillow.
I bend down lower and lower
to see the face under the flop of fringe,
and tell her what I am doing.
"I'm going to pull you forward Siobhán -
and make you more comfortable" I begin optimistically.
And so I brace the chair against the radiator with my bent knees,
and on a count of One, Two, THREE.....
heave the small stiff body of my Mother forward
and then try to hold her,
and the pillow,
and pray to any God in the Universe
that I am not hurting her back
or wrenching her arms out of their sockets
as I lay her back,
feeling the cool pillow behind her shoulders,
and hugging her a little,
now that I can.
One night in the middle
of this manipulation
the door opens quietly
and the deaf man on the stick who comes to chat,
stands framed in the backlight,
and watches as I lean into her,

lifting her,
holding her
and taps his way back down the hall.
"Hold me" says Michael Harding in his new book.
I read "Staring at Lakes" last year in a single sitting,
and this year,
watching him talk about the loss of his own Mother
on the Late Late Show,
- how as humans we crave to be held,
ran out the door nearly knocking people
over to pull
"Hanging with the Elephant" out of the box in the bookshop.
"I never held her" he says of his Mother
as she made the last uphill trek,
"Hold me" he says to the Beloved all over the world.
Hold me.
Sometimes at the end of warm nights,
when immobility has stiffened her limbs,
I watch the twilight sky, the images of us reflected in the glass,
cumulous   clouds collecting us,
allowing through the mirror
the memories of that other time,
of us as children in Carlow in our Nana's house,
of Girly, and Handsome, and Tawnish,
of Duck Arse & Dickett & Keyhole Kate,
Blind Bill and Birds Custard and the Long One
of nights in the Club and County homes
when it was her
leaning into the big chair,
bracing and placing and holding,
her own.
Some nights the memories and emotions weave such a spell
that I stand with bent knees, braced,
holding her,
looking into that other time,
between my Mother and my mind,
between my tearful snuffling and her strength,
and look at the Montana sky that holds us both -
Drifting.

Sweden Summer 2014 - Year 9

Tangled Mornings

On tangled mornings
When we woke
Ashes in the red wine
Lipstick on the glass
that broke
Entwined in limbs and satin sheets
Your warm hand splayed
Across my spine
Bent knees under mine
As like a child
I sat
On your lap
While we slept in
Charcoal glass dripping morning
Knowing then that it would end
On frozen mornings now
Turning, turning through a sleeping haze
Comfort blanket flung
On a fake wooden floor
A telephone that won't get rung
No head around the door
Chocolate stains on a white lace pillow
A beaded roselight dripping
Calling you beneath a Swedish Willow
While the days of us keep slipping
Away

January 2015 - Year 10

One morning you will find you are googling images of an Alzheimers brain split down the middle.
Your eyes will watch an autopsy on youtube.
Your mind will try to process and retain the fact that a human brain resembles a bowl of cooked pasta bake that has been left in the back of a fridge - a heavy plate of cold ham on top - and consequently it has formed a brawn of its own volition. Pressed Pigs Head. Pressed Head.
Our Father who art in Wexford made it for us as children in Carne.
Forcemeat.

Your ears will hear the voiceover mention that the weight of a healthy brain is approx 3 lbs. and that it feels like a jelly just about to set, firm but with a little give.

Your mind will try to process and retain the fact that what the Scientist is holding in his blue - gloved hands is the piece of pink meat that controls the body, the personality, the conscious and sub conscious.

You will remember the theatre sister with a lisp announce at Sunday lunch that cutting into a fat person is like "thlicing roath pork"

Never seen so much meat without gravy.

You will notice that as he cuts it with a large silver knife he exerts the same technique and force as a Turkish man slicing a head of red cabbage to dress a kebab.

You will notice and retain that an Alzheimers brain resembles a raw cauliflower that has rolled to the deepest darkest corner of the vegetable press and when you are finally alerted by its decaying odour and extract it on your aching knees - seeing shriveled florettes and the shrunken stalk - you will remember the desiccated brain, the hippocampus reduced, as have the frontal and temporal lobes, and they are covered with sticky blobs of plaque, and tangled neurons that have shut down and now resemble the creeping fluffy fur on a jar of strawberry jam that has been sealed under a double circle of greaseproof paper and an elastic band while it was still warm.

You will remind yourself that you tell people the difference between vascular and alzheimers dementia as the former being like a kink in a bicycle tube, a narrowing of arteries carrying blood and oxygen to the brain, like standing on a hosepipe, and then stepping off, and that the latter is like a layer of limescale building up on a kettle element, and the sticky proteins shutting down the areas of the brain one by one, lights winking out on a Christmas tree.

And that it is a bastard.

You will watch a man at a bar order another afternoon round and his words will hover in the air like dust motes in sunlight, about nobody knowing enough about this fucker of a disease, and you will raise your glass and think, actually he's wrong.

You know enough.

You will think to yourself - as you watch the scientist place the healthy and diseased brains together to compare - this is in my Mothers head and your hands will fumble for a lighter, the soft grey ash coating the keyboard like a delicate dusting of icing sugar.

October 22nd 2014 / 50th Birthday/Spiegel Tent

In the dream, She is walking-
with my Father and her sister
at the waters edge
of a golden beach.
I know I am asleep and that this is what is referred to as "Lucid Dreaming"
What it feels like is that I am behind glass.
I need to retain the information,
I need to remember,

I need ..... Oh Christ, I'm so needy..............

It was a miracle I made it onstage.

I won't bore you with the ins and outs

the whys and wherefores

but I was like a woman possessed by the time the camera crew followed me up the quayside,

the smoke of the fireworks hanging over the thousands of adults and children who made their annual pilgrimage to the waters edge.

I almost fell over one of them, on camera.

Siobhán was diagnosed with a kidney infection and prescribed anti-biotics and was slumped,

unresponsive -

her head hanging,

in the Stephen Hawking chair.

My default setting is hysteria and so I react and spend nights sobbing alone in the small kitchen filled with pages and pages and pages of memories and photographs,

images of a life, memories unbidden and unbound, unravelling.

I fear it is me who is unravelling.

My public awaits ....

I march in, squeezed into the red velvet frock with an arse like 2 puppies fighting under a blanket and the high black boots as if I am ten foot tall and bulletproof,

drag my aching bones onto the stage,

squint into the spotlight,

and am almost undone as the crowd starts to softly sing *Happy Birthday*,

starting in pockets,

and spreading slowly but surely around the red drapes of the velvet roof ,

the bobbing balloons,

the portrait of me,

the frilled Swedish apron lying across the back of a chair.

I had forgotten it was my birthday.

Well, I had shouted it from the rooftops and then blacked it out.

It would have been impossible to "perform" if I let my grip falter.

2 Weeks and 2 sets of anti-biotics later I am standing in her room last night,

having not seen her for a week as I was laid low with a bastard of a flu or a complete emotional collapse.

Or both.

Or neither, an ability to not only empathise with every single situation, but to actually feeeeeeeeeel the others mood and pain have blurred the lines so much that I am at a loss to know anymore.

With a red flaky nose, a crackling chest and a cough that sounds like a foghorn, I cry as the ice-cream pools in the corner of her mouth and trickles down her chin like chocolate tears.

I re-fill the syringe with cranberry juice and measure the drops that I aim at the back of her throat, watching the muscle bobbing in her neck, that indicate she is swallowing.

I use the Turkish head massager to stimulate the pressure points on her scalp and then lay it down and place my hands gently on her head to do a bit of Reiki in the hope that it may help,

that I may harness the energy of the Universe

and channel it through me into her,

under the scalp, through the bones of the skull, and into the small pink organ that has white protein growing all over it,

this parasite of a disease.

The only thing taking my Mother away from me

- little by little -

is a growth of a white protein on a small organ nestled at the top of her head.

We are meat.

We are meat, and flesh and bones,

We are meat, and flesh and bones who build machines.

Last night it hit me like a ton of bricks and I thought of all of us and our little pink organs, and how they shape and define us and make us who we are, and compel us to do as we do.

On stage I had to do the piece about Siobhán in a packed Spiegel with a camera on my face, and one to the left and one to the right, and try to remember and not collapse.

The prayer I sobbed in the lonely kitchen all that week was -

"Mam, Pleeeeeeeeeease don't die, not now, not now, I'm not able......

I'm not able"

I'm not able....................

In the dream, behind the glass, I jump up and down and get excited and try to make phone calls and call people, and she smiles calmly at me, as if to say

what's all the palava about,

cool your jets there,

and she turns her eyes to mine,

the eyes that are so rarely open now,

and then only for a moment,

she turns her eyes to mine,

and they are not glassy, and opaque, with ointment on the lids to serve as artificial tears for a blocked tear duct,

they are as china blue as a birds egg,

or a summer sky,

or the bottom of a lagoon,

or the hull of a wooden boat hauled up onto a warm sandy beach,

and in the dream she smiles at me and tells me she has accepted it and is aware, and knows we are there, all of us, and what is said,

and KNOWS that we are there ....

and I wake sobbing again at 4 in the morning,

as once more the dawning, woke up the wanting,

in me.................

I have no need of artificial tears.

The crowd in the tent,

in the booths,

in the tiered seating,
on the extra folding chairs,
and the ones standing at the back rose as one -
when I said the words she spoke for my spoken word performance -
"Stop it, she said. She said *Stop it*
and they stand clapping in a spontaneous sustained ovation
and over the brightness of the spotlight I see my Father getting to his feet in his best suit,
and know it has been ok
the film crew decide to close the show with them filming me walking out so I ignore the
outstretched hands and take the directions,
and slump at the hoarding around a tree,
like a balloon someone has just stuck a pin in -
It has words scrolled across it in painted gold, this hoarding,the words say -
"***Do not forsake her***"
And we put it on youtube for all the world to look.

November 2014 - Year 9

She looks across at me from under her glasses -
the orange lights reflecting on the soft sheened road -
glistening.
I have been even more batshit tonight than normal.
This woman I have known for three decades,
this woman I went to school with,
whose bedroom I drank flagons in,
(whose Mother will only watch "a pitcher with a woman in it"
and who let us clog up the sofa every night for years,
eating rissoles and making toast-)
this woman who I worked with,
danced around Majorcan bars with,
and met her husband the same time as she did with,
this woman who has tried to help and heal and console
the fractured manic presence that is Michelle,
and who has been a solid calming presence
and quiet rock of sense for an aeon,
while ferrying the beloobas broad who orders her around
and expects her to sit on a door with a biscuit tin,
and listen to the ranting and sobbing and manic laughter that happens by the minute.
This woman knew.
She knows that there is a performance side of Michelle.
The loud, funny, smart- arse who plays to the gallery and would knock you down to get a
microphone in her hand standing under a spotlight,

or the insular moody hysterical woman who lies around in 4 cardigans,
with the curtains closed watching "Grand Designs",
and who won't answer the door unless you ring,
and maybe even then not....................
She knew that "*The Eff Word*" knocked me sideways and that I had to lie down for days,
hiding on friends and family,
not even turning up to things with my lovely Swedish people who flew over and never got
inside the door,
I KNOW.... right?
refusing to go out or engage,
feeling it was all too much,
that I had splashed the insides of me all over the floor,
and stripped myself naked with a zip,
while they laughed,
and cried,
and clapped,
and I fell apart.
"I feel like I've been kicked in the back"
says I as I tried to walk up the planks of the Quay
carrying bags and a music stand, and my broken heart in my hands.
My Mothers mouth smells like wilted hyacinths.
"I know you look in the mirror when you cry" says Hewhomustnotbenamed.
I do.
"What do *you* want?" says this woman as she indicates to join the merging traffic which
she has ignored for 20 minutes, the indicator clicking persistently as she watches me
fidget,
drawing in ragged lungfuls of air and trying to exhale.
I have been in bed for ten days with a chest infection and my hair is wet on my neck.
"The Book" I say and instantly know it is true.
the hands tapping tentatively at the glass,
the silent walkers in the halls,
the sticks tap tap tapping along the skirting boards,
and to the woman who inspired it,
who humbles me on a daily basis,
and who in the midst of the whirling ravages of an unspeakable illness
illuminates and enlightens me with her silent presence,
and her love,
and to the woman who drove me to print out the draft,
Literally.

The Scourge - 1973

We had a new cinema in town.
For decades Wexfordians had horsed up and down the South Main Street that housed "The Capital Cinema",
where we had been brought since we were babies.
My younger brother screeched and bawled on his first time
when the opening music of "Dr Doolittle" blasted out of the speakers and Rex Harrison gave it loads a few technicolour feet from him.
He had to be placated and consoled in the foyér and promised chips in Graces on the way home.
One Saturday afternoon we queued with half the town for a cowboy pitcher and right at the top of the queue a big boy poked me in the back and said -
"Your Da's over there" -
and I led my brother away by the hand with my heart in my mouth to see him jump into our spot and walk in laughing, leaving us to re-join the disorderly mob at the very back and get in when the main film was on, standing in the chewing gum and fag butts in the dark, wondering where would we sit, while the man in the rumpled suit rubbed his head and said
"Ah, lads, will yee STOP" in a tired voice as the Matineé crowd ran amok.
There was always 2 films on and ads in the middle, where they would show a photo of a pub with a smiling barman handing a tankard of Bass across a counter with big glass ashtrays and the whole cinema would whoop and holler while the voice over said -
"For Best drinks - After the show".
"Yah, right" someone would shout and throw a banana skin at the screen.
Years later Hewhomustnotbenamed would take a toddler to the cinema and when the music started the child stood up on the back of the seat behind him and shouted -
"Out of here I have to get"
On the night Siobhán took me to the cinema I had been gatching around the house, probably with my brother in a headlock, or terrorising my 3 year old sister with a flat faced doll named Roberta or locking her in a press.
She swears I did both.
That night Siobhán got my coat out of the cupboard under the stairs where the gas meter was and buttoned it on as she told me to be good and quiet as we sneaked out of the house leaving the others behind watching "Opportunity Knocks" and a "Clapometer" that someone was obviously pushing with their finger.
We went to see a movie in the new cinema in Georges Street, - "The Abbey".
It had what my Father referred to as "bucket seats" but which were most usually used as courting couches.
He took my Mother to see "The Sting" on the opening week.
"Are you sitting in the doubles?" the young ones would ask each other in the queue outside as the freshly shaved farmers on motorbikes from Broadway came in to watch "Scanners" 3 times in the one week as there was nowhere else to go.

For Feck sake.
The bit where your mans head blows up though.
I don't know how Siobhán knew about the film.
Maybe she read it in the Papal Peeper.
But she brought me and me alone.
It was the most heartbreaking film I ever saw.
And I was 9 years old.
In the end a child dies in his fathers arms -
(while a thin trickle of blood down his nose signifies to the entire audience to wipe their own with a sleeve of their jersey) -
On a Carousel.
While the saddest music in the world plays.
Siobhán has a kidney infection and is on an antibiotic and is taking drinks with a syringe which my Father insists on washing and wrapping in a piece of tissue and placing in the top drawer with a note.
41 years after I sat in that cinema, pretending not to cry while my face was wet, I find a clip of the film on youtube tonight.
The title stayed with me all my life and so by the miracle of internet when I typed "The Last Snows of Spring" into the toolbar, something that I had thought was only a distant memory or a dream came to life on the laptop and the music that had been only a whisper, a half remembered snatch of notes, a nun singing in a quiet church, a whiff of perfume in a warm room, a shaft of sunlight on a faded couch, a ring of children with fizzle sticks on a fireside mat, becomes tangible and immediate and yet more ghostly than ever before.

January 2015 - Year 10

The room is warm and cosy,
the radiator hopping,
Siobháns face is flushed.
I open the window to let a breath of cold air in,
and place my hand on her forehead and behind her neck.
A kidney infection (U.T.I.) has seen her take a number of different anti-biotics over the last few weeks and be given drinks with a syringe.
It is left in the glass with a tissue beside it when I come in.
My Father, Little Thomasina, leaning over the big chair to offer the purple Cranberry or Ribena to his wife,
after he has painstakingly fed her the ice-cream he stops for every day.
The medication Siobhán takes for her Parkinsons and Alzheimers means that the jerking and tics are largely absent,
presenting usually with a few small sudden twitches, mainly in the left side.I move her from one side of the chair to the other,

alone,

bolstering the giant memory foam pillow behind her back to cool it, placing a cushion under each small socked foot on the foot rest, a cushion under the left elbow, and a cushion under the right.

This living doll.

The enormity crushes me some nights so that I can barely see.

"She wouldn't take the ice-cream today " says he on the phone when I call to ask how his day was.

I call him first thing every morning, and last thing every night, and on numerous other occasions during the day, mostly to enquire about the possibility of lunching.

He is always watching Primetime or listening to the Death announcements despite my protestations.

He is missing the company of his friend, his old neighbour who lives in the room down the hall, whom he used to talk to every afternoon.

The two of them are as deaf as posts.

He calls to him in the hospital every evening now on his way home, a bag of Werthers Eclairs in his pocket as he walks the miles of corridors to his bed.

His energy humbles me as I am usually exhausted just negotiating my way around this tiny brimful house.

"The lad opposite him is stone deaf, and so was his visitor" says the Da on the mobile in the car, pulled in to take the call, the seat belt warning beeping going off unheeded, as he has rushed to answer the phone.

I visualise the 4 deaf men shouting at each other in the white ward

That night the sister drove me over after dinner, and we lifted and bolstered together, one wiping, one lifting, one petting, one talking.

And then a spasm went through Siobhán -

like a scene from *The Green Mile* -

knocking the syringe from my hand.

Her eyes are wide and she has literally jumped a foot upwards in the chair.

I turn to my sister and watch as her eyes mirror mine, wide open -

in shock.

And then it happens again.

And then it happens again.

"I'm getting a nurse" says the sister.

"Leave it" - I say, and she sits back on the bed and we witness.

In my head I didn't want Nurses coming in,

talking loudly,

saying "*Well, Siobhán*"

or opening her blouse to place the scope on her chest,

turning on the big light,

or doing things.

Anything.

It happens again, and although I have her small hands in mine, she is moving me with her.

The strength.

It happens again.

- Get the nurse - I say and she leaves.

It doesn't happen again when they come back.

At my late night call the Da casually talks about this and that, and what he will cook for lunch for his daughters the next day.

At the very end he says -

"Mam frightened the heart out of the girl in the kitchen by talking again" and my heart almost stops.

- Name of Christ and you tell me NOW - I roar.

Did I mention he was deaf?

She said "*What are you at*"

And I wonder what she knew.

And I wonder what she knows.

She keeps moving me with her strength

January 2015 - Year 10

I'm still in here,
but not for long.
I know they are here,
I hear what they say,
and how they care
and I love them for it.
I never told them enough.
It was just my way.
I love them all,
No favourites,
Except Crinos...................

"Oh, Peggy Gordon, you are my darling,
Come sit you down upon my knee,
And tell to me, the very reason,
Why I am slighted so by thee"

December 2014

"Are you all set for Christmas?"
they ask as they throw the rotting pumpkins and Witches costumes in the bin.
Our year appears to have morphed from a collection of seasons, endless times when looking into it was half the pleasure of it,

and a man could lie across a 5 barred gate staring off into the middle distance,
at the changes in the evening sky.
into an insane hurdy- gurdy where we play catch up,
running breathlessly from event to event,
never catching,
never up, our faces glued to the blue screens filming our lives as they unfold,
Mother of God.
Now we have an endless round of Hallmark Cards and newly thought up festivities.
As I type they are preparing to slash the price of selection boxes and wheel out the Valentine hearts,
the pallets of Easter Eggs already leaving the depot.
Pass me the factor 30.
Blue Monday. Black Friday.
Trick or Treat.
The 6th Christmas Siobhán has been away from home looms.
The first one that a massive bus with a solitary occupant bolted and belted to the floor, will not be driven across the green lanes of the mountain to deliver my Mother home on a Christmas morning.
"Don't jump up and down" says the Sister after dinner last week when the point was mooted. Everyone has repaired to the armchairs around the fire and I am left alone at the table, scrolling through my phone, Paddy Last again having talked through the entire meal.
It's a whore of a job trying to book a wheelchair accessible vehicle on a day like that, and after I fruitlessly call the regulars who due to the state of the lifting mechanism or the sobriety of the driver will not be available, a friend, with a purpose built van, offers her services.
"It's invasive and intrusive, and awful to send her back out in the cold again" says the Sister and she braces herself for the expected onslaught.
It does not come.
I sigh.
And agree.
I can barely keep up with stuff myself.
The kitchen table awash with doodles,
half finished sketches, hand made Christmas Cards, scraps of paper with great tracks I have heard on radio jotted on,
teacakes,
marbles, candles,
dogs bandanas,
a half written play,
a half edited book,
and a thousand phone numbers.
I know what the journey is like.
The winching, the hoisting,
the placing and wheeling,
is something I am au fait with.

I have been pushing wheelchairs since I was a child.
One time heroically volunteering to push a fellow Girl Guide in the Patricks Day Parade,
all around town,
to much hilarity on Georges Street as I stretched to my full length about an inch from the
ground to gain purchase uphill.
I pushed my Grandmother in the loan of a wheelchair when she came to Carne, down the
stony road that led to the beach while the adults shouted -"*Will you MIND*"
and knew how to go up and down steps without tipping the passenger out onto the road.
I pushed my Mother in the Stephen Hawking Chair,
as wide as a bed,
through the front doors of the mountain house,
without shaving too much out of the woodwork,
for dinner by the fire.
And I wrapped her again to bring her back.
Unable to get her arms into a coat, we pile capes and blankets around her and wrap her
head like she is going in an open topped car.
Thelma & Louise.
The interior, the only moving light down the black hill back,
though all the scarlet porches are flickering,
the lamplit windows lickering at,
the shining Santas and Snowmen in the sky.
I booked a room in the Nursing home,
just big enough for the chair,just small enough to hold us,
which I will faff about dressing up while the herculean efforts of the sister will be employed
in the cooking and transporting of Turkey & Ham.
Mary & Martha.
Mother & Daughter.
Mother of God.

Christmas Day 2014

I did my shopping on Christmas Eve.
I always do.
Most people are either falling around the roads scourging pints
or at home getting scourged with relations.
I had to get wooly jumpers for two men,
the only gifts that weren't home-made or a piss take,
or both.
The shops were pleasantly empty, one person ahead of me in the queue, a roll of wrapping
paper reduced in a basket beside it.
Result.
I took a cab home and swore I'd wrap everything that night.

I swore again in the morning when I realised I hadn't.

Apparently, it was far more important to eat half a box of Roses looking for a toffee, watching crap till all hours.

Then I decided to sketch and paint 7 Christmas Cards.

I was half way through the 4th one when the Brother rang.

"Are you right" says he.

"Christ, I'm in my tights with nothing done, go ahead and send someone down from the mountain for me" -

The people carrier full of people leaves.

I paint 3 more and start wrapping and he rings back.

"Ten minutes" says he.

The children look at me with round eyes as I talk my way up the hill from the back seat, the trailing bags of unravelling ribbons at my booted feet, my hair damply steaming in the waves of heat.

Holy Lord Lantern, I have become a caricature of a mad aunt.

I even have a *ronnie.*

All I need now is a hanky up my sleeve, and a roll of silvermints and I'm away on a hack.

Any minute now I expect to start reeking of piss and biscuits.

Siobhán is waiting in the rest room.

The table has been set and there are candles on the window sills and I throw the presents under the small tree, angling them in with the toe of my boot, as God forbid I should bend down.

Mams lunch comes in on a tray, something something mashed, something something blended, and a bowl of something soft.

Our lunch comes in the window on tinfoil platters.

The Quiet Leitrim Man was in the first wave of the assault on the Nursing Home, where we are spending our first Christmas, although Siobhán is in year 7 of her stay there.

We thought it would be easier and less disruptive than trucking around the halls with giant flats of meat and veg, gravy in a glass jug, trifle, pudding, chocolate cake, champagne.

So we threw the windows wide and eased the food in.

Easy does it.

My Father is not himself.

"Leave it so, leave it, it's grand, can you not leave it the way it is, don't touch that, I said LEAVE it" until I shout in frustration.

Offer it up says the Brother.

Serve it up says the Sister.

Easy does it says I .... *easy does it.*

I fed her in the corner by the window, as the sun sparkled through the glass, and the green field with the horses darkened through the lilac evening, and the faces around the table softened in repose and relief.

"Close the door on it" says the Matron when she pops her head in to see how we are.

We cleaned up anyway.

The Quiet Leitrim Man and the "*child*" took the dishes back out the way they came in, the sister scraped and stacked and loaded the dishwasher, the Father folded the table cloths

and dragged the chairs back, and the brother knelt, and dustpanned the entire carpet.
I watch him on his knees.
We left the way we came -
Quietly.
Easy does it.

Little Christmas 6th January 2015

The Nursing home is closed to visits
- due to a bug -
I can't go out there this night.
to dispense my usual hug,
Although my thoughts
 are in her quiet room,
my cold cold fingers typing,
typing in the candlelit gloom,
other memories from long ago nights
and so I am lost in reverie, and sights
of other Little Christmas Lights,
On the Women's Little Christmas -
"Nollaig na Mban"
from long ago
a day revered
by women as their own,
and they gathered all these women,
to each other,some alone,
without Father, husband, brother,
to sisters and daughters,
to nieces and aunts,
and especially the Mother,
to show how much they love her,
and they celebrated quietly,
with a minimum of fuss,
and sliced the white- iced fruit cakes,
and told the memories of us,
and drank strong tea from blue rimmed cups,
and prayed for all our sakes
And my cold fingers are type type typing
in the glooming candlestanding
Can I steal a kiss miss? On the Little Women's Christmas
In their shawls, spending shillings in snugs,

singing hoarsely as they filled up the jugs,
Other memories from long ago nights
So I am lost in reverie and sights
of other Little Christmas lights
On the Little Women's Christmas

Little Christmas - 2002

Little Christmas when we were late for the dinner coming home from Carlow and the scourge had been cooking all day at home as a surprise, about seven courses cooling on the table, she had rung Toms mobile about a hundred times but he could not hear her. I walked past her and all the food and sat down at the corner of the table with a sad face on me like a Mother of Sorrows and she says -

- "What is it, what is it eh? What is it….
- "They've gev Ollie 2 weeks, there was blood all over his bed, he wouldn't go, he wouldn't go to the doctor, he'd rather die of embarrassment, blood all over the mattress in the hospital, and he caught the hand of the nurse and said let me go, let me go out of this, and let me home to get the place painted for the priest, and then from his bed in the little room downstairs where I slept as a child with Keyhole Kate,while the child papered the walls, he sat up on the pillows and rang the Scourge who was sailing into a sunset as her ship left port.

She stood on the top deck with her arm held up as she tried to hear his voice travelling from cold towers , pulling in the signal and his words as he called to say - put the white on the window, Bye bye.

Bye Bye.

On the ship she watched a Maitre'd so drunk he waited a table in his underpants with his trousers folded across his arm like a tea towel.

She shaved a mans head to fix the mess the boys had inflicted on him after he came aboard to say hello to his brother and was passed out at the wrong lighthouse when they docked.

She lived in fear of a baby built like a tank who wore only a heavy gold chain and a heavier nappy and ran amok in the duty free, smashing perfume and eating **toblerones** twice a month.

She held hands with a stranger as they lost power in a perfect storm, as the waves broke over the bridge, and the tug chains snapped.

The tallest man on board had signed in with the crew and had the saddest face she ever saw. He was the clown.

Every day he dressed in his cabin and made his features different with make- up and lipstick, drawing on a smile, presenting himself to the world and the children he was paid to please. He blew up balloons and fell over and took pies in the face and all the time when she passed him she could feel it, the palpable sense of otherness from him, the lonliness , a feeling of being cut adrift, loosened, all at sea. All at sea. She watched him sit alone at the table staring out at the gunmetal waves while his meal cooled in front of him. He was polite, with a refined accent, and a mild stoic air. She tried to include him or engage, but was too busy drawing on her own face *and presenting herself to the world.*

They only noticed he was missing when the children went berserk and ran riot and someone had to be paged to hoover up the popcorn and wipe down the bulkheads.

"That bleedin' Clown is missing and the place is in a jocker below" says the small chef when she walked through the crew galley dragging a gash bag after soojeying a cabin. She ran to his cabin and knocked. No answer. She knocked louder. Then called out but the only sound was the roar of the engines and the sea. She took out her pass key and opened the door.

The entire cabin was pink.

Her eyes scanned the small space, the intrusion, the violation as he laid there. His clothes strewn around, wallet and papers on the deck, vulnerable and laid bare, the minutae of a solitary mans existence displayed around the room, she entered his space and stepped through the pink substance, and walked to where he lay on his back and cradled his giant head in her hands. Beside her at the bedside was a glass of pink liquid like jelly, his teeth on the locker, pink gloop clinging to the shiny white enamel, and on one of his giant white shoes, a trail of the mottled crimson slime. It looked like a giant hand had upended a strawberry trifle all over the gaff. There was a scream from the door, a flurry of faces then the sound of pounding feet as they ran to get the Master At Arms and the Purser. She wondered if he felt the blood roaring in his ears as he bled out. She wondered if he felt his heartbeat in his throat. She wondered how his family would react coming to a port to collect the body of their son. He was going, then gone, but she stayed kneeling there, frozen in the moment, frozen in time. The next time she looked up the Chief Purser was standing framed in the door with a face like thunder on him.

"Madam" - says he, "what have I told you before about the gloves?"

January 10th 2015 - Year10

On a frozen night I sang "*All my Exe's live in Texas*",
as I gave Siobhán a Jemmy,
swaying the medical recliner with my knees.
I think She smiled.

JANUARY 15th - 2015 Year 10

She looks older and smaller in the bed.
Siobhán has been winched from the Stephen Hawking chair and retired early as she has another UTI (Urinary Tract Infection) and I am shocked to see the giant empty chair -
without her small shoes on the cushioned footrest,
the multi-coloured wool blanket I knit for Christmas,
around her shrinking knees.
She is running a temperature as the anti-biotics try to fight the infection and her cheeks are two Carlow Poppy scarlet slashes against the white pillow, her white hair.

I run a flannel under the cold tap and gently wipe her face,

murmuring who I am, watching as the whites of her eyes roll up,

like the eyes of the plaster saints with the powder blue veils,

as I whispered childish secrets,

when I was small and lighting candles at their statue feet,

without putting money in the box.

"Go on out of there" said the man in the flat cap who had been whispering his rosary to an unseen one, a prompter from the wings.

My cheeks burned like my Mothers with mortification and shame as I crept down the vast silent church.

I fill a syringe with flat 7-up and place it at the corner of her mouth.

"You feel bad because you have a touch of flu" I tell her as I explain that I am giving her a drink, and she must help me hydrate her and I watch her neck bobbing as she swallows so that I know when to stop and give her air.

I only ever fed my Nephews and Niece, and sometimes a random baby that someone was deranged enough to leave with me.

"They all think I am a mules tool , prancing around the roads every time someone opens an envelope, getting my phisog in the paper, being tagged here there and everywhere, and falling home at 4am"-

I tell her as I try in vain not to drench her chin, or soak the towel.

That is surely how they think I fill the hours.

I measure the amount of fluids as she takes them.

20 ml per syringe.

I fill it 15 times, moving on to orange juice when I think the fizzing may be too much on an empty tummy.

"Would you like some cream for your strawberry cheeks?" I ask as I rummage on the shelf amidst the unopened jars of beautiful face concoctions ruefully and consider stealing one for myself.

I open the window to get a breath, turn off the lights, light the candles, mute the soaps, put on the radio and we listen to the blues.

In the name of Christ turn off the news and the bullshit I say to anyone who has ears and play music, music, music.

She is listening I say.

She is listening.

And then I tell her secrets.

I don't tell her that I have nightmares every night and wake crying.

Or that I sit slumped in an armchair wrapped in a throw at 5am - watching repeats of interminable shows where plastic people who hate each other, sit on a panel with frozen smiles and talk about nonsense for an hour.

Or that I read an article where a woman said she would throw herself under a train before she was found wandering in traffic wearing a nappy.

I imagine them laughing and dancing in the bar at my friends party,

I imagine the sounds of the orchestra tuning up in the theatre around the corner, the one lit by the floodlight lilac spot,

I imagine I can see and smell the fragrant crowd heading in to hear the singing tonight at the Arts Centre, the buzz of excitement, the smokers at the door, and then realise with a start that I am not imagining this but that I have inadvertently walked the 2 tiny dogs into the throng and am being asked by every single one of them why I am not going in.

I don't tell them that I am going to light candles at the foot of the bed of another angelic statue,

without putting a shilling in the box.

I fill my hours with words and syringes.

"Go on out of there" said the man in the flat cap.

I left the cream.

Kidney Punch January 27th 2015 - Year 10

Death is the baby that is born with us, and walks with us through a life.

it is the chink where the light comes in, a hairline crack in the giant Universe that allows us to ease our tiny souls in and out.

It is our shadow self.

I am telling the Matron that I subsist - when not fed by others - on a diet of caffeine, nicotine and chocolate, when I realize she is also telling ME something.

Important.

Listen to this says the small voice in my head and my eyes fill with tears as I hear her explain that Siobhán is being called home.

To be present, to be in *THIS* moment, I find that I am rhythmically punching myself softly in the right hand side of my lower back, again and again.

And as I notice I become aware that I am punching myself and so her words seem to come from a long way off, as if she is whispering through wet newspaper.

She has also noticed the punching.

It is impossible to stop.

Her calm voice is a million miles away, and I smell the cinnamon candle from the visitors toilet mingle with the hot lilies beside the radio, incongruously playing pop music.

A matter of time.

I sit in my Mother's bedroom holding her hand and crying while the radio plays Theolonious Monk's **Ruby My Dear**

And I turn off all the lights and sit in candle glow with the window open, and brush my Mother's hair.

She is deeply deeply asleep. In the new extension where the automatic doors shooosh open as you approach, I describe the various houseplants on the sills to the woman who loved plants and window boxes and deadheading primroses, and I stop at a plant that is so breathtakingly beautiful that I reach out to caress its delicate leaves, a fragile pink flower against an aubergine bloom, and I snip a stem with my fingers, and wrap it in her hand.

I do not know that she is dying then.

Or that this will be our last walk, the last time I will manouevure that bastard chair, or place a flower in her hand.

I do not really believe She is dying *hour by hour*

As we all are.

She looks frail as we leave, my sister and I, and I look back in at the small white head, leaning to one side and I have an ominous feeling of dread, a foretaste.

At home, I am unsettled.

Not knowing whether I need a shit or a haircut, I clean the house, tidying, and moving things, carrying armfuls of bedding and curtains upstairs from a hot press so full of tangled clothing from a tumbler that getting dressed is like playing Russian Roulette with the universe, over the joyous yapping of a pair of hysterical toy dogs.

I take a sleeping tablet and dream that I am woken by the phone with the name of the nursing home flashing on the screen.

I am woken by the phone with the name of the nursing home flashing on the screen

"It's time to come in" the Matron says and I have to get to my Dad.

I run through the streets with unbrushed hair.

He is sitting in the kitchen playing his accordion..

I look at the half cup of tepid tea on the table, the tannin stain inside the pink porcelain.

"You know that thing you have dreaded for years?" I ask and watch as he covers his face with his hands, and the accordion strap falls unheeded down his arm.

"Has it happened?" he whispers.

"No, but it is" I say and I stand behind him then and rub his stiff shoulders while he wipes his eyes with a torn tissue and from somewhere deep inside of me I hear a voice saying all the right things, about strength and acceptance, and doing it for her,

For *her*.

We are as alike as two peas in a pod he and I, needy, emotional, highly strung, liable to revert to hysteria as a default setting, so alone in the kitchen I feel the *Dooley* in me elbow aside the **Mahon** in me as if to say move along, nothing to see here, I got this and play a blinder.

My Father sits with her all day, holding her hand, sometimes talking, sometimes not.

And we listen to **"The Umbrellas of Cherbourg"** playing softly on the radio.

If it takes forever I will wait for you ....

In the quiet room Siobháns breathing is labored but there is no agitation.

Well, none from her.

The rest of us are up to high doh.

People come, people go, food comes, soup is made, things under tinfoil are left in the room where the scones and brown bread and cheese are left for a family when the bed is pulled out from the wall, and I realize with a start that it is for *us* now.

"Tell her you love her" I say watching him rub her wedding band.

"Aren't I telling her that my whole life" says he.

At 11pm he bows to the pressure of his children and takes his Grandson home with him to snatch whatever hours of unconsciousness he can grab.

My Sister stays in the chair beside her, while I vacate to a sofa bed in the upstairs office where I lie wide eyed in the unusual darkness listening to the screaming wind outside the sealed glass.

It sounds like a banshee.

I have to get up and sit staring out into the blackness. as the wind howls and wails, hurrying the clouds across the moon, *peekaboo, peekaboo*, and I think *this is happening, come to peace with* it.

I open the window a crack although it is icy, to allow the wind to sneak in, to remove the awful horror of the feral cat keening, to let it gain access to the interior instead of screeching outside to come in.

Brewing up a storm

Come in come in why don't you instead of screaming out there? and I look up into the mottled sky and think - *My Mother is going out there, out among those rushing clouds, that peekaboo moon*

There is a nest of some insect things caught in the hinge of the frame, unopened for months.

The polished ebony of a dancers shoes, a slash of metallic green on their wings, I am repulsed when I see them slither and move, tumbling over and under each other, until I realize they are not buzzing and alive, but merely blowing in the fluff that has harnessed them in a macabre dance of death.

Friday

The sister texts that she is leaving and I go back down.
My Mother is paler.
Her breathing has become panting.
I take a shower and reach into her wardrobe for some clean clothes.
People come, people go.
The carers and the nurses do their caring and nursing.
Leave the room they say as they get ready to wash and change both Siobhán and the bed. And only in the hallway as I stand staring at the door, wearing her grey polo neck jersey and a pair of soft brown fleece track suit bottoms that I don't know who owns, I come to terms with the reality of routine, and *of course* this is how things are.
In the real world, and not on planet Michelle.
My Father arrives back out, showered and changed, and I wipe a chocolate stain from the leg of his good pants with a damp cloth.
We sit together at the bed which has been pulled out from the wall.
My sister arrives back in the afternoon to bring me home and I go in to feed and walk the dogs and talk complete gibberish to a friend at the kitchen table, before she drives me back out at midnight.
I drag an electric recliner up the hall with a nurse, who unfolds a sheet warm from the laundry for Little Thomasina to lie back and snooze with his wife for the first time in years, and also for the last time in years. I split a sleeping tablet with him and throw a quilt over his knees and feet while he protests, but worn out from exhaustive emotion and thought he is soon asleep.
It crosses my mind that it is the first time since I was a child on holidays in a far flung B&B with beagles and huntsmen on placemats and a lace cover over a milk jug that I can hear my Mother and Father sleeping in the same room, her gentle panting, his soft snoring, the buzz of the airbed, the quiet beeping on the phone as another alert comes telling me that someone somewhere is thinking of us, lighting a candle, saying a prayer.

I am thinking of us too.
God give me the strength to do this, I think and wonder how I will be.

Saturday

Today as she climbed all the steps to the highest cliff
We held every part of her, as she once held the parts of us,
United and connected,
The balance beam of my place in the world is about to snap a chain.
Leaving me hanging, as my stomach turns and my knees buckle
And we reach out to touch and hold her,
Whispering soft things to the face on the pillow,
Curled as she is into a childs shape as if she is ready to be born,
My Mother is in labour with her unborn self, back to the womb of the consciousness is the
sole entry I wrote across the entire page in my diary.
a hand on a scalp, a shoulder, an ear, a kneecap,
a small hand under the crisp cotton sheet.
We lay down in the room on floors and armchairs,
on blankets, on rubber sheets and campbeds
for all the days and star filled nights
And all the while the wind raged and banged and slammed heavy doors and rustled the
geraniums on the window sills and tinkled the wind chimes in the hall
And her family formed a ring of steel
as we sobbed our flinty spangled tears all around the small woman,
encircling her in a mist of hope to bring with her to that other space.
Since I was a child I have watched the mourners in the top pew, and imagined,
and empathised,
and craned my head to get a look as the box slowly passes,
the muffled crying,
the broken ravaged sobs.
Now it is my turn.
To every season turn, turn, turn.
I take the chance of a lift,
to go home and feed my babies,
never knowing that the man in the corner was eyeballing a fob watch on a chain,
and that the sands of the hour glass were running out,
until as the car drove away and I put my key in the door, the dogs already barking with
delight
the phone rings and I have to go back........
NOW
My stomach turns.
I look wild eyed up and down the street.
I have forgotten how to call a cab.
And as I try to breathe -

in a burst of sunlight
so that I am dazzled,
a car slows and the window drops and a man's voice shouts
"How's Siobhán?"
And I say "bring me there" already getting in the back seat.
He takes off in a burst, fuming at traffic lights and I watch the grey streets and green fields
flash past from a detached calm space I am unfamiliar with, as I listen to him talk.
It is as it is.
Could the irony be that the Universe who has watched me document every step of her
journey, leave me absent from the finale,
They are all around the bed when I get in,
and She has waited for me.
"Read something beautiful " says the sister and hands me an extract from the Tibetan Book
of the Dead,
and through blurred eyes
I talk about the stranger who lives inside us,
and walks with us from the moment we are born
and whom we spend our whole lives running away from,
and Siobhán left us quietly,
left us hanging on a breath,
until there was none,
and my Father said "She's gone" and dissolved.
And the Matron called it.
5.31pm.
End of Life.
She was the sunset, and the moonlit sky, and the butterfly,
She was the smell of Lavender at midnight around my lonely brothers shoulders as he
stared into the fire.
She is the energy and the presence that nestled deep in the centre of me,
in the wide open spaces of my heart,
where the wind blew through.
In the end, Siobhán died as she had lived, - gently.
With everyone in the room that she had loved,
and who had loved her,
telling her.
And when she was gone,
and I heard the last sigh come as the sobbing started,
I opened the window and let the screaming wind take her spirit, and they blew away
together, and it became quietly calm and the sky cleared.
I raised the sticky bottle of **Jameson** used to make endless Irish Coffees to be fed to her
on a spoon, and drained it.
"Jesus Christ, there's floaters in that" says the Quiet Leitrim Man when he looks in his glass
and I shrug.
I open the door by accident when we are waiting in the hall and see the nurses place a

chinstrap on my Mother.

Some things can never be unseen.

And I think only of the shedding tarantula named Diana, for a princess, in a blue plastic ashtray and feel nothing but relief.

This is not my Mother, it is the banana skin, it is an envelope without the letter, it is what she has left behind as she stepped out of herself, to join the eternal consciousness we arise from, the Source of all that is.

I don't believe in a God with a beard who lies around on a cloud - judging us.

I don't believe he has to open the gates of Paradise for my Mother.

Or for anyone.

I do believe in a magnificent presence of compassion and light that is all encompassing, benign and loving and wants only miracles in our lives.

We have been taught to forget this.

Sometimes it can be hard to rationalise that loving energy with catastrophic tragedies and the ravages of **cancer**, **motor neurone**, or **Alzheimers.**

My Mothers soft breathing over her last days became the soundtrack to all our lives and a meditation for her entire family.

Quietly, gently, and with the strength and dignity she has exhibited her entire life, she softly panted her way to a re-birth of herself, in another dimension, where she has discarded her broken body to return to the heavens she came from. I have seen that Diana tarantula shed itself, leaving behind its empty twin, and have felt the heft of its weightlessness and realised it has not *died* but just slipped out of its skin and *instantly* begun a new life.

On the last day, I held her limp hand in mine, knowing it was the final time I would feel the warmth or aliveness in it, and wondering how in the name of God and all his angels I would be able to cope without this lovely hand to hold , this woman to love and tend, and trying to imprint every freckle, every vein, every wisp of hair, onto my fractured mind, to retain the memory of her, I scanned her minutely and noted that our thumbs are identical.

In the shower this morning I reached for shampoo and noticed the thumb on my right hand and realised that Siobhán is - always and ever - as near to me as my thumb , my right hand woman, my guiding presence.

In the silent Nursing Home Chapel where I had always said – "Hello God, it's Siobhán and Michelle", I crept across to her coffin to apply her make-up as my final gift to her, carrying my small cosmetic bag of creams and brushes and from within the centre of me bursts out a harsh sob that hurts my chest, bursts out like the stuffing from a fat couch,

"Do it first lads, and then we'll work out how"

And the man on the radio sang -

"What'll I do
when you
are far away
and I am blue,
what'll I do?"

Turn turn turn to the season, to every season turn turn turn, and thus it is fitting that Siobhán discards her battered body like a tarantula at the beginning of Spring, a time of hope and relief, a time of closing old ways and choosing new options, for the new vernal days, of green shoots and re-growth, adapting our beliefs, knowing that like the vacant spider it is not her being buried in cold frosty ground, but only what she left behind, what she has no use for anymore, - *what , this old thing, I have it the last 80 years* - and her joyful liberated self is free and easy and dancing with the pure energy of the stars, she has become one with that which formed and created her, and created so many blessings in her, and through her.

She gave me the gift of faith in a talent she said was wasted.

She gave me the gift of all the scraps, sketches, notebooks and photos she had been storing for half her lifetime, and all of mine.

She gave me the gift of time to learn and love and unburden myself
into her silent ear,

and then she gave me the gift of 4 days to spend holding her hand, and telling her how beautiful and brilliant she was, how the nurses called her heroic, and how I would be lost without my best friend.

She let me sleep in the chair beside her, my sister on cushions, and my Little Thomasina Dad in a recliner,

and she gave me the time to process the enormity of loss we would endure..

And the silent empty church where we had sat for so many hours and talked to God was packed.

And the silent church where she had sat for so many hours with her husband on the loveseat beside the piano was filled with memories and laughter as people called to see her and say their farewells.

More called to see her in the box than had ever darkened the door.

She was buried on Groundhog Day.

I was either in denial or having my 19th nervous breakdown but I was hilarious and flippant - ending most of my pronouncements with – *"on this the day of my Mother's funeral"* puffing out my cheeks like Marlon Brando. I couldn't remember which bit was which -   behave or perform.

And shook endless hands and kissed endless cheeks.

 At her wake, when the hot sobbing had ceased, I spot a madman smoking by the door.

"That lad is either a friend of yours or he is at the wrong funeral" say the children between sandwiches.

These Blonde Boys in Black Suits

Siobhán was driven slowly away from her 7 year home in a long black car, while a parade of women who had loved, nursed and cared for her stood quietly in the sun saying goodbye, the only sound the soft crunch of the wheels on the gravel as we walked behind her to the gates carrying a candle, and in the silence I opened my mouth and said "Thank you, thank you *ALL*"

Outside the small country church she was married in, a large crowd stood silent and bare headed at noon as the black car crawled up the hill, then followed in behind the black suited blondes and her son who carried her, to the sounds of a beautiful violin playing traditional laments.

She even ordered the weather, had a burst of incense uncoil out from under her coffin, fizzing out like dry ice, while a shaft of spring sunlight.illuminated the giant butterfly who flitted from whiteflower to whiteflower on the simple wooden box as the strains of *Galileo* floated around the high vaulted chapel ceiling, and she was carried by her Grandsons to the fresh clay under the trees, with a view of the snow capped mountains.

And so it is with disbelief and in a state of detached numbness I hold her wedding photograph handed to me by the undertaker in her black coat,

as the box containing Siobhán is lowered into the soggy clay,

the canvas strap being fed slowly through the hands of her son,

and She tilts,

as the woman in the black coat mumbles

"aisy does it, Let her down aisy, aisy does it"

until with a soft thump -

She is back in the damp earth, in the womb of the land.

And I turn in my black coat to face the outstretched hands, the hyacinth mouths, the procession of teeth and lipstick, the ring crushing handshakes and the fervour of the elderly man in the soft hat who nearly knocked me backwards into the dark yawning maw of the fresh soft clay.

"Lads, will yee mind the flowers for the love of God, will yee mind"

January 31st 2015 - Year 10 5.31 pm

I felt nothing but peace in the bed. Serenely calm,
as if I was about to finally arrive into a terminal from a speeding train,
and I could feel and hear them,
and when I let go, I felt the sensation of a bath draining,
then found myself lifting, gently,
weightless, floating, and I could see them below me
and I could feel nothing but joy even though they cried,
and I wanted to shout - that's only the skin of the spider,
but there was a ring of smiling faces waiting for me in the warm brightness
with their hands out,
and I floated faster and faster into the light,
into the light of love and home.
At last ....
I am here, there and everywhere.
Turn the dial on the buttery radio and I'm singing in the white noise.
Rise and shine, rise and shine, rise and shine.

Hidden behind your every fear about death is the face of your shadow self, your soul partner, coming to wrap themselves around you, and lead you gently home.

And so I turn in my black coat to the outstretched hands and the hyacinth mouths.

Siobhán stayed long enough to teach us how to let her go, and so it was on the last day of winter that the wind carried her soul back to the Universe it had come winking out from, and after all the storms and gales a spectacular sunset bathed the green fields and the empty white gate, and a full moon rose to a shining peak in the lilac sky.

Death is a tragedy that only time can heal,
Love, the only memory Alzheimers couldn't steal.
MDM

It is done.
Siobhán Mahon (*Nee Dooley*)
19.02.34. – 31.01.15.

The 9th Day - February 2015

On the 9th day there was always a tradition in the homeplace of honouring the passing of a soul from one realm to the other.

It was like a funeral, but more craic.

The pressure AND the coats came off.

There was an evening mass said that usually only family and people who had missed the main event attended, the rest of the hordes esconsced in snugs and lounges waiting for the frozen attendees to stamp in from the cold, throw a Cromby coat with a carnation in the lapel over a leather stool, order a Hennessy and give the nod to the waitress to come out with the grub.

There was turkey and ham with vegetables boiled so long they were uniformly grey- green, even the carrots.

Especially the carrots.

There was jelly and ice-cream, the only Irish Dessert for 50 years. And there were urns of strong tea that a spoon could stand up in by itself, poured by a harried waitress who was being alternately heckled, propositioned, berated and having her arse slapped.

On our 9th day I walked into the mountain house for dinner and saw Little Thomasina sitting by the fire and the conditioned part of my brain that operates by rote framed the question "How was Mam today?"

And before it could escape past my teeth I walked into the bathroom and had a moment behind the locked door.

Sweet Jesus.

A week after we laid her under the tree, I have to write her obituary with a word count, a list of instructions, and a photo, to a deadline.

On our 9th day Little Thomasina sits at the table and writes the details for me on the back of a piece of paper that has a sketch of a terrible bird I made in pottery class in school on it.

It looks like a large penis.

A fact that did not escape my sister who almost poured gravy on it while she rolled her eyes. I rolled mine back.

At least she made gravy.

It has been a tough week.

People grieve in different ways and although there are as many stages of bereavement as personalities, we seem to be embracing all of them simultaneously.

Thus we sit down with resignation, acceptance, denial, anger, trauma and clarity.

And that's only Me.

I often wondered how I would be.

I thought of nothing else for years.

I carried Siobhán around on my shoulders, in my boots, and especially in my eyes.

I woke from nightmares crying on a nightly basis and began to dread bedtime.

Now I wake calmly.

I often wondered if there would be a moment, a window of peace before the crashing realisation that my Mother was dead fell on me like a bucket of cold water.

Now, it is the opposite.

Tears come suddenly, but for moments only and the peace is extended.

I feel that her soul is released and peaceful and that she communes this fact to me hourly, allowing me to write a tiny sliver of her life, to describe her in bare flat lines on a paper page so that when my Father reads it he can describe it as a *"lovely write-up"* and fold it into his shirt pocket.

He did.

My Sister and I went to what I now call "*Siobhans Garden*" in diary entries - as grave is too harsh - and tore away the rotting flowers that had frozen and browned, the silk ribbons, the memory cards, and I saved the florists oasis to re-use, as my sister stamped on the soft clay to flatten it, and we danced on the lumps and bumps. She bent to place the primroses into the soil and I helped her by bending and scooping the overflow the men dug out with my bare hands, moulding it around the naked roots of the young plants.

As we drive away, I look at the clay from her burial space under my nails and still my peace is constant.

I feel Siobhán is returning the favour,

from out at the edges where the pale blue lines soften and blur, and that now,

She is minding me.

2 Weeks Later

February 19th 2015

It is my Mother's birthday.

In the hotel where we have gathered for lunch we sit uncomfortably, avoiding each others eyes, perusing menus and checking phones.

"To Siobhán" I say as I raise my water glass and the hands extend and reach across the table to clink.

And we eat.

We talk of grief and graves,

settling clay and headstones,

we talk of sleepless nights and loss,

woodstain, mulch and primroses.

"Petunia Vulgaris" somebody says, while I spread mayonnaise on a toasted bun, and I remember.

"Siobhán used to always sing "*I'm a lonely little petunia in an onion patch*" to make us laugh, member?"

And they smile in recognition of the woman we mourn.

I tell them about the soul who is born with us, walks with us, and leaves with us and the sister rolls her eyes to the brother who rolls them right back.

"Thank God I have no faith" she laughs.

And I tell them I walk a lonely path.

Down another lonely path we are standing at the newly decked ridges of Siobháns grave, Father and Son measuring and laying the small wooden fence to keep the clay in, to keep Mam snug.

I cried more at her chair than I have since she died.

I cried more sitting beside the chair, wheeling the chair, and photographing the chair than I did the day we buried her.

I cried louder when I saw the chair abandoned in the hair salon in the last days - when the bed was pulled out from the wall - than I did when I realised it was over.

"It was torture" I tell them today.

And they know.

I look at the small mood ring on my finger, the flickering blue and green, and imagine it winking up through the dark of the under space, on my Mothers little finger.

In the distance the hills are lilac, shrouded with faint grey mist and the fields are greening, emerald, lime, terracotta, and the corrugated roof of the farm shed is the shiny gloss of a childs train set on Christmas Day, and the woman at my feet in the womb of the earth has been loved for fourscore years and one.

Under an arch of trees we walk, them ahead pointing out names and dates on tombs, of friends and neighbours, while I photograph the hills, the fields, the sky, and them.

I am glad I never listened to the exhortations to put down the phone as I now have a catalogue of images to draw from, to love, to share, and to remember.

Surely that is the point.

"I have lost a Mother and a child" I say to the man at my kitchen table on a long afternoon measured out in coffee cups.

"Your inner child?" he asks as he stirs in sugar with a soup spoon.

"No, not her, actually, ... maybe her as well, but I have lost the baby my Siobhán became, so I have lost both Madonna and Child and my two hands are empty now"

I sing Peggy Gordon, when he leaves, for the day that's in it.

7 Weeks Later

49 days tomorrow since Siobhán went home.

I keep waiting for the deluge.

For flood gates to open and a perfect storm of biblical grief to overwhelm and batter me, carrying me off like a matchstick house................

I am in the eye of the hurricane.

In a quiet space, peeping out.

The outstretched hands that clasp my elbow and breathe into my eyes about how I must be in tatters have no effect in here.

They scan my face for signs of the breakdown they are surely expecting, and when all else fails they ask about my Da, Little Thomasina, who must surely be distraught, and prostrate and prone with grief.

"He is playing a blinder" I tell them, and not that he cried all the morning as he tried to collate images to make a memory card.

Memory Card.

The Wicked Witch of the West - who is wearing a fur coat -squeezes my arm so hard it hurts, telling me how lost and lonely and demented we must all be.

"Actually we're good" - I tell her detangling my limb from her grasp and moving up the path a number of inches.

I don't tell her that I said "Well, Siobhán, how are you now?" to what may have been the space station on a moonlit night.

Or that hot tears sprang to my eyes and my breath caught as it was the same greeting I used night and day to her for a decade.

The moon was so full on the night She died that it looked like the one Jim Carrey pulled down from the sky in the movie *Bruce Almighty*

I don't tell her that I have the basket of plants I gave her for Mother's Day last year in my bedroom window,

the ivy entwined and lit with little pink solar lights in the shape of orchids, that come out in the darkness and mind me at night

and wink out slowly when the sun comes up.

Or that I wake and instantly look for the pink light and say -

" Well, Siobhán, how are you this morning?"

They would think I'm nuts.

"Am I in denial, or having a breakdown, or completely insane?" I ask the handsome suited man at the table as he looks for somewhere to put down a glass.

"Michelle, you are the sanest woman I know" says he.

On her birthday last week I toasted her and told my family that what was, what she, what WE endured, was torture.

Pure and simple.

On my sisters birthday today Little Thomasina is sitting alone at a big table in a shaft of warm sunshine, as the remaining women in his life arrive, late.

His head is bent reading the menu.

He has ordered for us following a garbled telephone call.

The talk turns to the Months Mind, and flowers, and Memory Cards.

"Do NOT let them put some tack about roses growing around a door on a generic card in the name of Christ" I say as I ask the waitress for a gravy boat.

He tells a story about a man blown over the side of a cliff above a stormy sea, miles below, how he grabbed at a root of a tree as he fell and was hanging, suspended over the churning ocean.

"Oh God, oh God, oh Jesus, help me, help me" he begged as his hand cramped.

"HELLO" boomed a voice from the clouds.

"Who's that?" the man screamed.

"IT'S GOD, WHAT DO YOU NEED?"-

"Please, please help me" shouted the man.

"TRUST ME, ...LET GO!"

..................(Pause).................

(In a quiet voice)

"*Is there anybody else up there*?"

The gravy has gone cold as I listen.

And I wonder again at the joy of small things, knowing as one ages and we lose the people closest to us that every day is a gift.

And how it's all gravy from here.

"Look what is on the bottom of the menu" he says and hands it to my sister first,

(well, it is HER birthday)

and I read upside down the quote the hotel has printed today.

**"Some of us think that holding on makes us stronger -
sometimes it's letting go."**

Hermann Hesse.

And I think of the cords that bound Siobhán to the big chair in the small room,

cords of love, but binding nonetheless,

and thank the Creator that the wind blew her out of the shackles of dementia, and out of the chair

and carried her home on a breeze.

Months Mind on Mothers Day

I wake early to shower and see the clothes hanging on the back of the door. Apparently, I had placed them there the night before in some out of body space. They are all wrong, of course. So contrived and outrageous that I look like a caricature of a middle aged spinster, the trailing scarves, the full skirt too long, the layers too many.

"Will you look at the get up of the one" I imagine them saying in the church yard as they park. The more I try to blend in, to fade into the background, the more of a ragged bird of paradise I become. I wear them only because they are dry and ready and God forbid I should tackle the hotpress. Again. I share the car with 3 men. My Father driving, the brother beside him, Hewhomustnotbenamed staring out the window at the dappled fields in the icy cold.

We have all lost a Mother once. In the cemetary, I stumble across to the soft brown grave carrying a floral arrangement in a wrought iron jug that weighs a ton. The stiff pink tulips stand out frieze like as if I am advancing on Burnham Wood behind their rigid heads.

"There's water in that" says Hewhomustnotbenamed when he hears it sloshing around in the car. Well, obviously as I put it in there. Along with the brown spotted rain soaked daffodils I have plucked from the Friary door, the church where my Mother knelt in the silent white basilica of St Anthony and prayed for lost things.

A lost daughter.

As the wind sharpens the people hold their coats closed and I press my hand to my hat to keep it on the mess of tangled wet curls and proffer the small book of yellow post-its and a blue gel pen to the mourners and ask them to write a message to Siobhán on Mothers Day. They look at me askance. And then I tell them that they can seal them with the sticky side and the message will be private, and I imagine the small yellow flags fluttering in the breeze, like prayer flags on mountains, and high rocky places, attached with the tiny pink pegs in the glass jar that someone gave me once. The bell tolls from the doorway, the deep red studded black archway that I am so familiar with from their wedding photograph, and the bell that married her, then called her home, rings now to call us from her graveside with the flickering lemon leaves. I sit between my Father and Brother, noticing the disparity in height as we kneel. And I let my mind and my gaze wander to the heights of the pillared ceiling and see the butterfly in the captured light from the cantileverd stained glass windows, flitting in the spangling sun. In front of us is a family of ringleted children, relics of *aul decency*, belted coats, fancy white tights and patent shoes, and at the blessing for Mothers, the smallest one leans into hers and whispers into her ear, clutching a tiny dimpled hand around her neck. The Mother whispers back into the ringlets and they smile.

One minute I am visiting my Mother, the next I am eating roast beef at her funeral.

"We offer this mass for the repose of the soul of Siobhán Mahon" says the lovely Priest into his Garth Brooks mike.

And he tells us the responsorial psalm.

"*Oh, let my tongue cleave to my mouth if I remember you not*"

And I think of the small woman slumped in the Stephen Hawking chair, the one who suffered a decade of the ravages of dementia and whose voice I can only remember from dreams, the woman who was bound by cords of love like steel ropes to her sentinel, and who stayed long enough to teach us how to let her go.

And I think of the small curly haired child I once was, who knelt beside her Mother in the Basilica and read the prayer to the saint with the curls, asking too for the gift of lost faith to be restored and am shocked to find it never left. My Father, who told me that St Anthony brought him Siobhán in answer to his own prayers hands me his message with the words facing up, unsealed.

And God help me, I read it.

And the bright lemon leaves flutter goodbye as we drive away.

Flutter by, Butterfly.

3 Months Later

One morning you will find that you are lying, in bed, staring at the headlights of cars as they criss cross the white ceiling of your room,
the shadow play and chiaroscuro of light and shade.
One afternoon you will find that you are standing, staring at the names flashing on the phone ringing to voicemail and you will not call them back, and you will realise that it is days since you spoke or left the house, and that you almost wore shades to buy smokes.
One nightime you will find that you are sitting staring at the TV and your racing mind will project lights and squares and colours all around the room, off to the right, in the corner of your eye, and even rubbing or closing them will not remove the dancing lights and you will think you are having a turn.
It is 3 months since my Mother died.
I type the word *"died"*and my stomach flips.
Her quiet breathing over the days of her leavetaking became the soundtrack to her end-of-life
A week later - the frost bitten bouquets, the soft wet clay that clings to my red boots as I tamp it down.
Stilnocht became my lover.
Again.
Bouts of crying, spontaneous, unheralded.
I write her Obituary and then dance in the kitchen, alone, with the music blaring so loud a speaker falls off a shelf.

Diary Entry - Monday February 9th

Feel very calm today, as if am slowly moving towards new beginning, fundamentally organically altering.
I take a call at 2 am to tell me the pups are born in Drumeela.
My mood varies between flatlining or visualising myself giving an acceptance speech at the Oscars for best screenplay, where I have to be played off stage, still forgetting to name the people to thank.
A woman stored on my phone as *Mary Meat* walks my dogs.
And now we dream of her.
My sister dreams that my Mother is driving all over town, parking anywhere she likes and flouting all the basic principles of motoring.
My father dreams that my Mother is in the kitchen at home, cooking, and that the house is full of visitors she is serving up meals to.
And I dream that I am throwing a party in my kitchen and have run out of shot glasses for vodka and when I ask her to wash some, she hands me a block of *HB Raspberry Ripple* Ice-Cream.
As loth as I am to engage, I need to be near people so leave the house and sit near humans

to hear them talk.

I wear a hood in the house, and eat crisps, and peep out the spyhole ignoring the bell.

I cry when my father tells me his back hurts from bending at the grave, his small figure crouched over the wet clay, balancing rocks in the jug he puts the flowers in, so the wind cannot blow them away.

My Mam blew away in the wind though.

Mood = Numb.

I google the side effects of opiate abuse.

The house looks like Beirut or *The Hoarder Next Door,* but I can't seem to muster the ability to care.

I dress in what falls out of the hotpress.

Even the buzzing of the fridge gives me a headache.

My bracelets feel heavy on my wrists.

I stand in corners of rooms staring at nothing for minutes.

I snap out of it and sit staring at the screen for hours.

I cannot write.

I sit staring into space like a pig pissing.

Diary Entry February 26th.

I get up at 4am and write 12,000 words till 9pm.

I send a Bio and some features to Press about my Easter show.

A firelog falls out of the fire onto the mat but I am alerted by the dogs barking.

Thank Christ.

My Mothers clothes are in bags and boxes in my sisters house and we cannot open them.

I dream that she and I are in the piano room in the Nursing home, and that she wiped her hand across her face, and smiled and said - *I am not gone anywhere.*

One day you will try to tidy the house and you will realise after 12 hours that you have only moved stuff from one room to another, and you will stand by the sink and eat left over chicken, cold, from out of the tray it came on. One day you will open your diary and realise that you cannot read your own writing and that there are several blank pages in a row.

On her Months Mind on Mothers Day I make my Father drive me back to the graveyard in the evening to take the photo I forgot of the flowers with the pink pegs and the prayer flags fluttering in the breeze, that I insisted they sign, and the men watch from the car as I kneel on the wet muck to get the exact shot, and they think - "She's losing it"

Diary Entry March 17th Patricks Day

Wake at 5 am. Spend an hour de-tangling dreads from hair with bottle of coconut oil. Eat a biscuit. Wonder how my Father can go to Mass in the Nursing Home every week, passing her room, without seeing her bent head in the chair, sitting there, the empty space by the piano where she was wedged in. I walk on the Quay taking photos of children in bumper cars and huge grey skies. I meet my dogs brother. I buy a reduced box of Black Magic and a firelog and watch the worst Irish Film ever made. I give my Father a book called *The 10 things that happen when you Die*, and implore him to read it.

I cry in the Quiet Leitrim Man's car all the way to town while he carries on talking about politics and ignores me wiping my nose on my sleeve. My Father telephones to say he is making stew. I tell him I am going out as I can't form words. He rings while I am on the street outside a restaurant smoking to deliver it.

"It's in a bag" he says as if that is important.

Diary Entry April 1st

I inhabit my grief like a coat. It has turned down my mouth and the dogs don't know me now. They bark and bark and reverse away from me in the hall. It rains and rains and rains. One of the pups from Drumeela takes a shit in the kitchen and we laugh when my Da says it looks like toothpaste. The Quiet Leitrim man throws a spoon in the sink. I have to go into the jacks to bawl. I see my Mother look back at me from my God-Sons eyes, the pale blue of the bottom of an upturned boat, a porcelain sky.

My Sister tells me it was too soon to go back on stage and that I was too vulnerable and upset to do the show, to perform **Kidney Punch** for an audience while we cried. She said she had nightmares all night.

I dream my Mother is sitting in the back of the church, wearing a lace blouse, smiling. I tell my father exactly which seat when he asks. I do meetings and calls. I do a radio interview with an Australian Channel where the Interviewer burst out "*but you're MAD*" in the middle and a man described it as like listening to someone after doing a bag of coke, or several.

Diary Entry April 20th

Got up sometime. Did some stuff. Ate some stuff. Washed up some stuff. Took some drugs. Slept.

You will watch endless episodes of Tipping Point and The Chaser with the curtains closed. One day you will experience a cosmic shift, a sea change and one of the tiny cogs in your racing brain will fire a different synapse. You will still your mind with meditation and EFT. You will remain present and awake and aware and you will cold turkey yourself off the *Stilnocht* sleeper and so you will do a week long retreat, alone and silent. You will be easy and gentle on yourself and and eat only what is in the house, whether it be stale bread or rice. You will become a character from a Claire Keegan short story who washes her body and throws the feet water out the back door, and cleans the house from pillar to post. Your old mantra of *do it first lads, and then we'll work out how* will be uninstalled and you will run a new programme called *"Do it like you mean it"* and you will borrow a working hoover and your soul and your mind will be washed as clean as the tiles and you will remember you can write, and that you can do this.

I am clean.

I can write.

I'm getting there.

You will remember not the woman she became but the woman she was.

You will recall before the days of silence and immobility, nappies and beakers, enemas and hoists, and you will remember her quiet fortitude and her gentle laugh, and you will write it all down.

And the smiling image of Siobhán, a woman who had the tremendous effort of will to try to disguise the fragmenting of her personae and an illness that would become a prism refracting death into a spectrum of its parts, will wave to you from a far away curtained room, across a divide that is as vast as it is minuscule ,misty and voile like, pale blue, out at the edges where the lines soften and blur, from where she is returning the favour and carrying me.

Mouth Piece

"How did you get on with your man"
says she at the kitchen table - rolling a cigarette -
this woman who has minded and held and picked up after for me for 48 hours.
She is referring to a gentleman caller I had the evening before.
"Grand" says I and allude to the fact that I am alternately numb or high,
and that he probably wanted to see for himself whether I was falling around the roads or
ready to hurl myself over the quay.
I am neither.
I tell her that he said to keep going,
no matter what, and to keep writing......... as I am her voice.
Her voice.
I am trying to put a hundred things in a bag,
so I can finally leave the building,
spinning in a circle in the permanently dark kitchen,
wondering where the hell anything is in this ship of a house.
It's a big ask - I tell her - finding the phone charger with the tiny teeth marks in the socket.
How much more can I write? I ask.
Can I tell the absolute truth about this?
I am high and speeding,
still racing on the adrenalin of the previous week,
head spinning, body aching, eyes swollen
and yet strangely at peace.
I have felt Siobhán around me and beside me in the last days more than I ever felt the
lingering physicality of her in the massive chair, as if the separation was entirely through
the metal panel.
She licks the paper and adds a filter.
"You know you can do this" she says as she flicks the lighter
and curls her lip around the smoke to talk.
"She would want you to".
And I look at the wall.
And I see the light on the photo..............
orange and purple and vivid,
and it drops from an eye,
across my cheek,
and then to lips,
and then it stays.............
"hand me the phone" I whisper and we look together
there is no light, no reflection, no prism, no mirror, we wave our hands, and stand in the
way, and look at the ceiling,
and still it stays
and for a moment in my eyes,
I see Siobhán look back at me and smile,

and I take the photos, 23 of them over 4 minutes,
and the tears that had stopped came again,
as the woman whispered,
"*She's telling you to be her voice*"
and a tear drops from an eye,
across my cheek,
and then to lips,
and then I smile.

September 2015 MDM

Acknowledgements

I wish to thank all the following people who assisted not only in the writing of this book, but in the living of a life.

My family - Little Thomasina (Tom Mahon) & The Skin & Blister (Nicola Rawle) for their loving support, lunches, lifts and loans of paper folding money. The Lesser Spotted Brother - Barty Mahon, The Quiet Leitrim Man (Des Rawle) Josie Mom Bosie, Corey Mom Borey, Eoghan, Adam, Sophie and Yvonne Mahon for being themselves.

Siobháns sisters Keyhole Kate (Madge Sweeney) and The Baby (Ann Brennan) for their memories.

Mary and Nicola Doran and the entire compliment of Nursing, Caring, Kitchen and Housekeeping staff at Knockeen Nursing Home for their diligence, kindness, patience and loving care of Siobhán in her other *home*.

Dr. Grainne Pinaqui, Derek Fehily MPSI and Sr. Theresa Bookle.

The Drivers who ferried me in and out for 7 years in all weathers and moods –
Keishy Rawle, Mary Waddell, Clair Whitty, Celestine Murphy, Patricia Robinson,
and Tony Reck for driving me on the last day.

Fr Noel Hartley for blessing my parents every week, and our lives.

Colm Campbell - of **Riverbank House Hotel** for being a total gentleman in all situations.

Edna O Brien - for her gift of words and her best wishes.

My readers panel – Paul Bell, Mary Waddell, Declan Dempsey, Dominic Williams, Jackie Hayden, Jennifer Traupe, Tishani Doshi and Theresa O'Brien.

Valerie Kennedy for heroism in the face of hysteria, Gordon Barry for *Aeroplane*,
Laura Way, Barry Doyle, James Bell, Pavlina Kubelkova for the filming at **Spiegel**
Nuala & Johnny, Danny & Theresa, Zen, Frock, Elizabeth, Helena, Amy, Denise and Ollie

Denis Collins and Sheila Gallagher (Alzheimer Society Wexford Office)

The entire 148 funders of the project on **fundit** who pledged to buy this book without seeing a word of it.

My extended family and friends.

And Ronan Furlong for his supportive encouragement and friendship, and buying the laptop.

And finally, Siobhán herself, who not only birthed and raised me, but stood at my shoulder over many a long night dictating the story - in her own words - *Rise and Shine*.

With many thanks to my Mother and all of you, with much love –

The Scourge.
MDM © September 2015